ALLEN COUNTY PUBLIC LIBRARY

ACPL IT

DISCARDED

Y0-AAH-632

FEB 12 73

In the Middle of Things

PREVIOUS BOOKS BY MICHAEL RUBIN

A TRIP INTO TOWN

WHISTLE ME HOME

IN A COLD COUNTRY

AN ABSENCE OF BELLS

In the Middle of Things

AN EXPERIENCE WITH PRIMAL THEORY

by Michael Rubin

G. P. Putnam's Sons, New York

COPYRIGHT © *1973* BY MICHAEL RUBIN

*All rights reserved. This book, or parts thereof, must not
be reproduced in any form without permission. Published
simultaneously in Canada by Longman Canada Limited, Toronto.*

SBN: *399-11095*-X

Library of Congress Catalog Card Number: 72-90807

PRINTED IN THE UNITED STATES OF AMERICA

1725563

In the Middle of Things

Sunday

I've been here at the Marin Center for Intensive Therapy for only fifteen minutes and already want to run away.

When Rhoda, the woman who's to be my therapist, showed me to my room, she said a repairman might be in during the week to patch up the circle of crushed wallboard behind the door. At first I thought the door itself had done the damage. Now I can see that the knob would hit somewhat lower and at least two feet away from the point of impact. Some lunatic's fist then? Seems too low for that. Maybe the madman tried to kick down the wall.

I hate the mustard color of the thick rag rug, though the size of the room surprises me. Fifteen by fifteen, maybe larger. A long deep closet. Sparse furniture: the daybed I'm sitting on, a night table and lamp, a dresser, two chairs, one a flimsy modern rocker, and a narrow five-foot mirror that probably belongs behind the closet door. I miss a desk, pictures. The walls are bare. The curtain over the single set of windows a neutral white.

Rhoda said, "Don't look out." I promptly did. My room is on the first floor front of this big pseudo-colonial house. While my friend Stan was here—friend? roommate? lover? god-knows-*what* these days—while Stan was here for his three weeks a couple of months ago, he learned that the building once belonged to a large hillside estate. Since then the land has been subdivided on all sides; the elegant stone stairway beyond the macadam drive runs right down into the rear of a motel. At least there's traffic for me to watch along the avenue. I could easily spend the rest of the day counting cars cruising by, or gazing at the eastern hills. Anything, anything at all to keep me from myself, right?

The bathroom's going to be a problem. It's around a bend down the hall. That's okay, but one of its two doors adjoins the bedroom across the entrance foyer, and already I'm in mortal fear that whoever's living there now will barge in while I'm on the pot or in the shower. There's another john upstairs, but Rhoda told me it was verboten for bathing or showering during the day. As usual I'll be forced to work my bowel movements and urinating around the routines of others.

There's a third bedroom on this floor, connected to mine, though the door between us is locked. I heard footsteps in there awhile ago but couldn't tell if they belonged to a man or a woman. Then on my trip to the john I saw him standing in the center of his room. Did he open his door to get a glimpse of me? He must have heard me unpacking my suitcase and the inordinate noise of the dresser drawers as I put my clothes away.

He merely stared. So did I. About 5'8", stocky, or at least his brown beard, as full as Tolstoy's, gave him a chunky look. Don't know if I'll see him again during my three weeks of "intensive." Don't know much of *anything* right now. Wonder what he thought of me parading by in my sneakers, T-shirt, and old Bermudas. Feeling so bloated from a week of drinking and overeating, I had to get out of my trousers.

Rhoda said, "No writing, no reading, no excessive eating, no drinking—including wine." Does she take me for a connoisseur? Or a conniver who'll look for letters of the law? Before my three weeks are through I'll lose ten pounds, no doubt—and hopefully all of my past.

I don't think I like her. She was very standoffish, official.

But that might be "technique" here. Stan said they tend to be stern at first, then begin to relax once you get into things —if you ever do. Rewards of love for good behavior? That would be defeating the purposes of therapy, wouldn't it? She reminded me of a Catskill summer camp counselor whom you're surprised to see pressed into city clothes at the winter reunion.

The sounds in the hall are driving me up the wall now. There seems to be so much coming and going even on a Sunday afternoon. It's an act of will not to rush to the window and press my nose to the glass to see who's on the stone veranda. My writing all this down is probably very wrong too. An escape route. But I won't stay at it too long.

When Stan dropped me off at one, he said, "Make yourself miserable and you'll be closer to things tomorrow." Impossible. I've been so miserable so much of my life, I can't call up on cue what's already second nature by now. Where did I read that the neurotic *thinks* himself full of real feelings when he's merely being defensively emotional? Janov's *The Primal Scream,* no doubt. In reality, his emotions are only a cover-up, a struggle against *true* feeling. Then all those years of tears were for *nothing?* I can't believe it.

3:30 P.M.

I've spent the past two hours performing a dozen irrelevant tricks: trying to sleep, peeking through the curtains, doing RCAF exercises, trying the bathroom again, up and down, up and down, feeling nothing but irritable about being here now. And once more fearing that nothing at all will come of this method for me, that by now I'm frozen in too solidly for help. I can't bring myself to explore my childhood as Rhoda suggested I should. I've been through it too many goddamn times before, looking for reasons *why,* trying over and over again to understand what turned me into the mess I am, and making so many abortive attempts to come to terms with all my misery, all my mistakes.

I hate being here and I'm *bored.*

But that's what they want, isn't it? To make me hateful of it, bored—no, *anxious,* but without recourse to the usual ways away from that anxiety. If I were at home and feeling this low, by now I would've made a dozen defensive trips to the icebox, read half a novel, jogged, showered, washed my hair, jerked off, mixed a drink. Even now my stomach's registering hunger long before mealtime. I'll have to be tough on myself. No supper until seven, damn you! Otherwise I'll have too long an evening to kill.

Fewer noises now. Nothing next door. Has he gone out? Run away? I feel funny about exercising here. I'm afraid he'll hear me at it and laugh or tell me to stop. Is this his first day too?

I'm not certain how many live-in patients the house has room for or who's assigned to the local motels. First come, first served, I suppose, according to how many therapists are available. Stan discovered that if someone leaves before his three weeks' "intensive" is done, the Center quickly finds a replacement from its waiting list. A thriving business, I'd say. Well, there's lots of sickness around to thrive on.

There are at least four of us in the house now anyway, I know, because on the way back from the john awhile ago I noticed a middle-aged lady in a dressing gown drifting across the hall toward the second-floor bathroom. Blanche Dubois. Worn out, terribly sad. Does that mean that the process is working or that it *ain't?* Shit, despite the glimmer of new hope that brought me to apply here for therapy, I'm suddenly certain that this latest brand won't do any more good for me than the last one I bought.

That mirror against the wall. Should I put it in the closet? It's not a good one, distorted, but to *my* advantage at least. I almost look thin in it. For the sake of illusion I'll leave it out. No doubt I'll have a fine old time appraising my naked body—disapproving as usual.

Rhoda said, "No masturbating," in the same breath as "No excessive eating," and I had to stop myself from delivering a deceitful oh-I-never-do-*that!* look. I beat Alexander Portnoy by a mile.

The room is cold. Or is that me? I have to pee again but that'll be the third time and he might be listening through the door, or the lady in the bedroom adjoining the bath might get annoyed. (Why do I think it's a lady? I've no idea if it is. Might be important.) She might have left her latch off or the door ajar; I'd have to lock both hers from the bathroom side and the one leading from the hall; then as I leave, make sure to *unlock* hers. My God, I'm beginning to sound like some paranoid loon out of Edgar Allan Poe. But, God help me, that kind of self-consciousness is what's always going on inside my head, *always!*

5:30 P.M.

More of the same shenanigans: sitting on the rocker awhile, examining myself in the mirror (clothed), lying down, fixing a towel on the back of the chair, making a project of pissing, pacing, peeking out the window. For an hour at least.

Maybe it will help if I ask myself just who I am one more time, why I'm here—the old useless sorting-out routine:

NAME: Michael Rubin
AGE: Thirty-six. *In medias res.* Smack in the middle of my life.
BORN: February 17, 1935
PLACE OF BIRTH: Brooklyn, New York
HEIGHT: 5′10″, just.

WEIGHT: Around 165, at last, depending on supper and mood. Once tipped the scale at 185. Hovered at 170 until last year.

HAIR: Brown—and thinning too fucking fast.

EYES: Brown—soulful and wicked by turns.

COMPLEXION: Dark. A Jew.

PHYSICAL HEALTH: Okay. Minor thyroid deficiency; prone to colds, which the San Francisco weather doesn't help.

FATHER: Henry

DATES: July, 1907–January, 1964

PLACE OF BIRTH: New York, New York

MOTHER: Charlotte

DATES: September, 1910–October, 1962

PLACE OF BIRTH: Pittsburgh, Pennsylvania

Both of them dying so goddamn young . . .

SIBLINGS: Sister—born January, 1938, married 1959; mother of three, a daughter eight and one half, twin sons five and one half; and though younger than I, a surrogate mother to me.

Brother—born December, 1944; unmarried, *comme moi.*

CHILDHOOD RESIDENCES: All in the Flatbush section of Brooklyn:

Years

0–1: An apartment house, so my mother said.

1–3½: Upper floor of a two-family house, only a sun porch and long flight of steps remembered.

3½–7½: First floor of a two-family house on 15th Street. Family friends upstairs with a boy about a year older than I.

7½–13½: First floor of my father's parents' two-family house on 13th Street. They lived upstairs, as for a time did one of their married daughters, her husband and son, one and a half years older than I. I hated the place.

13½–16½: Our own house on Avenue R—which I loved.

16½: The Great Move: Hollybrook Farm, Brewster, New York. Fifty miles north of the city. A small farm and estate converted into a bungalow colony as a family business. (No comment. Not yet, not yet.)

CHILDHOOD SUMMERS:

6,7,8: The Hermitage. Walker Valley, New York—a big old boardinghouse and farm in the Catskills.

9,10,11,12: Camp Roosevelt, Monticello, New York—"for the discriminating." Ha! Shit on it.

13: Brooklyn. Stayed home in our new house. Adolescence paralyzing me.

14,15: Back to Camp Roosevelt. Less unbearable with counselors to fall in love with.

16: Our farm. Spent the summer stringing barbed wire around the fucking place.

And after? Is that at all important? The details of the rest of my life? Choices seem so predicated on the problems of the past. Bard College, a Fulbright year in Australia, tramping around Europe, Columbia for another degree so I could teach high school English in order to write fiction in order to help pay for the analyst in order to stick too damn close to home . . .

Amazing how much one can accomplish despite or *because* of one's sicknesses!

Symptoms, symptoms, you bastard, go ahead:

Chronic Depression—Blues that sweep over me for days on end, inexplicable and all-consuming, unleashing tears of amorphous self-pity, suicidal slumps. To some extent the worst of these depressions have dissipated during the past three or four years, only to be replaced by a kind of nattering resentment and all the more urgent yearnings for which I've found meaningless, if not utterly self-defeating outlets in flesh and fantasy.

Self-Hatred—There's a little man who sits inside my nasty head. His job is to hound me to death about my looks, my feelings, my thoughts, my actions. As long as I can remember, he's never let me be. He hates my voice, my weight, my face, my body, my writing, my teaching, my loving. Achieve some small degree of success, and the troll will find it false. Find me no longer disparaging the shape of my nose or the sound of my name, and the mean little bastard will discover thinning hair to despise, age to enrage him, wrinkles to worry me with. Good work scarcely done, and it's already less than best. A decent class concluded, a passage of prose I'm proud of, and it's not long before he's cursing me for my vanity, *me* cursing *me* for imagined failure or failed imagination.

Paranoia—Evil spawn of the troll. Everyone's looking at me! Looking at me! And I must find all my cues for living through the eyes of others. Autonomy? Never heard of the guy. I'm David Reisman's other-directed man, ogling reactions in order to calibrate my own. This one's laughing at me. This one finds me attractive enough. That one loathes what I'm wearing. That one's out for my blood. Often I've fancied that I enjoy looking at people because that's a writer's job—to search for revealing details of character. What I reveal by the search is the lie of my own.

Conversely, I also suffer from an angry withdrawal from all critical and prying eyes, effecting a furious determination to go my own way, to write, read, teach as I please—until anxiety grips me again and I fawn after approval.

Grudge-Bearing—An incessant need to blame my ills on others, to hold them responsible for my misery. Hot unspoken but potent anger against the significant people in my life for the slightest infractions against what I feel due me for my fidelity. No matter how deeply felt (albeit wrongly) an unwillingness to tell them, to *let them know,* which further feeds my grievance with silent spite.

Competitiveness—Not the open kind, no, no, not this hypocrite. But subtle and insidious. A mean streak of envy for what I feel are other men's greater value, better skills. And a secret steady operation to win favor away from them (from whom, from whom?) if only in the comfort of a daydream.

Guilt—Guilt for it all. Always. For everything!

Loneliness, Lovelessness, and Other Sexual Thrills—Homosexuality for one. Variety circa 1950. One whose quiver of shame has been dulled to grudged resignation for the last few years, an old-fashioned faggot who's still afraid to be found out and is dead sure everybody knows. And the lovers looked for? No perverse specialties or totemic color of hair. A preference for the two most popular types: (1) the comforting Older Man—to make up for Daddy, of course, of course; (2) the handsome all-American Boy—to make up for me. No whips and leather; the fraud's too patent (ha). No wasp-waisted queens; they're slightly more pathetic than I find myself. But the straight-looking, oh, yes, the well built, the ruggedly handsome, the understated, affectionate, wise. Why not? It's *my* wish fulfillment.

Heterosexuality? Sure. Nothing exclusive about me. Several affairs, and two or three lingering liaisons never properly concluded. Often we wind up being Great Friends. I'm so understanding. Such a good guy. I get invited to all their weddings.

Why won't I stick with the opposite sex? The usual crap, I guess: fear of what a sustained relationship might mean. That's true with the boys too, though there the escape clause is generally part of the contract. But with women I'm always afraid I'm doomed for life, panic-stricken at the prospect of failing to please, fulfill, entertain, intrigue. Whenever a deepening involvement is imminent, there rises in me a sense of suffocation, an anxious fear-ridden dread that she'll want more and more, much much more than I'm able to give, that my whole life will be sucked dry by her, that I will not be allowed my own—what?—integrity, my own *life!*

Well, I've never laid claim to being very original. And despite eight or more years of orthodox psychoanalysis I don't think I ever really got to the root of those fears at all. Time and again I learned that all that useless, fearful garbage was only in *me,* and that whatever its cause, as long as I realized that those fears were unfounded, I could use such sane knowledge to fight off my anxiety and finally walk in the gardens of heterosexual health. So how come I couldn't?

Add to the above a lingering dose of that good old American clap: "Sex is evil!" Women—sinners or saints. Their bodies—verboten or vile. Resolved somewhat with experience, but I still find it part of the unconscious equipment that allows me to camp more comfortably in other hunting grounds.

And while I'm on the subject, for good measure I might as well throw in my problem with premature ejaculation— with either sex. Habitual now, this disgusting inability to sustain myself long enough to enjoy a fuller sense of sensuality. Much of it has to do with the person I'm with. With Laura it was really getting to be good. But if it's Numbers Night at the Turkish Bath, I'm in and out and adding up the score along with the best of them. If it's some man or woman who might mean more—hell, the fear of finishing too soon is often enough to finish me.

After I'd disappointed her four or five times one night,

one kind girl once begged, "Think of other things." The trouble was, I was.

More? Sure, more.

Overeating—Vestigial remains of childhood's major compensation. But instead of the constant pillaging of mother's full refrigerator, or the stealing of bread to hide under my pillow for nibbling alone at night, nowadays it's binges—the virtue of a strict diet rewarded by a massive splurge. Abstinence, then just desserts. Oh, well, it keeps the weight down. I like to believe that my metabolism was inalterably damaged in infancy, that Mother fed me out of an excess of love. But something's always made me doubt that.

Urine Retention—An inability to urinate or move my bowels in public. No, not on street corners. But in public rest rooms, summer camp, college dorms, men's rooms around the world, any place where I can't be assured of great privacy; often not even a closed stall is enough protection if I feel someone's listening in on the sound of my shitting or pissing, waiting for the noise or the smell to start. Not even in private homes if I feel the presence of people beyond the door, fear they're within earshot. Funny? Very funny. I've canceled vacation trips, refused evenings out, weekends with friends because of it. One summer, commuting from the farm into New York City for a factory job where only open johns were available, I used to piss at 5:30 A.M. at home, then not again until I returned around 7 P.M. God knows what damage I did to my kidneys.

Assorted Little Joys

A voice that often pitches too high to whine and beg, afraid even the simplest request will be rebuffed.

Unctuous smiles unfelt but forced on my face to please.

A laugh added to my own punch lines in order to cue an audience in on the appreciation I crave.

A penny-wise/pound-foolishness.

An excessive fear of physical pain or risk—that my body will kill me with its clumsiness or the ease with which it might bruise.

Compulsive planning, organizing, clock watching.

The automatic recourse into fantasies of future success, holding incessant conversations with myself, fashioning letters, speeches, seminars, stories—"creative" to some extent, but such an obvious way to compensate for and control my present reality. Sigmund Freud says that thinking is really a form of rehearsing. I spend so much time rehearsing that I never know when I'm already onstage.

So much for symptoms. Causes? Cures? Shit, I've certainly had my share of help in trying to find both. Doctors and textbooks galore filling me with descriptions, prescriptions, dicta, doubt:

My Frog Pond

Dr. E—Family physician. An attractive and troubled man who was dabbling at the time in psychology and assorted nurses. I was sent to him by my parents after we moved to Brewster. At age sixteen I was terrified of starting my senior year in a strange high school, scared enough even to confess to my folks my fear of homosexuality, though not the rest of it: my depressions, suicidal urges, urine retention, *et al*. Dr. E saw me once a week all through that year. Pleasant discussions. It was good having someone to talk to at least. But now, the only distinct memory I have of those sessions was my eyeing in the waiting room a handsome college jock who saw Dr. E the same evenings I did. For monkey glands, right?

Dr. H—At college. A psychiatrist whom I shared for a year and a half with the rest of the nuts on campus one afternoon a week. We assumed he was an administrative stooge who reported all our neuroses to the Registrar. He looked like Ernest Hemingway and told me that once upon a time he'd worked as a cabin boy and was slapped hard on his ear by the captain for eating freshly baked bread. Fresh bread is hard to digest, I gathered, and no man could be spared for a bellyache. I never ate freshly baked bread again.

I also remember trying to get him to tell me the name of another student whom he mentioned he was also treating for homosexuality. (It was still that time in my life when I thought there was only one other gay guy in the world, and he lived somewhere near Paris. It was thrilling to learn of a third.) Outside of some guilt-ridden and uninspiring mutual masturbation with the boys in camp and with a classmate in Brooklyn, I'd never been to bed with anyone. Dr. H wouldn't comply. Soon after that he sustained a heart attack and had to give up his afternoons. The college never hired me any more help.

Dr. X—Fifteen minutes. At my draft board examination. The nicest shrink in the world:

"I see you have listed yourself as homosexual. Is that true?"

"Yes, Doctor."

"You practice it?"

"Whenever I can."

"You cannot control your impulses?"

"I don't rape little boys in the street, if that's what you mean. But worse than that, I can't urinate in public. I suffer from terrible urine retention. Here's a note from my family doctor."

"Ah, I see. You know, I don't think you would be very happy in the Army."

"Neither do I."

"Funny, you don't *look* queer."

"Why, thank you."

"But I can see your point. You are 4-F. I suggest you find

an analyst, though I don't know what good that would do."
That was in 1958. Few were conscientiously objecting to
anything then. Today my excuse could be moral. In those
days it seemed rank cowardice. With repercussions. Those
"private" reports of my 4-F status were somehow allowed to
be seen by the New York City school system, which caused a
long delay in my getting a city license (one which I never
used anyway) and an embarrassing interview with another
analyst who said I looked awfully nervous but since the city
needed teachers, he'd let me through. Worse than that,
three years later I was turned down by the Peace Corps.
NFA. No faggots allowed. Oh, Gay Lib, where were you
when I was a boy?

Dr. M—1959-67. On whom I was bestowed as a clinic patient while he was still a resident at the Psychoanalytic Institute in New York. An awful union lasting far too long for
both of us. Deep psychoanalysis four times a week for three
years, three times a week for two, two for three more, and
more. On my side a stormy love/hate relationship that ex-
posed to me my worst patterns of behavior without helping
me modify them at all, which made me hate myself all the
more thoroughly for being such a failure.

On his side? Should I dare suggest he had his own problems? He never admitted to any, of course. But I *still* suspect he was the kind of shrink that Allen Wheelis writes
about in *The Quest for Identity*: the guy who becomes an
analyst in order to have his emotional distance validated
and kept intact. If body language tells anything at all, Dr.
M walked around looking as if he had a pole shoved up his
ass. Splayed teeth indicated either an inveterate thumb-
sucker or a baby trying to save himself from choking to
death on his tongue. Rapid balding suggested poor blood
circulation and a crummy sugar-loaded diet.

Am I bitter? Yes, I am bitter.

Toward the end of our liaison, when we were both pretty
much disgusted with so little to show for so many years of

effort and strain, in a rare moment of open honesty, Dr. M confessed that I often reminded him too much of the worst things in himself, which had continually made him feel uncomfortable in the "analytic situation." *Now* he tells me! After eight and a half years!

Why did I stay so long? I was desperately unhappy, damn it! I wanted to get *better!* (No matter *what* Freud might say about resistance. I couldn't have been *that* sick, to use all that time, money, energy just to prove to the world that I couldn't or *wouldn't* get well.) Besides, since I was a clinic patient (and subsequently, a legacy to his private practice), the cost of my treatment was cheaper than I could ever find elsewhere. On my teacher's salary I sure as hell didn't have the money to look further afield. What's more, the alternatives always seemed second-best. I mean, after all, there I was being *psychoanalyzed,* wasn't I? Not by any fly-by-night clinical psychologist or some cheap psychiatric *social* worker. I was having my life redone by the bona fide thing. A *doctor* with all the right degrees. And finally, I was so emotionally tied up with Dr. M, I couldn't abide the thought of leaving. Misguided compassion on his part, probably, to indulge my fear for so long. But I suspect I was also his personal test case, his toughest nut to crack. Occasionally I still wonder how he takes our failure. Win some, lose some, *tant pis?*

After our final break (there were several brief attempts during those years) I deliberately refrained from keeping in touch with him. Recently I heard he's now an administrator in some geriatric hospital on Staten Island. He deserves Staten Island. But I pity the old folks.

Dr. L—1967. Dr. M sent me to him. One visit.

"A homo, eh? Well, I'll have to see you twice a week at thirty-five bucks a shot, plus two evening group sessions which'll run you twenty apiece. Don't worry. I'll give you the fathering you need. In three or four years, you'll probably be okay."

Better sick than sorry, I never returned, although at his request I'd already taken a series of comprehensive psychological tests for $150 from:

Dr. J—Who concluded I suffered from "severe emotional deprivation." Oh. "From suicidal tendencies." Do tell. "And a penchant for relating more fully to fantasy than to reality." It's true, it's true! But could *I* help it if I kept seeing Helen Hayes in a funny little hat on every goddamn Rorschach card?

Dr. T—1967-68. One and a half years. Not long enough. But all the money I could spare before running West. A kind and good man recommended to me by a cousin who'd been in his care. "Existentially oriented," whatever that means. Anyway, a man who had the sense to let me sit up and look him in the eye, to talk back to me and register emotions like a human being rather than hide behind Dr. M's traditional analytic couch and silent stone-faced wall. A sympathetic man who wanted very much to ease my agony. He tried hard to make me feel better about myself. Supportive, encouraging, *there*. But ultimately it seemed to me a mere "holding" action, a survival ploy, a *coping* rather than a cure. I still wonder, though, if I might not have done very well with him if he'd been my analyst from the start.

Nor can I forget my intense and/or spotty attention to the following assortment of wise old lizards and self-deluded little newts: Sigmund Freud, Alfred Adler, Carl Jung, Harry Stack Sullivan, Wilhelm Reich, Erik Erikson, Rollo May, Abraham Maslow, Victor Frankl, Karen Horney, Allen Wheelis, Bruno Bettelheim, Alexander Lowen, Gordon Allport, R. D. Laing, Carl Rogers, Fritz Perls, Arthur Janov, Alan Watts, Paul Goodman, William Schutz, Eric Berne, Rose Franzblau, Abigail Van Buren, Ron Hubbard, and Maxwell Maltz.

I pray with all my heart that the therapists here at the

Marin Center for Intensive Therapy are not just more frogs
for that overstocked pond.

Of course I'm probably looking for miracles. Last year
when I read *The Primal Scream* by Arthur Janov, I was
overwhelmed. Here was this guy claiming what I'd come to
suspect: Therapeutic insights are worthless unless part of
an *affective* experience. Connections between your craziness
and its cause have to be made not through the intellect, but
through your deepest *feelings*. Symptoms will only truly
settle themselves when you allow yourself to relive the
impact of their original pain, symptoms really only being a
struggling denial of that pain. I immediately saw myself
lying there on Dr. M's couch all those stupid years *talking*
my way out of my body, out of my feelings, mind-fucking
my way out of my sick life, and getting sicker for it.

Unfortunately, when I applied to the Primal Institute in
L.A., I discovered a waiting list over two years long with no
guarantee of acceptance. In the meantime I learned that
this place in San Rafael was doing similar work. I managed
to get an interview here only to learn from Dr. Rosen, one
of the directors, that there is no professional connection between this center and Janov's institute. Primal theory, he
explained, has been evolving out of the work of many important contributors—Ferenczi, Reich, Lowen, Janov,
among others. There's no patent on it. The therapists here
use the techniques of primal theory as well as certain prin-
ciples of Gestalt psychology and the lessons of their own
professional experience. Dr. Rosen made it clear that they
were not out to promise any magical mystical cures. Nor
were they selling "birth primals" as the ultimate experience. Cures? Hell, he made the goal of their work here
less than appealing: *to come to be totally in touch with
one's basic feelings.* That's what I'm supposed to start
fighting for here. And even if I win my way there, the place
ain't gonna be much fun. Nor, as far as Dr. Rosen is concerned, is it likely that I'll ever finish the fight. It's unrea-

sonable, he warned me, to expect a patient to emerge from this therapy or any other completely whole again, absolutely anxiety-free. The therapists here refuse to claim this method to be a political revolution or the messianic answer to the world's ills. All they hope to do is bring a patient closer to an open acceptance of his shortchanged reality and all the pains that forged it.

Shit, and here I sit still hoping it won't hurt.

8:40 P.M.

Jesus, some woman—Blanche Dubois, I guess—is screaming her lungs out upstairs, right above my head, stamping her life out on the floor! It's horrifying. An awful repetition of: "God damn you! I hate you! I hate you!" Such rage. It frightens me to think I might have to do that soon too. But I'm also scared I *won't* be able to get into such a deep expression of pain. That's what I'm *supposed* to do here, I know. But it's unbelievable—that witchlike croaking.

Suddenly, right now, I feel disconnected from it. Almost . . . amused.

Since supper I've been lying around finally getting into some remembrance of things past. Writing out that long nasty history helped. But now it doesn't seem to mean much. My childhood disassociated from my life. More suitable for fiction, if anything.

She's still screaming. As though she were dying.

I wish I could be more terrified by it. My defense, I guess, is to think of it almost as comical. I feel cold and numb now. Clinically interested but unaffected. I wish I could be with her up there, to hear more closely what it is that's killing her, what she can rage against like that.

What is it in me that scares me from doing the same thing if they tell me to, what is it that I *can't* rage against?

Oh, sure, sure, I remember wishing my father dead dozens of times. I hated him from the start. I feared him, resented him, *loathed* him. But he's dead. It's finished business. Finished? Shit. Psychoanalysis convinced me that my excessive attachment to my mother led to my resentment and fear of my father, à la any old Oedipus complex. Dad was a threat to my security with Mom. Okay, I buy that. I *bought* it. Then why in hell didn't it *help?*

Now some guy upstairs has joined the shrieking cat. When I went to the john a couple of minutes ago I saw him coming into the house carrying a cardboard sign reading: BERKELEY. He must have hitchhiked over. He hurried up the stairs and went into one of the vacant offices. But I can hear him all right. He wants to die. He keeps screaming that out. An unholy racket. Banging, banging on the floor. Blanche still shrieking. The hitchhiker screaming. A lunatic asylum.

I had trouble urinating too. I was so sure that the girl in the bedroom adjoining the john was listening that I had to run the tap, and even then it was a struggle. It *is* a girl. I saw her earlier on my way out to supper. She knows me now. It'll be so damn rough. I'll be constipated for days.

Are there private sessions here on Sunday night? I don't understand this: Just now through the corner of the drape I spied on a therapist (at least I *think* she's a therapist because she parked her roadster in the small parking lot next to the house) coming into the building. A young redhead in a maxi-coat. I'm in a madhouse run by teen-agers! Well, if nothing begins to happen in a day or two, I'll leave, that's all. Fuck the money.

He's still banging his heart out upstairs. If all that screaming won't cure him, what will?

The diner across the way—part of another motel along the avenue—is awful. Stan told me the food there was pretty good, but he also admitted that during his three

weeks here his sinuses were so clogged up he wasn't tasting
very well. I told myself I'd start a diet tonight and, instead,
wound up ordering french fries with my hamburger and ice
cream for dessert. I'll have to do better tomorrow. Keep up
with my exercises too.

10:10 P.M.

I'm tired and bored and haven't been thinking about
anything but how deprived I feel. Can't even find it in me
to blame anyone for making it come to this. "That it should
come to this!" *Hamlet* Act I, Sc. ii (*sic?*): "Oh, that this too
too solid flesh would melt—and mess up the stage."

Amazing how distracting that window can be. Movement, color, the slightest change registers like a seismo-
graph. A cat crossing the road is 8.5 on the Richter scale. A
sunset—the end of the world. I think of my father now,
chained to the dark in his blindness, and how subtle his
hearing became.

Awhile back the crying stopped. Failure, impasse? Must
the guy now hitchhike home uncured?
  I've got gas. I'll have to relieve myself after taps.
  I wish to God I were home in front of my color TV.
  "Oh, Lord, won't you buy me a Mercedes-Benz!"
  Shit, I've got to take this anxiety far more seriously.
  I'm not sure anymore what this waiting is expected to *do!*
I can't stand this damn isolation. I can't just go over and
over and over again that fucking childhood of mine. Such a
waste. All those years of useless psychoanalytic review. I feel
more detached than depressed right now, though.
  God, I wish it were morning. Maybe tomorrow night I'll
be able to scream myself to sleep.

Monday

Slept in twenty-minute stints all night long. Up at 5:00 or so. Feeling neutral. Worrying about the john as usual. Went at 6:00, washed, no bowel movement—and probably woke the girl early by not doing it all later when good people do.

Some dreams, but can't remember. Think my mother was involved. Am still reconstructing events in those Brooklyn houses, the neighborhood, my crummy times there. Recalled for the first time in years the look of a front sun-room on 15th Street and the light through yellow lace curtains. That was the room where Larry from upstairs threw me against the radiator and cracked my head. Traumatic, I guess. Blood. I have the scar to prove it. And now I also remember the time that tinker toy piece rammed down my throat. My own fault for running with it in my mouth. Gushes of blood and guts, the doctor coming. My throat was sore for weeks. Maybe that's where it all started: one minute happy while playing a game with Mom, the next my insides coughed up like shreds of rubber.

I remember the Mortimers on the corner. They had hollyhocks and Christmas trees, and their house smelled of graham crackers. Mary Mortimer was in my class at school. I played with her and Eddie, her younger brother. The other two, Jackie and Billy, were older. Jackie was the one I had to impress. A hard thin kid. I was a butterball. Can't remember ever feeling comfortable with the boys on that block. Preferred being with Mary Mortimer or with Margery Langsam across the street. Only Alan next door was nice to me, took me to Saturday matinees and baby-sat for us. I was scared of the mythical 14th Street gang around the corner and the teen-agers in the middle of the block who teased us about having to pay a toll to get down to Kings Highway. I was afraid of everyone.

That puppet show: afraid to sit with the other kids down front in the dark. My mother allowed me to stay with her, but I knew I was doing something *wrong*, that I should've gone off with the other kids. Shades of Proust. But where did that fear originate?

I can't remember my father during this time at all. Just my avoiding him and his damned menacing presence.

1:05 P.M.

All the preceding seems irrelevant now.

Rhoda knocked at my door at 9:30. Asked me to come upstairs. Immediate dislike for her noncommittal sternness —a professional manner she's probably learned from some goddamn textbook, or finds necessary to keep her protected from the maniacs. Dr. M all over again! She introduced me to a trainee—a black girl, ha! having to listen to my middle-class white Jewish problems.

The girl's presence didn't disturb me, nor did Rhoda's until she—wait.

In the semidarkened office she tells me to lie down on a black leather mat, a box of tissues nearby. She asks me to breathe deeply—arms spread out, legs spread out, making me feel awfully vulnerable. Always dutiful, I do as directed and feel myself beginning to get dizzy from so much deep breathing.

Does she sense it? She says, "Say 'Mama.' "

Like a baby doll, I say, "Mama."

She says, "Again."

"Mama," I say. Then again. And again.

I don't know how or why, but eventually I begin to say it for its own sake, and at Rhoda's suggestion, louder and louder: "Mama. Mama! Mama!!"

And before I know what's happening I find myself weeping and then screaming it out, calling for her: "Mama. Mama! Mama!!"

Rhoda tells me to pound the mat.

I scream louder. I pound. Pound. Pound.

Eventually she asks, "What are you feeling?"

I have to think, to define the heat and the constrictions in my body. "Anger," I tell her, though I'm not sure *why* I feel angry. "Fear," I say, though I'm not sure why I should be feeling afraid.

"Let it out!" Rhoda shouts. "Feel it. Feel it!"

I try to feel that anger and fear more intensely. It comes out as more screaming, more pounding, more calling for my mother.

But it only proves a mere preamble:

Soon I begin to find myself writhing. I can't believe this is me! *I* don't writhe like this. I break out into a deeper sweat—hot, burning. Steaming! I'm wet from head to toe.

It doesn't go on too long. I relax and find myself crying softly. I chance to say something, mentioning an early misgiving (I can't remember what now) but Rhoda cuts my talk short. She tells me to call for my mother to come to me. (Yes, that's what the misgiving was—something about waiting for my mother to come.) I do as she bids and find myself—God—*begging* my mother to come to me, begging like a little kid. Suddenly I'm feeling like the kid I once was on those nights when I called to her out of fear that there were robbers in the house, and I was the only one awake listening to the creaking floors. I call to her as I did one night while suffering from an awful toothache and she slept on with my father in their room, leaving me alone to suffer alone in the dark. I become overwhelmed suddenly by a terribly sad feeling that my mother won't come to comfort me no matter how long I cry for her. Rhoda asks me how that makes me feel now.

Angry. Angry. But I'm muttering it to myself. More sad about something than angry. Then feeling angrier for my mother not coming to help me, to tell me there are no robbers, to stop my tooth from aching.

"Say it!"

"I'm angry. I hate her for that!"

"Tell her!"

"I hate you for that! I hate you!" I'm telling my mother I hate her for that! My dead mother. I've never told her that before! Never! Never even *thought* it before, I swear!

But I say it again and again now—on and on and on. Pounding. Writhing. Screaming out my hatred for her not coming to help me, for her never coming when I needed her! Losing all sense of time and place.

Still, in spite of all this intensity, I sense a certain hesitation, an inner reservation, an unwillingness to let myself go utterly, to admit something even worse, to feel something that goes beyond my sudden, almost all too easy hatred.

I insist on talking. An escape from feeling more of this? I mention to Rhoda how I always felt forced to be the "good" one in our family, not like my sister, who was always getting punished for being bad. I'd do almost anything to please my mother. And then, out of the blue it occurs to me: "But it never seemed to be enough for her."

"Tell her!" Rhoda shouts.

"It was never enough for you! It's never enough, Mother!"

I'm amazed by this, never having ever been at all conscious before of so little reward for all that work to please my mother. Of course! Always I had to do more and more to prove my love, to prove I was *worth* her loving me!

"How does that make you feel?"

"It makes me—hate her."

"*Tell her!*"

"I hate you, Mother. I hate you!"

And worse: "You killed me! You killed me!" I find myself screaming now.

Then there's a lull. I feel spent. I tell Rhoda that I want to get back to a time when I felt okay.

She startles me: "You never had a chance to feel okay, Mike."

I begin to suspect she's right. All these feelings I'm having as I lie there on the floor seem to be going back so damn far, far beyond a time when I was even conscious of *trying* to be a good little boy to win my mother's love. But Rhoda's blaming it on her now, so fast, so easily, makes me feel I have to protest, to defend my mother. I don't say anything, though. I'm just feeling the unfairness of that blame inside me.

Then Rhoda says, "The Jewish Mother did it."

I rear at that simplistic idea and insist that my mother was more complicated than that old cliché. I hate Rhoda then. Hate being on the floor. Being here.

I try to explain my mother's problems to her.

Rhoda immediately asks me how that feels too.

I say I feel sad for my mother. But then, without even bothering to ask myself why, I suddenly find myself beginning to blame my mother for making me feel sad too, for making me identify with her nervousness and her sad, sad eyes in order to win her approval. My God, incorporating all her problems into me! Making myself over to be just like her. To *be* her! Feeling so guilty if I wasn't just what she wanted me to be! I begin banging and writhing and screaming and sweating again. Terrible, terrible. Then my stomach begins to ache like hell. I tell Rhoda.

"How does it feel?" she wants to know.

Damn her, *how does it feel?* "In knots. Knots!"

"Your mother tied you into knots like that."

She asks me to scream out my rage at being tied into knots. But the pain in my guts is so fierce I have to stop. I feel I'll vomit, that I have colitis all over again, the way I'd suffered with that and nervous stomachs all through my adolescence. It's unbearable. Hot twisting knots in my guts. I want to curl up, sleep, but Rhoda insists that I remain face up, spread-eagle, that I *feel* it. I can't! I can't dare feel any more of this!

I rest a minute. We try again. Instantly the stomach pains recur. I'm scared out of my skull. I see stars, think I'm dying, that I'll throw up. I begin gagging.

"That's a feeling. *Feel it!*" Rhoda screams, but I have to stop, I just have to. I've felt it, haven't I? Wasn't that *enough?* Do I have to feel it *more* deeply? I can't see *how!*

She says, "Look at your hands. What are they doing?"

They're clutching the ends of the mat. I say, "I'm afraid to lose control."

She says, "Let go. Let yourself go!"

But as soon as I do, my stomach aches too much and I want to vomit again.

For some reason the tightness I feel makes me mention my trouble with pissing, how I always have to be quiet about it.

"Sure, a quiet, good little boy. No noise."

Rhoda lets me relax a few minutes and announces that we'll stop there today.

While I'm picking myself up off the floor, she sternly adds, "You'll have to decide to feel that, Mike. Otherwise—"

In tears again I mutter, "If I feel it any more there's going to be vomit all over the floor," and run out of her office trying to slam her goddamn door to let her know how she's hurting me.

God, I *hated* that pep talk, but I was in no condition to complain about such absurd ultimatums. My head was aching and I was still shaking in a sweat, my stomach a basketful of snakes eating up my guts. As soon as I got downstairs, I scrambled into bed and desperately sought relief in sleep. Didn't doze, but remained immobile until after noon.

Then I took a shower and dressed. Those stomach pains are still with me right now. Fine. Just fine. All I need out of this is a colitis condition again.

I'm writing this in my room now after lunch. Ordered a lot of tea to soothe my hoarse throat. Couldn't eat much. It feels a little less raw, but not that dull aching in my guts—that's still there. And I feel woozy. I seem to have a permanent headache. No aspirins allowed. I'm supposed to *feel* my headaches too, I guess. Shit. All I feel is washed out, hurting, and scared stiff of the impact of those stomach pains if they really get going again.

As I walked back from the diner, I saw Dr. Rosen coming up the driveway. I imagined his saying, "How's it going?" And my replying, "You've given me back my colitis, damn you!"

And immediately I saw just what I always do to people—blame them for *my* pains. But with this astounding new connection for me: in the same way my mother subtly indicated that I was responsible for hers!

Still, I'm not absolutely convinced that the stomach pains weren't brought on by my current constipation or the simple pressure of all that screaming and banging. Whatever the cause, I don't want to feel them anymore! I don't!

Must I? Oh, shit—*Must I?* I'm sitting here remembering now the number of upset stomachs I had as a kid. My major childhood complaint. If Rhoda's right about it, was I calling for relief from those knots even then? But my mother was *best* to me when I was sick. It was easy to be her good little boy when I was sick in bed, being nursed by her. Sure, sure—for the time being I didn't have to *show* her how good I could be, being nothing but her thankful, helpless baby again.

Now I remember that sometime during the session I told Rhoda how I often used to hide bread under my pillow to eat at night.

"Taking to bed a piece of your mother—" she said.

Very Freudian. Very smart-alecky. The bitch!

But *true,* damn it, true. I heard the same thing from Dr. M. Yet today it seemed a completely fresh revelation. It made me cry so. I *felt* what that meant. For the first time I felt what it must have meant, to have to steal bread to take to bed because I'd never get enough of my mother. Oh, shit. I'm crying over it again right now.

I also recall now mentioning my clumsiness to Rhoda, and trying to analyze it for her as I'd been so long trained to do.

"That's all in the mind," she said abruptly.

I stopped. God forbid you should *think* or *talk* about things around here. Feel them. Feel them. Feel them. But I'm still so damned afraid—

4:35 P.M.

Yesterday I was listening to every sound in and out of the house, gathering clues like a blind man to establish my cues for conduct. Right now I couldn't care less. I avoid the window, hardly hear the hallway sounds. The screams get to me from upstairs, the pounding shaking the ceiling, the agonized shrieks. But not essentially. Maybe they should. But I'd rather shut out the world now, feel blank.

While lying here these past few hours one of a thousand thoughts involved my "David Susskind Complex" as a friend of mine calls it: my need to lead the classroom discussion, to maneuver the living-room conversation, to *shape* reality to some satisfying conclusion as though I fear what would happen if it went its own way. Is that part of this stomach thing? Some certain fear of pain if control gets

away from me? A possibility. Either it's effective organization or total chaos, and with chaos—what?—*pain?* And if I
let myself *feel* that pain and no one comes to *relieve* it, then
what does that mean? Oh, shit. I can't even write it. I don't
dare. I can't. I can't!

I just remembered the word "colic." When I was older,
my mother told me I'd been born with colic. Gas. She said
it had made me cry a lot during the first few weeks of my
life. Did she also suggest that I'd been troublesome then? I
seem to hear that somewhere inside me now. An unspoken
indication that I had been a troublesome baby. This is farfetched, but is it possible that instead of feeling I was crying
for my mother about a toothache or imaginary robbers in
the house, I was actually feeling the terror of an even earlier time—a time when I was still in my crib, crying for my
mother, or at least for some comforting mother-thing, and
never *did* get enough of a response from the creature who
was supposed to care for my life? Maybe she never managed
to ease that physical pain in those first days outside of her
body, or couldn't, or wouldn't, or didn't know how!
Oh, shit, how can I blame her for being unloving? Yet
now, for the first time in my life, *for the first time,* I *must*
reckon with her inability to stop that pain no matter *when*
it might have hurt. Why else would I have felt forced to do
all those good-little-boy things to win her caring, or at least
to remain assured of it? God, in over eight years of analysis
I never got into any of this at all.

6:25 P.M.   1725563

Tonight I've been asked to leave the house between 7:30
and 9:30. There's the regular evening group session at the
Center, and Rhoda told me not to attend this first time.

Stan mentioned how terrifying they could be if you're not ready for them—twelve to twenty patients doing in concert what I did alone this morning. I don't mind postponing that little pleasure. And by going out tonight at least I won't have to hear the ceiling coming down as it did all afternoon, or listen again to the pathetic boy who crumpled down on the carpet outside my door to moan "I need you!" for half an hour. Not *me*. Some mother. Some father. I tried to feel that with him, but couldn't. I've become a somnambulist again.

As a matter of fact, right now I feel that, outside of that colic insight (if it's at all true), my whole afternoon alone was a waste for me. I didn't dare feel myself into any new pain. My stomach's still twisted and my head still aches. Enough for one day, Rhoda! But with so much time in which to do some "serious feeling," I know it's been a loss. What's more, I'm already working on the assumption that Rhoda hates my guts for not feeling *enough* up there this morning. I feel guilty for not pleasing her, and angry enough over *that* stupidity so as not to *want* to work at this. Nothing new about that craziness!

I'd like to complain to her about all this, but the therapy seems so antitalk, I'm afraid she'll just shout, "That's bullshit!" the way Stan told me she shouted at him during one of his group sessions. In her own way she's just as demanding as my mother. That's important to talk about too, but will the bitch allow that kind of exchange? How do they reckon with transference around here?

I'll see how I feel in the morning. If it still rankles, I'll tell her!

Oh, sure, now I just realized that I'm only desperately trying to say, "Mommy, don't let it hurt so!" Maybe I should start from there. Because, damn it, it's really *hurting!*

I still haven't been able to move my bowels. At 7 tonight I'll leave for a hot time in the swinging town of San Rafael.

Maybe I'll treat myself to a laxative. Or isn't that allowed either?

9:30 P.M.

9:30—returned right on the dot. All too punctual, as always. Lots of shoes and sweaters in the hallway, but little sign of life. Oh, oh, I can hear some mild weeping upstairs now. Stan told me that the last half hour of these groups is spent in some sort of discussion work. I guess I'll find out about that soon enough.

After a crummy meal in a True-Western-Style-Ranch-Type-Barbeque-Serve-Your'n-Self-Cafeteria, I shuffled around San Rafael to stake out the territory. The restaurants open at night seem few. Stan said there was one Chinese place that was okay, but with his taste buds gone during his time here, who knows? I'd better find some decent food soon. My face'll soon be breaking out from all these goddamn french fried potatoes.

Later on I found the Montecito Shopping Center. A laundromat and supermarket I can use. I bought myself an apple to help along tonight's bedtime treat of Ex-Lax.

But as I walked around the area going nowhere, killing time, I was caught short by an overwhelming sense of desolation, a terrible need to cut out of here. I almost did. I just didn't want to go on with any more of this.

And I still feel so damned *alone* with it right now. I want Stan to be here to comfort me. But I blame him too for not telling me just how *awful* this would be. And I blame myself now for not being more thoughtful to him after he came back to our apartment after his three weeks here. But how could I? I didn't know the pain he must have faced.

Except for the stomach agonies (I notice I write "the" instead of "my." I'm always doing that, disassociating myself from *me*) the suffering—*my* suffering today has now dissipated itself into a general misery that I usually narcotize with food, booze, books, TV, sex. "I left my props in San Francisco. . . ."

The crowd is leaving. Very quietly. Comforting.

God, again I just *hate* being here. I feel drained and so damned depressed. Lonely as hell. I want to run away. I can't stand this emptiness and the threat of more agony tomorrow. This is no way to run an airline.

Tuesday

No wonder Stan told me he lost all interest in sex during his "intensive." After one of these sessions you're too dead to do much more than lie around like a sick dog. Shock treatments and shots of heroin probably do the same. I've been totally spent since my session ended around 11.

Rhoda knocked at 9:30 again and was already halfway up the stairs before I even got out of my room. That damned professional distance! I didn't care. Or maybe cared too much. Anyway, I was still too miserable from the hour or more I'd spent on the floor of my room trying to feel through yesterday's session again—and fearing the onset of that stomachache—to let her mean tactics intrude.

As soon as I lay down on the black mat, I told her I was angry with her, but it gushed out with tears. She was asking more than I could give! I insisted. I was furious at her for wanting me to suffer more of this pain. And before I was finished, even without her saying a word, I had to admit again that it was really Mother I'd been furious with since yesterday.

"Tell her," says Rhoda with her limited vocabulary.

"I'm angry! I'm angry, Mother. Angry! You're hurting me! You're making my stomach ache!"

And away I go again—pounding, sweating, screaming it all out.

Such a mixed bag of emotions: Anger for my mother making me suffer so. Pain in my gut instantly returning (though not nearly so intense). Sadness at not wanting to blame it on her.

"Why not, Mike?"

"She wasn't guilty. Her sadness was real!" I weep as I recall to myself the obligations and strains she put on herself —tending my father in his blindness, taking care of her aging crazy parents, three children, that goddamn bungalow colony.

Then as though I've been explaining all this out loud, I suddenly shout: "But it wasn't my fault either!"

"That's right," says Rhoda. "Tell her."

"It may not be your fault, Mother—but it's not mine either! It's not mine that you suffered! It's not my fault! It's not!"

Boy, it's so hard to account now for all that went on during the session. So much was experienced unsaid, *seeing* it instead in fleeting images, feeling it without words.

Somewhere during the hour I remember I got a sense of my awful childhood fears of being alone in the dark. My old terror of being kidnapped. (While walking back to the Center last night I'd momentarily felt as afraid of the shadows along the avenue as I ever had been of running home in the dark after Hebrew school in Brooklyn.) I told Rhoda how, after a bad kidnapping dream, for about a year I'd carried notes in my pocket which I'd somehow try to drop if I were stolen from home. "I'm kidnapped," the note read. "But don't worry."

Wow, that "don't worry" suddenly got to me.

Don't worry! I was telling my mother not to worry because that was all I *could* say to get her to love me! Don't worry, Mom. I won't make waves! I won't vomit! Not like my sister, who was always vomiting and throwing tantrums to tell them how she was feeling when she wasn't allowed to tell them straight either! "I won't piss! I won't shit!" I shouted. "I won't make noise! I'll be good! I'll be quiet!"

My stomach begins to grind again.

"Let it out, Mike!"

"You bitch! You bitch! You bitch! Nothing was enough for you. Nothing!" On and on, howling it until my throat's raw again and I'm drenched with sweat.

Rhoda lets me relax awhile. I feel my stomach pains ease. I tell her so. "How does that feel?" she asks.

"Good."

"What was in there?"

"Knots."

"Years of knots," she says. "It feels good to get them out." (Thank you, Dr. Ginott.)

But I begin to cry softly, feeling so guilty now for betraying my mother with this sense of raging freedom. I plead, "She wasn't always doing that. She did good things too—"

"I know," Rhoda says with surprising kindness, and a kind of sadness of her own.

Of my own accord I add, "But it wasn't enough."

"That's right. It was never enough. Tell her!"

I begin screaming it out again. And again. And again. And again! Pounding it. Pounding! My stomach pains begin to disappear only to lodge in my chest. They rise to my throat.

"Let it out, Mike!"

I gag, but try to keep with it this time, my head bursting. But I *do!* I keep with it, with the pain, the nausea of it all—until in a lull again I find myself calling for her: "Help me, Mommy! Don't let me be afraid! Be there! Let me be with you!" And then I cry: *"Let me die with you!"*

After I recover from that awful feeling a little, I tell Rhoda that I suspected that my mother, who died of leukemia at the ripe old age of fifty-two, had really killed herself; that is, she'd *let* herself die from distress over her responsibilities. It was the only way the poor woman had of getting out of her sad mess. It had been too much for her. Her life *always* had. That poor sick woman. Too much for her. (I'm crying again now as I write this. I can't help myself. It was too damned much for her.)

"How did that make you feel?"

"Like—she wanted to leave me too."

"As before."

Still in tears, I tell Rhoda that I spent the year after my mother's death weeping for her, but never about this awful possibility—that she had let herself die to be rid of *me*, of *all* of us. I was part of the mess she'd made for herself, and she finally just had to quit it all by dying.

"Don't leave me!" I begin to scream over and over again. "I want you! I need you, Mommy! I need you! I need you!"

Suddenly I'm almost floating. My blood's beating through my body like an electric current. I'm breathing like a hurricane. I can't do anything but lie there caught by it, astonished.

"I'm tingling," I tell Rhoda.

"How does that make you feel?"

"I don't know. Like my blood is in my fingertips and toes and I've never felt it there before."

I lie there practically *hearing* my blood running through my body. Breathing more deeply and fully than I can ever remember. All the controls I've been practicing for years to keep my stomach in, my chest high—believing I was holding in my gut when I was really only holding down my rage —they're all suddenly loosening! I've never breathed with my stomach like this before. Usually only with the upper part of my chest. All this ranting and raving seems to have pushed it down where it belongs. Where I must have been born breathing.

Rhoda asks, "What are you feeling now?"

"Mad—because I couldn't do this before."

"Do what?"

"Breathe this way. So completely."

"It feels good to let out all these buried feelings. Tell her."

"I feel good to feel, Mother! I won't let you do that to me again! I won't stop feeling! I won't spit it back! It has to come out! There's nothing wrong with that! I'll feel it, damn you, *I'll feel it!*"

Again my blood sings. Rhoda asks me if I want to stop. It surprises me that so much time must have passed. I feel too spent to go on now. She suggests I sit up for a few minutes. I feel like rubber. I can barely control my arms and legs.

When I recover, she reflects my feeling again: "It feels good to get that out, doesn't it?"

I nod. All I can do is nod. It's enough. It says it all.

Rhoda tells me to take a walk this afternoon and attend the group tonight.

My body was still flying when I left the session. My stomach didn't hurt, but my head was aching again. I lay down on my bed to rest, then took a shower at about noon and walked the mile to the center of town, still trying to breathe as fully as I had upstairs, not caring if my stomach might be sticking out.

As I walked along I continually mulled over the morning's hard work and felt awfully sad for myself in a way I'd never seen it before—for all my mother's sad mismanagement and my sad collusion, trying to get from her something she scarcely knew how to give.

From psychoanalysis I'd learned that I'd spent too much damn time pursuing my mother for neurotic love of her, but never until today did I ever dare approach a sense of how utterly *useless* it had been to try to win that nonexistent prize.

Once, soon after my mother died, I had hysterics in Dr. M's office. I refused to leave. I cried and screamed on out in his hallway at the hospital. I wanted him to give me something he couldn't; I wanted him to bring my mother back from the dead. But if only he'd *listened* to me, allowed me to scream out that need—for his help, for *her*—I might have come to feel the futility of it. Instead he asked me if I wanted to stay in the hospital for the night. Either that, or

I'd have to control myself (like a man, of course). He looked panicky, I'd accomplished *that,* at least! But I finally had to stifle my pain and leave, resentful of him, and still looking for what never existed.

After lunch I found the park that Stan had mentioned, and from a bench at a shady table where I've been writing all this, I'm also intermittently watching the kids at play. Stan had been encouraged by Dr. Rosen to do this too, to try to see himself in the children here, and to observe the mothers and fathers in action. But I'm too tied up inside myself to see much. All the kids seem relatively content. No tears, anyway, ten or twelve of them playing in groups— some of them in an imaginative game around a wooden structure that could serve as a carriage, a ferryboat, an ark. Awhile ago they turned the playground into an ocean and spotted great white whales (very literary for seven-year-olds, I must say) and schools of sharks, octopuses, assorted sea serpents.

Suddenly I'm skeptical about that breathing business this morning. Couldn't it just have been a physiological reaction due to my wild exertions on the mat? If so, then I don't suppose the effect will last very long, that I'll go back to shallow breaths all too soon.

In response to a letter I wrote to Dr. T telling him I was going to try a therapy based on primal theory, he suggested that the problems with some of these current notions are that they provide marvelous but only momentary catharsis. As soon as the sensation diminishes, the old neuroses rush in again like piranha. Maybe he's right. I've had the same good kind of physical experiences with some sensory awareness groups—which lasted all of an hour and finally seemed awfully superficial to me. But maybe Dr. T didn't know how deeply into physical feelings this therapy would plunge me. Neither did I. Besides, people like Reich,

Lowen, Rolf, and Janov have presented pretty convincing arguments about the ways our deepest feelings are translated into our body structure, our fears into muscular rigidities, etc., and how releasing these tensions can effect deep and permanent psychic change.

God, I sure as hell *want* to believe that but, having grown up with that traditional sense of a mind/body split, can only *intellectually* agree that they're one: MIND-BODY-BODYMIND. It's very hard for me to believe that the way to a man's stomach is through his heart.

Yet now I'm also wondering about the subtle kind of suggestive hypnosis that might be going on here. There on the floor I'm in such a vulnerable state that I seem willing to accept any explanation from that disembodied voice above me. Rhoda started the whole process too by saying, "Say 'Mama.'" Right from the start it's been her ball game, hasn't it? I follow instructions: "Feel it. Let it out. Tell her. Pound it out." And she often agrees with what I say in such a conclusive tone that I eagerly jump on it like a trained seal, accepting corroboration for truth.

What's more, I'm not sure now if she, out of her own faith in this method, is only hearing what she *wants* to hear. Or if I'm not giving her what I *sense* she wants to hear because I wish to please her. It's always been so easy for me to pick up cues for passion from other people and to learn the catchphrases of the crowd.

And suddenly more doubt: A couple of times this morning I felt immersed in some intense kind of method acting exercise. Maybe that *does* lead me to where the real pain truly lurks, but couldn't any good actor manage to *simulate* this and purposely drive himself into phony hysteria? Were *all* those witchy kids at Salem or the bitchy Nuns of Loudon driven by their own personal demons? Or for some was it just a little empathetic acting out that produced their frenzy out of a mere playful willingness to join in the fun for a few fantasy kicks?

9:15 P.M.

When I left my room at 7:30, I found a dozen or so people waiting to go upstairs for group. Their quiet talk grew solemn as someone above began to weep (an afternoon leftover?). I sat on the stairway too panicky even to wonder neurotically what kind of impression I was making. No one caught my eye or I his. However, I did have a chance to study the girl whose shared bathroom creates my daily traumas—a pretty, dark girl who ought to shave her legs. Maybe she's letting her hair grow for the duration as I am my beard.

Finally, one of the three therapists working that night called us, and very softly people picked places to lie down in the five large offices upstairs, three or four to a room. Pillows afloat like life preservers, jettisoned boxes of tissues. At no signal at all several people in the semidarkness began to drown in their own tears. The scene was straight out of Dante. What circle I can't recall, but those bodies lying face upward could have been stewing on beds of hot coals eternally doomed to moan their spirits away.

Not that I lingered long on *that* conceit. Another, more appalling image crossed my mind. I was in the baby nursery of a maternity ward, one of fifteen infants who all miraculously had grown-up larynxes and limited but potent vocabularies to use for howling out our lungs. "I hate you!" "I need you!" "Mommy!" "Daddy!" "I don't want you!" "I'm afraid!" "You're killing me!" "Let me live!" "Let me die!" "Oh, this pain!" "It never was enough for you!" "Love me!" "Don't hate me!" "Leave me alone!" "Where are you?" Bedlam—with a baby imprisoned inside every madman's body.

Enough picture making, damn it. I got into hell tonight more quickly than I'd imagined I could. Rhoda, who was one of the therapists working this evening, helped me get there fast. As usual she asked me to start by breathing deeply, then she simply said, "Let it out."

It came. Oh, it came. My weeping, howling, cursing, and exhausted pauses lasted close to an hour and a half. I started by calling out my need for my mother again. Felt my gorge rise. Got angry and blamed the knots on her once more. Asked her again how much I had to hurt to make her know I loved her? Why didn't she return it? On and on. The same stuff as this morning, but just as deeply felt. Tissues, damp and crumpled tissues everywhere.

Then I began to realize—no, to *feel*—that everything, all those childhood fears of mine were the result of not having had enough of her. I begged her for more attention, more love, screamed with rage when I couldn't have it. And this new insight: All the crying I'd done during childhood, in adolescence, on into my twenties and even after her death had come out of that one damned theme: my original unfulfilled need of her.

Why else did I feel such misery all my life or go to such extremes to try to believe she was mine? No, she was no Jewish Mother as Rhoda would have me think. I was not her Little Man. She didn't smother me. But I clung to her, all right! I clung to her because I was never sure of ever *having* her!

Later on I started screaming again about her death, that bitter way to abandon me. I cursed her for it. Called her to come back to me. On the day she died, I recalled, I wanted to tell her how much I loved her but was afraid it would cause her more pain and wound up by saying she had a beautiful nose. Never, not even on her deathbed was I allowed to tell her my true feelings! How much I still needed her. God, how simple it would have been if only she'd responded enough at the start! I cursed her for not being able to! Then wept for the both of us. No, for myself. *For myself!*

Then I got angry again for her making me choke it all

down. I breathed as I had this morning, and began to float, to feel my blood again, my nipples growing hard.

Cried then, and cursed my mother for having made me hate my body so. I feel I want to get into that more with Rhoda tomorrow. We barely touched on it this morning. That utter self-loathing for what I look like, for the way my body behaves.

Finally I wound up—and I can't believe I staged it—weeping to myself in a childhood curl, and, yes, Goddamn it, shoving my thumb in my mouth and sucking. An overwhelming urge. I felt what a baby must feel sucking his thumb or an easing teat. That's all I wanted, and to sleep. The noises of the weeping and wailing around me almost disappeared as I crawled into myself for comfort.

A lamp snapped on, bringing most everyone back from his trip. People slowly gathered in the largest room. An informal circle formed while in another office two or three patients went on with their agonized screams.

Duncan, one of the other therapists—a handsome man with a long red beard—waited for us all. I began to study the people—mostly in their early or late twenties, though some older ones too in their forties and fifties. Having shared tonight's baptism made me feel comfortable with them.

I can appreciate the value of the group experience now. Listening to the cries of others so easily helped to continue triggering my own all evening. I imagine that those most truly involved with their own grief wouldn't need that kind of stimulus, but several times during the session it helped me get to that point of departure again.

Since no one seemed willing to talk very much during the wrap-up, Duncan suggested we adjourn.

I'm exhausted. My throat's so raw. But I feel happy for having survived this evening's ordeal. Now, tonight should I or shouldn't I suck my thumb?

Wednesday

Rhoda just told me to take the night off but not to talk to anyone. "Don't talk away these feelings, Mike." I suppose I shouldn't be writing them away either, but I'm feeling so much even as I write this down that it seems impossible to do so. Right now I'm shaking like a leaf with cold, and crying, crying as I hear someone upstairs screaming for his life as I just now screamed for mine.

It's true. God, at least it *feels* so true! I can't recall any order to all this now, but I know we started today by my telling Rhoda about my feelings for her last night (something I didn't even admit to myself yesterday while it was actually happening); that is, my angry feeling of unwillingness during group to share her with anyone else there, the jealousy I felt when she went away from me. And then when she came near me again, the immediate resentment for feeling called on to *perform* for her to keep her there. Mother, Mother, of course—instant transference. Rhoda made me rage at that. Then to call for my mother's love again. Call. Rage at its never coming. Call again. Rage again for having to earn attention by performing for it. Call for it. And rage. It was endless, endless, but I didn't want to stop.

Somewhere during the session I flashed on a scene from Fellini's *8½* (still relating more readily to fantasy, I guess, than to life). This was the scene in which Guido as a little boy is being carried from his bath in a large white towel.

How good that made me feel during the film. Mother had carried me that way in from a bath once in a while. I felt loved by it, my body acceptable to her then. Rhoda asked if I remembered other times like that.

"No. But I see her hugging me for a photograph in the family album."

"Sure, special occasions," Rhoda says and I know she's right, God damn it. Only on special occasions did my fucking mother do that! I weep and scream again in pain and longing and rage.

Then once more I find myself insisting that my mother had *real* grief. I saw it in her eyes. She was a terribly unhappy woman. And I always felt so responsible for adding to her misery. But then I'm suddenly angry again because it was *her* grief, *her* sick life, and not my fault at all!

Rhoda asks about my father. I tell her I don't want to get into him yet. I keep insisting on my mother's sorrows. Rhoda's wise enough to suggest that's what makes my problems so much harder to sort out: I can't fully resent my mother's lapses of love for me when I know she suffered from lapses in her own life.

I remember then how often she used to go to the movies alone in the afternoon when I was a kid. Somehow I sensed she always went when she was unhappy. At the time I could only assume—or did she somehow imply it?—that my sister and I had made her miserable and driven her away. We were her grief. We made her unhappy. But of course I could win her back again by being extra-specially good to her when she came home, couldn't I? Always the good one, being what she wanted me to be, being *her*, God damn it, suffering *her* pain instead of my own!

Rhoda asks if I ever cried at the movies as I'd seen my mother do sometimes when she took me along with her. Instantly I recall the final scenes from the original version of that Fanny Hurst tearjerker *Imitation of Life*: While watching her dead black mother go by in a hearse, the daughter, who's been passing for white, breaks out from the crowd to scream, "Mammy! Mammy!" and begins tearing at the coffin to get to her mother.

The memory makes me roll on the floor in agony. When I first saw that movie, I'd wept my heart out. But I was only around ten at the time. Already I must have felt a complicated identification with both figures—the daughter, guilt-ridden for having hurt her mother so, and the mother in the coffin who had suffered her daughter's cruel denial of love. I was both mother and child.

But when I tell Rhoda this, she says I was crying for *myself,* not for the daughter, not for the mother—not even for my own dead mother. We can't really feel anyone's pain but our own, she insists, and I denied this by taking up my mother's grief as my own, the movie mother's for mine.

More tears. More tears for the God-awful truth of that.

Again we go into my mother's death. I admit to feeling somehow *glad* that my sister, her husband, and I were the only ones in the family who'd known she was dying almost up until the end. Not my brother, or my father, or any of a thousand relatives. In that way she was finally a little more *mine.* We were alone. I could protect her. Share her agony with an exclusive kind of suffering. My faithful concern would show her how much I cared. And I begin to cry again, again, *again* at the terrible futility of feeling I'd lost a woman I'd never really ever had.

I can't go on writing any more of this.

12:45 P.M.

I'm sitting in the park again feeling awfully depressed.

I'm watching the mothers and children. Everything seems okay, I guess. A picnic nearby with four mothers, six kids. I've the urge to deliver a blood and thunder sermon on child care. Mothers, beware! The Primal Theory Maniac stalks the park!

Shit, a kid just cried after tripping on a rock and called for his mother, who was walking slowly along with her younger child. Is this the moment when all the sickness starts? She didn't show the proper signs of sympathy, I thought, merely saying, "Oh, Jeff," almost with a smile. He stopped crying. Was it her knowing her own child well that allowed her to do so little? Or *not* knowing him well enough? Certainly it would have been foolish to gush concern because the boy was not indicating too much distress. But what if he needed just that slight edge *more* to assure him of her love and comfort? He stopped crying, yes, but was that because her minimal show of concern, her "Oh, Jeff" was enough for him, or because he'd long ago learned that's all he could expect from her? Has he already turned his true feelings aside in order to survive without the destroying sense that his mother doesn't care enough?

Who can tell? Neither mother nor child. Not now anyway. Maybe only Rhoda—twenty years from now after the poor young man comes crawling up to the Center with assorted soulful-body-aching ills.

Christ, that fucks up my mind with so many unanswerable questions. If, as I'm beginning to feel here so profoundly, Mama is where it all starts—and who can disbelieve it?—then doesn't that somehow reduce the rest of the world's ills to mere symptoms of the prime crime? That is, if the loss of Mama, or the experience of her early mismanagement, or some unsatisfied need for her less-than-adequate love is the genesis of human personality, don't all our contrary systems of philosophy, all our sociological studies, all our political and economic theories become mere sound and fury signifying nothing but man's self-preserving attempt to obscure that deeper truth? Is Nazi Germany due only to Hitler's mother's tough nipple, and to hell with the Treaty of Versailles? Is the entire Protestant Reformation—as Erikson and Norman O. Brown suggest—at bottom only the end result of Luther's lousy toilet training, his constipated cry for love? Economic exploitation, power politics, religious faith, hereditary rationales, Jungian horrors—are they only feeble explanations called into being because men called for their mamas and Mama didn't come quick enough?

How the hell should I know? Mama's own life is shaped by *her* mama's, the politics, the poverty, the plague of the time all decisive factors. Chickens and eggs. But if there *is* an element of truth in Mother as cause, then aren't we back to the old birth-trauma idea, the *inevitability* of separation and loss, the essential tragedy of parturition? And if *that's* so—then, wait a minute—then it simply cannot be avoided because it's the nature of the animal never to get the perfect mom. There are none! So long, Marx and Marcuse. No social system is going to produce the perfect lady for your lovely little boy. She will not, cannot exist! Not for any child! No matter how wealthy and healthy you make her!

So where does *that* leave me? Not willing to recognize this awful reality because that recognition jeopardizes the newborn organism's very reason for being, he is forced to mask his pain, to turn it inward on himself in guilt, in shame, in self-contempt, or outward on the world in anger, with fists, footballs, guns. Damn it, that means that a certain degree of "neurotic" illness must be in the best of us and as inevitable as death. Is it the given of our biological selves? Can there never be healthy men? Is neurosis the survival mechanism designed to keep us going even against our own inborn suspicion that it's really not worth the price?

I remember reading so much misleading criticism while preparing to teach *Lord of the Flies* to my high school groups. So many critics concluded that Golding was saying "man is basically evil," when it seemed to me that in the clearest allegorical terms, he was trying his damnedest to show that man has the potential for both good and evil (if one needs value judgments at all) and the causes for the arousal of "evil" are the archetypal fears that man is subjected to: the dark, his aloneness, his helplessness. Those are the awful elements that drive him to survive at the expense of others and, of course, at the expense of himself.

Hell, isn't the autistic child one of the most tragic examples of this possibility? Isn't he, as Bettelheim believes, dying in order to save himself? If he had the wherewithal he'd probably blow out his brains. Since he can't, he can only withdraw, shutting out the world, trying not to hear it or see it—oh, the tremendous expenditure of energy it must take to do that!—and, in effect, die—though that dying, that withdrawal is so obviously its own pitiful cry for help, just as all our neurotic defenses seem to me now to be ways of saying—how does Tommy say it in the rock opera?

> Hear me, Feel me
> Touch me, Heal me . . .

I just recalled a moment this morning while I was telling Rhoda how much I'd loved my mother and wanted to kill my father in order to have her all to myself the way in which I so easily shut off that feeling by sniffing and muttering, "Who needs this Oedipal crap?"

"What do you mean?" she asked.

"I mean I sound like a goddamn textbook!"

"It's just a feeling. It's a feeling. You felt that about your mother. You feel that."

"They're dead, damn it! It's all buried!" Flash: "Inside me! It's still all there! How much crying do I have to do to let it out, Rhoda?"

"You'll never be free of it, Mike. Not that feeling. It's hopeless."

"Then what's this goddamn therapy all *about*, damn it?"

"To help you feel that you can't defend yourself against that sense of hopelessness. That you must feel it to be free of the defenses you construct against it."

Oh—as the kids say these days—wow.

Hell. Another mother just turned off her kid here in the park. This time it was a serious show of annoyance with him for bothering her.

"Listen, lady, can't you see, you simple-assed fuck-up, that that kid of yours is asking for something you've never given him *enough* of! He wouldn't have to whine otherwise! Sure, he might be complaining about nothing. But it's a complaint—a *call*—he's calling you, you turd, and you'd better listen! Or *can't* you, you shithead? Are you that fucked up yourself that you can't understand your own son's whimpering for help? Then watch out, lady, because someday in order to be heard he's going to bring the house down around your *ears*. That is, if you haven't already turned him into some twisted burning block of ice by then!"

(I should've told her! Yeah, and gotten my teeth rammed down my throat for it. How can you tell them they're wrong about their own children? It's an attack on *them*. They'll be *forced* to defend themselves.)

Having just rejected Karl Marx, here I am thinking up new societies of my own—and still feeling how futile they all might be. Communal-kibbutzlike rearing, for instance? I don't know. Mothers—*exclusive* mothers—seem too important to me now. Maybe we should make all mothers pass a scream course before issuing licenses allowing them to have a kid. I'm not kidding. Even if some degree of neurosis *is* inevitable, as I'm feeling it is this afternoon, how else can you at least *reduce* the damage to new life?

Thursday

8:35 A.M.

No session until 4:30 this afternoon. Is the change in schedule calculated to break a patient of the defense of routine? To keep him on edge like French hangmen coming when least expected? Or to allow him to wallow on his own for a longer stretch in order to create a healthy sense of independent agony? I've heard that Janov tries all sorts of tough stunts: waking a patient up in the middle of the night, wrapping people in wet packs to stimulate birth primals. During my intake interview Dr. Rosen told me that the Center doesn't go in for any elaborate gimmicks like that, but from Stan's experience here I did learn that his appointments were sometimes shifted around in a further effort to cut into his resistances, and once Dr. Rosen even kicked him out of his office in order to scare him into some more intense feeling. Rhoda's warning on Monday was like that for me. "Feel it, kiddo—or get lost!" Hell, maybe she just has a dental appointment today and can't make it before then. Why should I begrudge her clean teeth?

Last night and earlier this morning I found myself drawn back to feeling my pain through a number of tedious old horrors again. My preoccupation with time, for one. For long as I can recall, I've had a sixth sense about the time of day and am always conscious of its running on—and out. I'm rarely if ever late for an appointment. Generally far too early. Aware as I am of it, I've never been able to break the pattern except by an occasional great act of will. Dr. M con-

demned me for it. He said it was a form of tyranny. And I
believe he was right. I recall my fury once while waiting for
two junior high friends at the Kings Highway subway stop.
I'm there ten minutes early and am angry as hell even before the appointed hour comes around. When the boys
finally do arrive, notoriously late by ten or fifteen minutes
—and oblivious to it—I'm ready to call off our trip into
Manhattan. I continue to fume to myself, holding it against
them inside me all day. They've abused me! I'm the good
one, I'm the early one, I'm better than they! And I'm getting nothing in return for it! No special deference, no extra
love. They are responsible for making me suffer so!

Yes, I believe there was tyranny in that. But now I can
see more to it—and I don't feel so abominably guilty about
it because I'm better able to get into how all that started:
Good old Reliable Rubin proving his sweetness and worth
by being the first in class to raise his hand, get on line size-
places, lick his platter clean, open the door for ladies, and
keep no one in the world waiting for him. Certainly not
outside the bathroom door. Go pee early before Mommy
and Daddy are awake. Disturb no one! Make room! Make
room! Be as quiet as a—they called me Mickey as a kid—
Mickey Mouse. That's the way they'll love you. That's the
way you'll reap your loving reward! No wonder you feel
like seething when it doesn't come!

The sequel: I'm also usually the first to leave a place, a
party, the first to feel the evening's wearing down, my
performance to please weakening, fearing I have nothing
more to give, nothing more to *get* in my endless search for
some facsimile of love. Shut down. Disappointed. Ready to
go. "Good night, everyone! I've got to be up early tomorrow!" In order not to feel the panic of not finding what
can't be found anywhere, or at least never existed for me.
And taking the blame: "It's *my* fault, dear. I've nothing to
give you, you see. You won't be satisfied with me. You'll
want more. And there'll never be enough of me for you to
love." Oh, shit, the struggle in all this!

And all so obvious in the bedroom. How rare it's been for me to feel as though I'm performing well there. But *performing* is such a God-awful judgment on myself. The inevitable anxiety inherent in having to put on a good show. Look, Ma, no sex act! My all too often premature ejaculations. "Now, now, this won't hurt a bit—did it?" All the fear in that to commit myself fully to another person, or to the sensations of my own body in terror that it won't be acceptable, or I won't be able to give enough, won't know what's expected of me, will fail to please—and sure enough, I do. This is incomplete. I have to think more about it. No, *feel* more, damn it!

What I *did* feel more about last night while walking back to the Center after my Rhoda-sanctioned movie was a keener sense of my mother's responsibility for turning me off women's bodies, making me feel ashamed and guilty for looking at them. Very, very early I knew it was somehow "wrong" to see my mother naked. If I happened to catch a glimpse of her in any way undressed, I quite voluntarily turned my eyes off. I can't even recall allowing myself to feel curious about her. Did I ever want to touch her breasts? God knows. I certainly wanted to hold onto her, but I can't remember ever feeling very good about it. Even the *need* for affection was somehow made to seem suspect.

I doubt if my mother liked her own body very much either. Is that where I picked up the idea of mine being unacceptable too—in my aggravated identification with her, in my need to be *like* her in order to get her to love me? She was a heavyish woman, always on one diet or another, and addicted to mineral oil for a number of years. A remedy for constipation, she told me. Did I pick up her stomach troubles too?

Anyway, à la Vienna and Queen Victoria, sex and a woman's nakedness were topics not on the agenda at our house. Once when I did see my mother's breasts and once the hair between her legs, I was more appalled than interested. Immediately I put it out of mind. As soon as imagined again, rejected. I had not seen what was forbidden! It was foul to want to. I didn't! I didn't!

When I was nine, going on ten, my mother was pregnant with my brother. She let me feel him kicking inside her a few times. And on one such occasion, when I asked where the baby would come out, she told me—through her behind. Babies were born through a woman's ass, didn't you know? *Why* in hell she couldn't have told me about her fucking vagina and its separation from her dunghole is beyond me. But that's how it was, Crazy Jane, and straight from the cow's mouth.

"No wonder your sister looks like a piece of shit!" one of the kids at camp said, snickering, when I delivered this superior bit of knowledge after lights-out one night.

In a rage I jumped on him and beat him up. (He was much smaller than I or I wouldn't have dared.) I was defending my sister's honor, wasn't I? And it was a way to put down my own visions of babies coming out all covered with dung. But though I've mulled over that incident many times, it was only last night that I realized for the first time in my life that what I'd really been fighting for was the preservation of my mother's "honesty." If I accepted what the other boys in the bunk were saying—that there was another place between a girl's legs for babies to come from—then my mother, my own mother had *lied* to me! I couldn't abide that. Even after our counselor, getting the drift of our argument, described the sex act and birth to us one breathless night soon after, I never consciously accused my mother of giving me false information. Nor did I ever once ask her another question about women again.

After that I recalled one more incident as deeply disturbing:

Once during the spring before that summer camp fight, I found a pack of dirty-picture playing cards in one of our closets at home. My sister and I looked through them: the usual variety of odd angles, tangled couples, threesomes. Vaguely, just vaguely I knew there was something "wrong" about my seeing them, that these men and women weren't supposed to be doing these things. But trusting Mother as always (and in my heart probably not trusting her for a second) I showed them to her, asking her in a frightened way what they meant. Instant fury and tears. She accused me of going through her dresser drawers. I hadn't. We'd found the pack on the floor of the closet in my sister's room, where my mother hung some of her stored clothing. She grabbed the cards and threw them out. But all that did was make me feel guiltier for committing a crime whose name I still didn't know. And worse, making my mother cry. Right now I can feel the same sinking feeling in my stomach that I felt then. My mother was in tears! I'd made her cry!

Some years later, during the time I was seeing the family doctor in Brewster, this incident was recalled, and I worked up enough courage to ask my father about those playing cards. I don't know if my mother had told him about the trauma they'd caused us that afternoon, but he delivered an admirably calm explanation: My mother was often hard to arouse, he said. The cards were used by adults sometimes to provide sexual stimulus and as a harmless joke (adding an edge to their bridge games?). I can see that now okay. But his explanation only added to the devastation of that memory. Just as I'd always suspected, my father had been making my mother do dirty things like that against her will!

And still one more, damn it: In junior high—age thirteen and fourteen (oh, that itching time when no kid should be made to sit at a desk)—dirty pictures and books galore were always being passed around. Aside from the worn and tattered Jiggs & Maggie jokebooks, Jiggs & Maggie with cocks and cunts, and a W. C. Fields-Mae West number (from what grandfather's bed table had those been lifted?), there was a "French" story titled "Percy." At the age of twelve Percy is seduced first by the housemaid, then by his aunt. I didn't mind that so much, even though I couldn't see myself in bed with any aunts of mine. Unfortunately, while they're screwing, his aunt delivers one crushing line of dialogue that made my head reel for years: "Don't tell your mother, Percy," she warns him. "She's been saving you for herself."

"No, no, no! Mothers don't sleep with Sons! They don't! It's bad. Bad! They shouldn't want to! Sons shouldn't want to! *I* don't. *I* don't. It's dirty, bad. *I* don't! I *couldn't* want that!"

I even stopped kissing my mother's cheek after that.

"What's wrong? Don't I get a kiss?" she once asked not long after. In a roomful of relatives, I recall. Would she have asked if we'd been alone?

"It's adolescence," said an aunt with a laugh. "They're afraid of us now."

Damn right, you dumb cunts!

But once again I'm mind-fucking by wondering if it's the nature of the beast or the nurturing patterns of our society that produce such fears. In his book *Nature of Human Nature,* Alex Comfort makes a pretty good case for the biological nature of the Oedipal struggle and incest taboo due to the primate offspring's extended childhood and the female's longer period in estrus.

During the early phases of adolescence so many straight guys go through the same sense of dread and withdrawal from their mothers as they become more acutely aware that both mother and son are sexual beings, so I can't see this as a strictly homosexual hang-up. My aunt had said, "They're afraid of us now." And her son is pleasantly married these days, the father of three. Generic? Cultural? Simply neurotic? Hell, all I know is it took me ages to accept tits and cunts. And even though I started sleeping with women in college, my inability to accept their bodies as something to be enjoyed freely, without inhibition, without a slight distaste, is still with me. Besides, by the time I was in college, my own body was drawing more and more strongly toward members of my own sex.

Hell, if my mother distorted my sexual nature, it must have been true of my other bodily functions as well—my inability to take much pleasure in the feel of myself or, more specifically, to allow others to touch me for long. How could I believe someone in bed might find desirable what I consider so vile about myself? God knows, enough men and women have tried to lay that specter to rest for me. But the ghost still walks. I still cannot lie on my back for long to allow any short-time lover to make love to *me*. I'm far more comfortable doing all the lovemaking, appreciating the other, performing like hell to do it well. To have a guy or girl start getting at vulnerable places—my belly, my thighs, all that criminal baggage—first becomes embarrassing, then almost insupportable. I *want* to like it, but am afraid it will turn my partner off—even though I can so often be turned on by the very same actions. Let them look too long in my eyes and I'm even more devastated that they'll find nothing in my glance to trust. Ah—like Mama again?

The best heterosexual experience I ever had was with Laura, a married woman with whom I was involved in my usual noncommittal way for close to three years. She seemed to accept me so completely, made me feel so much more accepting of myself. But it took lots of time to let me allow her to enter my sexual and emotional life more fully than I'd let any other girl. Maybe I was able to because I found *her* equally vulnerable. She didn't have the most beautiful body in the world; she seemed as much afraid to show it as I was (am) afraid to expose mine.

One night in particular, while I lay on my back, I remember she straddled me and rode on my penis in a beautiful way. In that position I had less of a need to come quickly and loved watching her moving above me, her breasts hanging down, sometimes rubbing against my chest when she leaned forward for another kiss, the look of ecstasy in her eyes, her deep moaning making me feel I was turning her on so completely. For a moment I wondered about the "passivity" of my position. Woman on top! Was this just another homosexual wrinkle? I fought down reservations with thoughts of *Love Without Fear* and *The Kama Sutra*, said, "Zit, zit!" to myself and loved every damned minute of it.

Oh, Rhoda, don't make me feel guilty (don't, Mama!) for diverting myself from my pain with that last paragraph. I know I'm involved in a pleasant masturbatory fantasy as I write this—more symptom than cause—and I'll get back to my pain in a while, but let me think about this just a minute more. I promise you I won't jerk off.

10:50 A.M.

A funny thing happened on the way to the bathroom just now. I found two cops talking to the black trainee in the hall. Apparently there'd been a complaint yesterday about the noise coming from the house. This is a mixed area of private homes, motels, communes, garden apartments, professional and semiprofessional offices built into older houses. With the windows opened to allow in the air, I'm sure we must sound gruesome. But then, so are the supersonic planes that break the sound barrier every half hour overhead, and the constant drone of the freeway a block off, ditto the motorcycles and automobiles along the avenue. (Something tells me we've unconsciously built all that noise into our machinery in order to drown out the sound of our grief.) Anyway, the neighbors are complaining.

One cop was beautiful: "I just finished my psychology course and I really approve of what's going on here, but—"

The trainee said that the house was to be air-conditioned

next week, which will allow us to keep our windows closed, and that double windows were to be installed. That should take care of the problem for the outside world. But then the Center will be adding its own inhuman hum to the rackets of the age. Shit.

The cop said that would be fine, but suggested until then we try to "keep it down."

I had to laugh. After they left I asked the trainee if that meant I couldn't scream anymore.

"Fuck 'em," she said with a wicked smile.

1:00 P.M.

Back in the park now, still waiting for my late session with Rhoda today and watching the kids again. I keep my fingers crossed for them all.

Mostly for myself, though, because suddenly I've been feeling a lot of doubts about this therapy again:

For instance, couldn't this process just be an elaborate diversionary tactic? Shit, I mean, what it seems I've been asked to do so far this week during my sessions is to focus on one or two basic causes of my trouble—and to keep focusing on them. Well, then, couldn't I just be funneling all my distress into a couple of convenient excuses for grief? Oh, sure, the grief is real all right, but why should my *feeling* the source of that desperation have any longer-lasting effect than, say, the pacification of a good crying jag, or a good screw, or a good Chinese dinner? Rhoda would probably tell me that we're *not* assuaging grief at the Center, that we're here to feel it in all its lovely pristine glory, but, my God, how often does it have to be felt in that pure unadulterated state before it's somehow incorporated into your system as an operative principle, and not just some new form of sublimation?

More doubt: Although Rhoda isn't intrusive, her quiet

corroboration of my feelings and insights sometimes sounds irksome to me with its subtle "I-told-you-so" air. This might be just the timbre of her voice hitting my particular eardrum, but it's what I'm feeling at the moment. When I mentioned the hysterical episode I'd had in Dr. M's office after my mother's death, and how I now saw the way in which he'd cut me off from an important and revealing feeling, practically forbidden me to feel it, Rhoda said, "What a waste." It *was*, sure, but I disliked that sense of a superior "We've-got-a-better-answer-here" tone in her voice. Religious and political fanatics sound the same note of certitude. I automatically distrust it. Eventually I might wholeheartedly feel that this *is* the cure for neurosis like Salk vaccine is for polio, but I'd like to get to that point without her proselytizing.

And one more worry: I'm in a house where the world hardly intrudes at all, except for the occasional cop coming along to tell us to lower our voices, and the girl whose bathroom (note: now it's *hers*) I'm forced to share. But what happens when I'm out in the big bad world again where all the old props exist, the old frustrations, the daily confrontations with myself in absurdity again? Well, I guess I'll have to wait on that one.

Meanwhile, I know I've already read into the face of the girl across the hall signs of hatred when she didn't acknowledge my existence as I passed her on the street today. "Do you hate me?" I wanted to ask her then and there. I was waiting to catch her eye and smile with the conspiratorial air of "getting well together" in the same nut house, but she never even looked my way, and immediately I took it into myself as *my* fault.

If I'm still so ready to do that, and an act of *will* is futile to prevent it, then how frequently, how many times, how much more deeply yet must I blame my mother for all these sins against myself before I can pass that girl without thinking one way or the other about her? Letting her be? Letting myself be?

6:20 P.M.

A full afternoon. Around three I took to the floor of my
room for a long warm-up before my session upstairs. Several
motives I see for doing this kind of preparation now: it
keeps me closely in touch with my pain. It also makes it easier to get into a greater intensity later on—again today I
went into Rhoda's office with eyes already streaming and
tissues to the nose. But I'm afraid that's where a baser reason shows through: Within me still is the neurotic little boy
saying, "Look, Mommy, look how hard I'm trying for you,
look how good at my therapy I am!" I want to earn my gold
medal from Rhoda. I want to be her model patient just as I
wanted to be my mother's model son. I did the same damn
thing with Dr. M, playing the good little analysand doing
his dream homework for his analyst's love. And, oh, how I
resented it when the reward wasn't forthcoming. But *knowing* that didn't stop me from doing it then and doesn't seem
to stop me from doing it now. It just adds an edge of irony,
damn it! If, maybe, this time I can feel deeply enough the
pain of so desperately needing my mother's approval,
maybe I'll find this less-than-helpful motive diminishing
more and more. Maybe, maybe.

Anyway, I went upstairs with a bagful of new/old memories, old griefs that would help me get back to their source.

I told Rhoda of the time when at the age of six or seven I
went out to play with the boys. Jackie Mortimer, skinny as
a bone, was shivering in the winter street. "You're lucky to
have so much fat on you because it helps to keep you
warm," he said in all seriousness, though one or two of the
other boys laughed. I was mortified, mortified! Already I
must have had awful feelings about my weight for the remark to hurt me so. It took no time at all for me to realize
how all these years I've been blaming myself for being fat,

and never the woman who'd allowed it to happen, who never let me tell her how miserable it made me. She was the one who was feeding me, wasn't she? She made me fat! She made food the only recourse to fill the emptiness she created! God, she should have known better! And all this time I'd been holding myself alone accountable for it!

I didn't need Rhoda to say, "Tell her!"

I told her. I told her!

And recalled again the night of that terrible toothache at the age of six, and what was worse, the next day's fear of the dentist's hurting me more. Since his office was on our street corner, it was nothing to tell my mother that I was going to the bathroom in the hallway and, once outside his waiting room, run all the way home. I hardly considered the consequences. Fifteen minutes later my mother came back down the street in search of me, furious for my running away and embarrassing her like that. *Embarrassing* her! Can you imagine it? When I was scared shitless! Couldn't she recognize that? Insult added to injury, she dragged me bawling like a baby back down the street to the dentist, forcing me to show my humiliation before the ever-present group of callous older kids along the block. A *Saturday Evening Post* cover? Hell, Norman Rockwell's worst crime against art was his willingness to make tragedies look *cute*.

I raged at her for that. And raged again.

And remembered next the time I urinated in our backyard on 13th Street. I must have been seven or eight already, much too old to do that. Maybe it was an act of defiance because I can't remember ever doing it outside before. I even recall feeling superior to a cousin on the next block whose mother allowed him to piss in the gutter instead of going all the way up to their apartment. My mother, I remember, once even justified my aunt's permissiveness by saying the distance he had to travel to the toilet was too great. Not *my* distance. No, sir! I got punished for it. Instead of a regular meal that night I was given milk and bread for supper. Suffering my shame, I sat at the table accepting this punishment and all its distress because I knew, *agreed* I'd been naughty. Wasn't Mother telling me so? Then, goddamn her, she allowed a little smile to escape her lips. The injustice of it! She wasn't taking my crime seriously! There I sat in an agony of humiliation, feeling deprived of my all-important meal, only to be laughed at for accepting the justice of my shame! What fucking hypocrisy! What goddamn stupidity!

Again and again for the first time in my life I keep coming up against this awful new sense of my mother's dishonesty. The countless times she promised to take me somewhere, then found reasons to break her promise by discovering some silly fault in me to blame it on. She didn't want to take me to that damn film in the first place. Okay, okay, so she preferred running away to the movies by herself. *Let her!* That sad, pathetic creature! But don't blame that misery on me! Don't make me feel guilty for being bad so that you can get off scot-free, Mother! Don't punish me because *you* stink!

And another movie came to mind while I was up there on the floor today. *Little Men.* One of Jo's orphaned boys does something wrong. To punish him, she gives him a ruler and asks him to hit her hands hard, to *hurt* her with the ruler by hitting her hands. He can barely lift the stick to do it. She insists. Slowly he begins to hit her and is crying out his heart for hurting her this way. Goddamn it, when I saw that scene in a TV rerun once long ago, I thought, "What a beautiful and fitting punishment." That little kid would never do that bad thing again, not when it meant hurting the only woman in the world he loved and who loved him! Oh, but today I suddenly felt the awful tyranny in it! Even now as I write it down, I'm feeling the brute injustice against that little boy!! The coercion, the emotional blackmail, the crime committed against his tenderness in the name of virtue! Up against the wall, Louisa May Alcott!

I told Rhoda that that was exactly the kind of pressure my mother practiced on me. And I *accepted* it, turned myself into a guilty sinner for her—for making her sad, for hurting her! Rhoda told me to tell dear old Mom. I did, again and again—screamed it out until I was sure she was hearing it in her grave.

"Your sadness has nothing to do with me, damn it! You're a sick sad woman! I don't want to see your sick sad eyes anymore! You gave it to me! You made me take it! You fooled me! I thought I'd have you if I were as sad as you! I never had you! Never! Only your goddamn sadness!"

Then, damn it, my rational mind intruded again. How could I blame her for it? How—when she was fucked up by *her* mother who must have been fucked up by *her* mother somewhere in the wilds of the Ukraine.

"A little kid doesn't know that," Rhoda said.

"That's right!" I shouted. "A little kid doesn't know that, Mother!"

Sure, sure, as an adult I can forgive her her sorry ignorance of herself, her awful misery. But as a little boy inside still, the little boy who's always been there looking for what he never had, I can only hate her for it still! Hate her!

"Why are you moving your legs that way?" Rhoda suddenly asked.

I didn't know I was moving them at all. It was a kind of running motion.

"I'm running," I said. "But I don't know if I'm running *to* her or away from her. I don't know!"

And then I also realized that my arms were once again wrapping themselves around my chest, almost as though I were incapable of keeping them vulnerably spread out as Rhoda has often directed.

"Oh, God, I have no one to hold onto but *me*, Rhoda. If I don't hold myself, no one will."

And that's when the worst of it began today. As I lay there on the mat I finally knew that I really had to hate my mother as fully as possible in order to let myself live on my own terms at last. The thought alone was enough to drown me in tears again.

"I don't want to hate you!" I cried. My God, to say "I hate you!" and *mean* it? "I can't say it, Rhoda."

"Why not?"

"It would be like killing her." Like killing my own mother! I never had her the way I needed her, I know that now, but I couldn't kill the little I *did* have. "But I have to —I have to—"

And then I swear my mother was in the room with me, looking at me with those sad sick eyes again, and I felt like a hatchet man getting ready for my own mother's execution.

I did it. It took time. Lots of tears and strain. Lots of excuses, tortured justifications. But with Rhoda pushing me, I cursed my mother again and again for all the needless grief she caused me. Screamed out my despisal of her. Wished her dead. Was glad she *was* dead. Because she made me hate my body so. Made me fear hers. Made me ashamed of my own human noises. Made me guilty for thinking I'd hurt her. Lied to me. Ran out on me. Never came when I called. Wouldn't hold me enough. Begrudged her kisses. Couldn't give anything. I called her every dirty name in the book. Believed it. Felt it with all my heart!

And when I was done, felt desolately alone. The aloneness that was always there, but which I could never admit to for fear it would destroy me. The aloneness I defended myself from with acts of piety, silence, obedience. Incorporating my mother into myself like some fucking holy wafer.

"Get out of me!" I cried over and over in one more frenzy.

An effective exorcism? The dybbuk removed? I don't know. I knew she couldn't hear it. Hadn't heard it while she lived, wouldn't hear it in her coffin. But I screamed it all out at her anyway. "Get out of me, you bitch, you silly cunt! Get out of me!"

When I lay there spent and sweating, Rhoda asked, "How do you feel now, Mike?"

"I don't know if there's any lasting value in this," I said, "but right now it's sure as hell therapeutic."

"More of it tonight," she said with a lovely laugh.

9:45 P.M.

Just had more. Not quite as intense, but intermittent and sustained. The afternoon's themes repeated, ending, unfortunately or not, in new feelings of guilt for betraying my mother by blaming her so for her false and incomplete love. This is *still* so hard for me to do. I have to keep the little boy in me alive to effect it. My adult mind is still so quick to defend her.

"Let me be inside you, not you inside me," I moaned up there, curling up like a fetus again. "Carry me, carry me, carry me—"

One thing that makes me suspect I wasn't tied in as deeply as I might have been tonight was my ability to hear individual voices at our Witches' Sabbath. Those shrieks from hoarse girls can be as spooky as Halloween. Crones. Banshees. Keening to put *Riders to the Sea* to shame. And one guy made me giggle as he went on talking to his mother in a perfectly reasonable way: "Listen, Mother, I really need you, you bastard, you cock-sucking son of a bitch." A certain confusion there.

Afterward we gathered for the wrap-up. Not too much said and, thank God, nothing in Duncan's manner to make one feel called on to perform. Some laughs. One guy said he'd remembered tonight how his father always made him feel like an incompetent little kid all the time; others corroborated, how often they still felt small and helpless. Duncan said he believed most people did. "Oh, God," said the

young man, "and I thought all those big guys had it all together."

"Boy, do I hate adults!" cried an older man.

Rueful laughs from all fifteen of us adults sitting in a
kids' campfire circle.

A good kind of communion for me. And the comforting
sense that all our sorrows are really so similar underneath
our individual symptoms. Sure, the particulars may be
unique for each of us—the stuff novels are made of—but
our needs come from the same common human core.

Didn't want to return to my cell. Sat on the stairs watching the people leave. The Girl of the Adjoining John did
too. Finally she said to me, "You're lucky, you've got two
more weeks here. I leave tomorrow."

I nodded, understanding the shit she'd be walking back
into out there again.

We traded bits of background. Finally (to escape?) I
said, "I feel guilty about talking to you."

She rose with a pretty Jean Seberg smile on her face. "I
know. I'm a terrible chatterer. I shouldn't break your isolation."

Is that why she wouldn't look my way on the street today? For *my* benefit? Wouldn't you know. More proof of my
paranoia!

Shall I knock on her bathroom door tonight? I think I'd
like to make love to her despite her hairy legs.

11:30 P.M.

Still up. Tried to sleep but lay awake worrying about
today's betrayal of Mother. Finally got up for a glass of
water and found myself sitting in the rocker by the opened
window, looking at the stars over the dull din and fleeting
lights along the freeway.

Don't mind this inability to sleep.

When I was first interviewed by Dr. Rosen, he said that even after his own intensive therapy, he still gets depressed from time to time—but at least he knows exactly what it is that's getting him down now, the connections it makes with his past, and is better able to live it through. I remember the miracles I first wanted, but now simply *being*—no matter how tough—sounds pretty good to me. No, Dr. Rosen didn't promise me any rose gardens, I recall. I no longer expect my hair to grow in because of this. But at least my stomach seems in the right place tonight.

One more doubt for the day: Why am I keeping this journal? It wasn't recommended. In fact, I was told *not* to write, which can be as emotionally withering as talk. But I'd brought a notebook along with me, entertaining the idea of keeping a log even before I came here. For several reasons: (1) I'm a writer and the experience promised to be important enough to write about. (2) I've never confronted my life directly through my writing. My novels and short stories have all been symbolic evasions. I thought it might somehow be valuable to try to write squarely about myself for a change. (3) A sick reason, I guess—that old sense of wanting to get something for my money. If I'm going to pay with suffering for this experience and also risk failing at it, at least I might have something creative to show for it, maybe to use one way or another later on to sell. (4) As I continued at it during the past few days, it became evident to me that the process of writing often takes me deeper into my feelings. As oblique as my fiction's been about my private life, it's never really taken me *out* of myself, exactly. I've always been aware of some kind of twisted confrontation in it. Madame Bovary—*c'est moi!* But now that encounter is coming straight and this journal helps keep me at it. I don't want that to stop.

Friday

In the Abominable Diner across the road a few minutes ago one of the morning regulars said "So long!" to the waitress, who called after him, "Be good now!"

"Be good now?" I wanted to scream.

"I'm always good," said the customer with a smile that defied her to doubt it, while inside I was still answering for him: *"Good?* Hell, what the fuck *for?* I'll be *me*—take it or leave it. I don't need to be good or bad or anything!"

You get that way around here.

I was up at 5:30 after a bad night's rest, and already out walking by 6:00. Along the avenue I picked a weed that had a nice flexible feel to it, almost like a fishing rod. Bouncing it between two fingers I suddenly thought: "Someone's going to accuse you of picking it! The ecologists will be after you! You've done something rotten!" Not in so many words. My guilt never needed syntax, my paranoia survives on the slimmest vocabulary. Oh, but that awful hounded feeling. It didn't take much to draw me to its source again, or to start feeling angry for being made the dupe of my mother's desires, to woo her with my goodness and become as saintly as she made me believe her to be. No place to scream it out on the street (we have enough trouble with the fuzz); instead, I found myself shuffling along down the avenue muttering like the village loon.

Question: Is that what the future holds then? Automatic sputtering rage at the Mama-Who-Isn't instead of the Son-Who-Is? Mere displacement? Or will I reach the stage where I can feel the pain of having had no real mother deeply enough not to have to keep looking for her or blaming myself for what never existed?

Hell, even now, just writing down the word "future" frightens me because that's so much how I've always lived my life, believing tomorrow would be better (could it ever be any worse?). "Tomorrow I'll be thinner. Tomorrow wiser. Tomorrow more loving. Loved. If that short story didn't sell, the next one will. Someday if I work hard enough, am good enough, and brave enough, I'll win all the rewards and the Wizard of Oz will send me back to Kansas." My *head* knows it's all bullshit. But that's not where *needs* reside.

Oh, shit, I can see it so much more clearly now, feel it straight for the first time—all the strictures and controls I've imposed upon myself in order to be awarded something vaguely like Mother's love. "Today, Michael, you'll write three whole pages. Tonight, you'll have broccoli for supper because you need your greens. Tomorrow you'll deserve time off to see a play." From morning to night I conceive inflexible plans for tomorrow, and am panic-stricken at any unforeseen disruptions from any routine. "Sorry, Tony, I can't stay out after eleven tonight. I won't be able to work well in the morning." "Oh, God, Laura's at the door wanting to get laid. I'll be in no condition to teach tomorrow." "Okay, Stan, we'll go to Europe two summers from now—if I work hard and finish my book." "Oh, hell, the newspaper didn't come today. *Now* what'll I do for an hour?"

And even here at the Center: "I'll do my warm-up to be ready for my session. Later I'll go to the laundromat. Dinner at the Chinese restaurant tonight. (I deserve that reward for being a good patient all week, and if I eat slowly enough it'll round out the night.)"

Every goddamn minute planned and accounted for—and why?—to delay anxiety, to make external order out of inner chaos, to fill up the Grand Canyon of uncertainty and longing, the fear of being alone with it—the instant depression when there's nothing in the offing, when all escape routes through work or perversion are cut off, those dreadful moments when my undefined misery looms up like a monster ready to make his evening meal of me.

Shit, is it *wrong* to hope for a more flexible life coming out of this therapy? "Hope" is such a dirty word around here. Yet I still desperately hope to find the means to unloosen those ropes I've tied around myself in order to win rewards that don't exist and to stop myself from feeling the futility of that incessant search.

12:05 P.M.

Warm-up time so quickly fills itself with forgotten bits of biography, so quickly reduces me to tears:

When I was about twenty, I went to a skin doctor because of a rash. While examining me, he noticed the striae on my buttocks and hips. "My God," he said, "you look like you've given birth to three babies." I gritted my teeth and smiled, once again blaming myself in silence for the shameful proof of a fat childhood. "You fucking bastard!" I should have screamed. "Don't you think those stretch marks have caused me enough humiliation? And what in hell can *you* do about it?" I didn't deliberately make myself fat! My mother should have seen what was happening! She should have known, damn her!

Joel was the only friend I had at the age when H. S. Sullivan prescribes every boy's need for a buddy. But Joel had enough friendship to give to more than one. How violently jealous I became of sharing him. One day I stopped speaking to him altogether, never letting him know the cause. When I didn't answer his questions, I saw tears well up in his eyes, but felt justified in my contempt of a friendship I'd have to split with others, never knowing until this very morning that I was asking again, as always, for exclusive love. Let *me* be the special one! And if I can't have it that way, I want none of it. Do you hear me, Mother? Do you hear?

I picked up a guy at a bar one night and we'd had a pretty good time in bed. He stayed until the next morning, and while we still lay side by side, I said I had to call home. There I was talking to Mom: "How's the weather up there? How are things going on the farm?" while this stranger, whom I never saw again, was holding me in his arms. What was I really saying to Mom? "Look what you're making me do! Look how naughty you're making me be! See—I can find love if I want. Help me, damn you! Get me out of this! Love me! Help me!"

I brought these things along inside my head today for my session, but as soon as I was on the mat again, I forgot them and began by blaming myself for wanting to scream the loudest at last night's group (suddenly finding my present feelings much more important than those of the past). I complained too about how I'd been trying to make connections with my biography in order dutifully to deliver up good little insights for Rhoda's reward of Mommy's never-love. But Rhoda wouldn't put up with that self-contempt. Instantly she turned it back on the right source, and once again we were off to the races. Deeper repetitions of yesterday. Howling rage at Mother. Howling rage for her turning me into her faggot slave fawning after her favor.

Sometime later Rhoda again suggested that I talk about my father, who'd cropped up in some previous association.

I still resisted dealing with him, repeated the catchphrase I've been using for years now: "I feared him at first, then hated him, and finally had nothing for him but pity."

I tried to avoid the whole issue by getting him off the hook: "He killed himself, Rhoda. A year after my mother died, he took an overdose of sleeping pills. He knew he couldn't win. He tried very hard after my mother was gone. He tried, but he was blind—he started going blind when I was around nine or ten—and he was miserable without my mother. He was so dependent on her. He couldn't do it alone!"

Still I kept talking, trying not to feel a thing even as I mentioned the guilt I'd suffered over his suicide, how I still held myself somehow responsible for not being able to take care of him. My obligation to my mother's memory made me move back to the farm for a while to help him out, but when I realized what I was doing to myself—trying to take my mother's place—I quit the house, that damned farm bought after he went blind only in order to help him pretend he was some great lord of the manor, to protect his ego at our expense, turning my brother and sister and mother and me into servants for *his* fear of facing life without eyes; keeping that damned failing business of a bungalow colony going in order to preserve his self-esteem, then unable to pull out even when he was ready to because all his savings had been sunk into that disaster; trying to make us into little farmers against our will, my mother into a businesswoman; always issuing orders and my mother giving those orders the lie as she hypocritically *let him believe* he was running the show, even though all the burdens had fallen on her! If he'd had any real feelings for her, he'd have known what he was doing! How I hated him. But how I'd hated him long before he went blind, his blindness only making me all the more guilt-ridden for hating him.

"Why guilt?"

"Because my mother loved him, wanted to protect him, made me keep quiet for him!"

"How?"

"Before he went blind he was a wholesale butcher in Brooklyn. As early as I can remember he used to get up in the middle of the night to go to work, but was always home by midafternoon. I always seemed to see him sleeping on the couch in the living room, and my mother saying, 'Don't wake Daddy.' "

"How did it make you feel then?"

"Don't worry. I had no intention of waking him. I was afraid of him."

"Why?"

"I couldn't trust what he'd do! Once, while I was waiting for him in the car, I played with the buttons on the dashboard. I must have been only three or four then. I didn't know what the buttons were for. Couldn't even recall turning any. When he got in and started the motor, the windshield wipers began to work. Like a shot he slapped me across the face. For what? I hadn't even made the connection between the button and the wipers. I didn't know what I'd done—and felt too surprised even to be outraged. But I hated coming near him after that."

"How did he look on the couch when he was lying there in the afternoons? See him there."

"I *couldn't* see him. I see his back. I can only see his fat ass."

"What do you want to tell him?"

"Nothing! I just want him to get up and get away from me!"

"Tell him that!"

"Get up off the couch, Daddy! Get up off that couch! Get up! Get up! Get up! Get up! Get up! *Get up! Get up! Get up!*"

I don't know how long my screaming went on, but when I saw stars I sank back on the mat breathing like some trapped animal.

"Let it out, Mike."

More.

"Let it out!"

And more. More. *More!*

Somehow during all this my grandmother, my mother's mother, displaced my father in my thoughts. Maybe I'd exhausted him for a time. Rhoda asked me about her. I had to laugh: "That poor lunatic should've been locked away years ago. She fucked up her two sons just as badly as she fucked up my mother. And she's going to outlive us all!"

"The way her own mother fucked her up?"

"Sure, and my grandmother's *mother's* mother fucked her up all the way back to Adam and Eve. So what's the *use* of all this, Rhoda?"

But then suddenly I remembered how much I'd loved my grandmother when I was a kid. It wasn't until she and my grandfather came to the farm after his retirement as a cabinetmaker in Pittsburgh that I realized what a fraud and a tyrant she was—a baby whom my mother was coerced by guilt into nursing—trying to get out of her what I was trying to get out of *my* mother!

"What?"

"*What?* Love—*love,* damn it!" Tears. Tears. Tears.

"Why did you love your grandmother?"

I had to think a moment. Of course: "She used to hold me a lot."

"The way your mother didn't."

"Yeah, sure—but there was a price. I had to listen to all her miserable stories about how bad her life had been, about all the people in the world who were against her. She was a lunatic, I'm telling you." But I also remembered *loving* to listen to her grief. Everyone she knew was a villain except her. Her sister-in-law was a whore. Her husband a miser. Her parents dead or alive in Russia somewhere, who knew? Her arm hurt. Her feet itched. Her eyes needed drops. "And I believed it all! She used to give me pennies to listen!"

"Buying you," Rhoda whispered.

"But I listened, didn't I? I could've left her lap, couldn't I?"

"Could you, Mike? It was all you had. Those pennies."

In the midst of tears over that truth I flashed on a penny story:

At the age of seven I made a bet with my cousin and some of his friends about the date of the day. I lost. After we checked the school calendar, I should have paid up. But when school let out I made a beeline through the backalleys for home. I wouldn't give them the penny. I knew I was wrong, but that penny was mine! In tears I ran into the house, but already the boys were banging on the side door. My mother made me pay them the penny and advised me not to bet if I didn't want to lose my money. She was right, of course. But what I never saw until now was how closely that penny—all my penny-wise miserliness—was tied up to my need for love.

I began to cry bitterly for so much self-deception.

I screamed in rage again for being forced to feel that those pennies meant more than money.

I don't know why, maybe the idea of love occurring did it, but another cruel memory rose up then: I told Rhoda that as a teen-ager I once saw my mother kiss my father in a way that seemed abominably voluptuous to me.

"Why?"

"I'm not sure. I never saw my mother kiss my father like that before. They kissed sometimes, but it was always—what?—familial, impersonal. The look I saw in her eyes told me she *slept* with him. It was sexual. I didn't want to see that."

"Why?"

"It was forbidden." Like the dirty playing cards, like her body. "She could do *that?*"

"Do what?"

"Kiss him like that."

"She was capable of love. You saw her capable of love."

"Sexual love. Adult love. None for me."

"*Love*," Rhoda insisted. "Giving. You saw her giving herself."

(Shit, I'm crying again all over the page now.)

"Love is love," Rhoda went on. "You're separating it into sex and something else."

And I knew I was. I knew I *always* did that. I mentioned the guy in last night's group who said how he hated adults. He was making the same kind of mistake: separating feelings—children's feelings from grown-up feelings. How we'd laughed at that irony, being able to recognize that adult or child feelings are *feelings*. I was crying again. Still am right now.

"How does it feel to be a child with feelings again?"

"Good. Why did they shut this off? Why? Why?"

Rhoda let me be. Eventually she whispered, "Feel the quiver when you breathe? Give in to it."

I tried, but my stomach began hurting terribly again.

"That's a feeling trying to come up, Mike."

"It hurts too much to feel!"

"Let it come. Let it come."

I struggled with it. I fought to let myself feel that renewal of physical as well as psychic agony—and suddenly I could breathe again. I lay there breathing more deeply and calmly than I could ever remember. Again there was that euphoric buzzing in my head, my blood racing through my body, my fingertips, my toes warm, my wrists almost hurting with so much blood in them.

"I've always had trouble with my circulation. Cold hands and feet. Always."

"Maybe you were too tied up inside to let your blood reach to warm them."

"Do you think this will grow hair?"

A quiet laugh.

I still lay there feeling that delicious sensation.

Eventually I said, "The work I do for a living—teaching,

writing—they're both supposedly *giving* occupations. Is it awful to do that? I mean, have I just been doing those things to get something like love back from it?"

"Maybe. But that's a feeling too, isn't it?"

"I suppose. But I mean, I *like* to teach. I like to write. I once worked—with pretty transparent symbolism, I guess —in a camp for physically handicapped kids. I *like* to help people. I always wanted to grow up to be the man in the information booth at Grand Central Station. Do I have to give all that up now because teaching and writing can't give me the love I crave?"

"Feelings aren't *bad,* Mike. You might still feel you want to do those things. They might still be right for you."

4:30 P.M.

Doubt assailing me again, even after so much deep-felt truth: Isn't this therapy too *easy?* You follow instructions. When Rhoda says, "Breathe deep," you breathe deep. Feel what she tells you to feel. Put your hands at your sides at her direction. Yes, you weep and you rage—but often on cue. For one like me who loves to follow orders like a performing seal after his bit of fish, isn't this less autonomous than any work with Dr. M, for instance, who would wait and wait and wait before grudging a word? A friend of mine once told me that she lay in her analyst's office for two whole years before she said anything at all. Her doctor *allowed* it. Until she was ready, he told her, nothing could be done.

I just killed my doubt: She indicated she was ready by coming to you in the first place, you dumb schmuck! All she needed was for you to say, "Breathe deep and say Mama!" All she needed was for you to ask, "What are you *feeling?* Feel it!"

Doubt: Shit, I feel too positive again. Have in me now Rhoda's sense that This-Is-It. I mistrust that. I feel like a crazy aunt of mine who discovers Zen one week and psycho-cybernetics the next. A desperate fanatic proclaiming this month's answer to her lifetime's depression until the next siege of misery overwhelms her.

The afternoon hangs heavy today. No more sessions until Monday at 10:30. Between now and then I'm to remain alone, allowed to walk, but not to talk unnecessarily, permitted to read a newspaper, but mostly to feel, feel, feel. The regimen seems a test of strength and goodness—a bad sign—that old *will* to do well rather than simply to be who I am, feel what I'm feeling moment by present moment.

9:50 P.M.

Rewarded myself with Chinese food as planned, damn it. But why must I see it as reward? Why not simply say I was hungry and for a change had some tasty Chinese food? Because Chinese food *was* always reward food at our house, what we earned for being good. I used to hurry home with those wonderful hot and pungent-smelling brown paper bags. And we'd all eat ourselves silly in the kitchen while listening to Jack Benny on the Sunday night air. It almost made life seem okay.

Boy, oh, boy, I never thought I'd ever wind up calling my mother a silly cunt.

As I walked past a local beauty parlor on the way to supper, I noticed a male hairdresser cruising me through his window. I didn't imagine it. I know those looks too damn well. Not my type, or I probably would have gone in and fucked him under his dryer. Instead, I shouted in silence, "I'm not your goddamn father! I'm *not*, you idiot!" and walked on as straight-looking as my ass'll let me.

Doubt: Hiked to San Anselmo after supper. (What for? To work off the pleasure I didn't feel I really deserved? Wouldn't put it past me.) Decided to take a bus for the three-mile return. Went into a hippie Indian-goods store, the proprietress with a monkey on her back (a real one), to ask where the bus stop was. As usual my old paranoia forced me to work up courage for the simple question. (I never underestimate my insanity; I can barely ask directions from a traffic cop.) And tonight, to force myself to do it, I said, "I'm afraid. I'm afraid I'll be rejected. Why? Because *you* made me afraid, Mother!" Fine. It worked. I asked my question, got my answer and a "cheep-cheep" from the monkey. But there's the looming doubt: Was that anger merely a touchstone and a talisman, "magic words" like the ones I say to myself while standing at a urinal in order to get myself to pee and keep my mind off my fear of making noise?

The Girl of the Adjoining John has gone home. I wish her luck. Since I know from Stan's experience that most people return for evening groups after their three weeks' intensive, I guess I'll probably be seeing her again during the week. The guy next door is breathing quietly. The house is as still as a stone.

Stars are out again tonight. It's almost the summer solstice. I'll sit outside in the rising wind awhile. If nothing else comes of this, at least I'll have had good weather.

Saturday

Slept well enough last night but found myself up at first
light. Immediately flooded by memories of Dad. The power
of yesterday's session? Tossed and turned on the verge of
tears but foolishly fought them back. The old survival operation.

Deliberately I searched my mind for good times with
Daddy: Trips to Prospect Park Zoo on Sunday morning.
Running between his legs to be caught and allowed to escape, then running in for the playful struggle again. Being
carried out on his shoulders into the "deep water" at Riis
Park or Brighton Beach. Feeling very secure and proud up
there. Climbing the highest hill in Brooklyn with him one
afternoon.

More: The day I refused to go to Margery's seventh-year
birthday party across the street when I found out I'd been
the only boy invited. Positive sign, eh? My father understood; he told me to take Margery's present to her house
and tell her mother that I had to go away with him. I loved
our sense of conspiracy. Ran across the street only to have
Margery's mother furiously throw my gift into the gutter. I
brought it home. My mother said she'd talk with Mrs.
Langsam later. I didn't care one way or the other. I was
going to the movies with my father!

Another: Getting up at dawn once to visit his meat sup-
plier up in Kingston. (Lucky I didn't see the slaughter-
house that day!) Riding with my father in his car and

watching the sun come up over the city. Eating fried potatoes at breakfast for the first time in my life.

His buying us similar leather jackets one Sunday on Or-
chard Street, then showing me the public school he'd at-
tended on the Lower East Side.

Jesus, I guess I wanted to be with him more than I've
ever admitted. It's enough to make a faggot cry. I think I
will.

One most important good memory: summer at the Hermitage. Age seven or eight. One Friday evening after the
daddies had come up from the city, mine said, "Let's go for
a swim." It was past swimming time and had started to rain
a little; no one else was in that pool but my father and I.
Delicious. Sinful. He was a great swimmer, although it was
my mother who'd taught me how the previous summer. My
father said he'd once raced Gertrude Ederle at Brighton
Beach. But I was swimming well and seemed to be impress-
ing him. God, it was so quiet there—just the two of us—
and that delightful threat as the rain hit the water. To
make him laugh I said, "Hey, we'll get wet!" And he
laughed. I never wanted it to end.

He'd had a younger brother who'd drowned in a pool as a
little boy. My father had been seventeen at the time. When
the other children who'd been playing at the forbidden
place came shouting that someone had fallen in, he raced
toward the pool, dived in, and went under again and again
until he came up with the body of the drowned little boy.

Once on Yom Kippur I went with my parents and grand-
parents to visit the boy's grave. My grandmother began to
weep and my father said that her eyes had been weakened
by all the tears she'd shed since her youngest son's death. I'd
never liked my father's mother, who always seemed indifferent or bossy to me and had a kiss that stung, but I felt
sorry for her then and imagined myself as the drowned little boy. Now, for the first time I'm wondering if I were

really quite so secure that day when my father and I swam alone together. Even then I'd heard about his drowned brother. If I'd fallen in, would my father have been able to save me? And if he came up with my dead body, would that have made him cry?

My life has always been filled with death fantasies and suicidal wishes. Several times as an adolescent I wrote suicide notes to square accounts with my father. And there were even two meager attempts at it: Once in Brewster I started the motor of our car in the closed garage until I got sick from the smell. Then, after my mother's death I tried it with far too few pills and phoned Dr. M, who phoned my brother-in-law, who raced across three boroughs to help me walk off a roaring headache. Futile attempts and fantasies designed to make my parents (whether alive or dead) and my analyst (more dead than alive) feel sorry for me, to let them know how they were making me suffer, to wreak revenge, to plead for help. They never knew what I was trying to say. Neither did I.

An aggravating sequel to that pool memory: We had a dilapidated leaky pool of our own on the farm which was constantly causing us trouble, but we had no money to finance a new one. During the last summer of my mother's life, when I was feeling most exploited by that losing proposition of a place but would do anything to keep her happy by fulfilling my father's wishes, the bastard decided we needed a new fence around the pool. Instead of buying a single-picket or wire one, my grandfather found a bargain at a local lumber mill for an unpainted double-posted fence. No wonder it was a bargain! It cost my brother-in-law and me endless weekends of work to paint it. The trickiest, most frustrating, time-consuming, groove-infested paint job anyone but a pointillist could have conceived. But we did it because my mother wanted it to sustain my father's belief in his bargain of a buy, and we weren't about to make my dying mother unhappy by telling Dad to go fuck himself or paint the goddamn thing himself instead of sitting on the porch directing traffic without any eyes!

Oh, it hurts so to write that. I think of his blindness and suddenly all of it gnaws at me to be forgiven. And once again I'm back in those deep feelings of guilt because I hated even to be seen on the street with that blind man. People were watching, I was sure! People were looking at him—and me! We were objects of pitiful interest—*I* was— the one who wanted to be invisible with no voice (and who loved to act and dance and sing and write and be patted on the head for performing). I felt so ashamed of him. Hated him for his blindness. And guilty, so guilty for that. Making me feel so bad again. Taking it *into* myself. And out on him when it was the fearful, repressed, good, quiet, little boy unable to scream out his hatred. Well, he had something to do with that too. It wasn't just my mother who preferred me not seen, not heard, who didn't protect enough. Your turn's coming, you bastard!

And now I recall again that awful fight I was forced into at the Hermitage. One of the other fathers deliberately goaded his son and me into a slugging contest. I saw him doing it. Even at the age of six I *knew* what that crud was up to! I could see the way he wanted to test his own son's strength against mine. But I had no doubts that I'd lose. That other little kid, my height, my weight, was a slugger, and I'd always been afraid to make a fist. I feared him. I hated his father. And my own father was nowhere around to stop it! He hadn't come up from the city yet. I *had* to fight! And was crying even before I was into it, raging inside at that other kid's father for doing this to me, raging at my own for not being there to protect me from it.

Did I also wonder if my father *would have* stopped it instead of beating up the other father for me as that son of a bitch deserved? I'm sure as hell wondering that now. Or would I have been made to fight my father's battle for him, just as that other little kid was being made to fight *his* fucking father's?

Still another: Age six or seven again, on 15th Street. One Sunday morning I was playing with Eddie Mortimer, a year or so younger than I. We often played together when I wasn't playing with the girls, whom I preferred playing with rather than with the boys my own age. We were chasing each other in a circle. Eddie tripped and began to cry. He blamed his fall on me and ran to tell his father. I raced into the house scared to death, and damn it, his father *did* come. Even now I can see myself slamming the back door in Mr. Mortimer's face when he came down our alley, and my mother hurrying down the back stairs to talk with the angry man. I hadn't done anything! It wasn't my fault! I *told* my parents that. But both my mother and father said I had to apologize to Mr. Mortimer, more for slamming the door on him than for accidentally making Eddie cry. The Mortimers, I recall, were going off to church. I had to walk to their car to say I was sorry even though I was shaking at the gross injustice of it. To this day I wonder why my father didn't defend *me* against that man. The Mortimers were Irish. We were Jewish. Maybe my folks decided it was the best way to keep the ethnic peace. Well, it also helped to fuck up your son, Daddy.

Hell, so much of this seems trivial now. So much a deliberate wish to make a *case* against my father. Every kid goes through similar trials, doesn't he? Why should I bring in so overwhelming an indictment on such slim evidence? It makes me feel fraudulent, ungrateful. Do I really want to get angry at these unavoidable disasters?

(But that little kid knew them only *as* disasters, Dad! "Be that little kid, Mike. Feel it as you truly felt it then," I hear Rhoda saying in my mind.)

Suddenly I'm back to portions of food at our kitchen table. My constant watchfulness for who was getting *more,* my sister or me. My eating quickly to get it all down in order to be able to ask for seconds even when I was already full with what I'd hardly tasted. My mother never denied us food. We got that from her, at least.

I still eat too quickly, still look for more. Still, damn it, *still!* "It's bad manners to take the largest piece of cake." Good little boy again coveting that large piece given to Daddy. Or given it for being the bigger child, feeling loved more than my sister and lording it over her.

I want to call myself reprehensible again, as I did for years with Dr. M, but now I'm screaming at the bastards who did that to me, slapping grievance on top of grievance, trying to fight down guilt again for this case-building, forcing myself in the most painful way imaginable to feel the hate I could never feel for fear of its consequences!

When my two-year-old sister came nosing around the table while my parents were having dinner one night, Daddy pushed a cupcake in her face. Little Mickey wouldn't snoop near Daddy's dessert like that. Not he. He doesn't want to be hurt by Daddy like sister was. He's older. Better. He'll steal a cupcake later when no one's looking.

"Let's find out what's inside the beanbag, Sister."

We open it together, and oops—the beans spill out.

"They're beans. That's interesting. That's what makes the noise and feels so funny."

Uh-oh—Daddy's coming. He doesn't like what we've done. He's sending us to bed.

"But we just wanted to see—"

He's coming at us with a strap now. He's hitting me with his belt—because I opened a beanbag!

Sister's throwing another tantrum and now Daddy is pushing her face down near her own vomit to make her smell her mess like a dog. Little Mickey will never throw up. He doesn't want his face in vomit. He won't scream like sister does. She's the bad one. Mickey's good. Mickey will be loved. Look how good I'm being, Mommy. Look, Daddy! Stay away from me, Daddy!

Daddy wanted to take me to a football game at age eight or so, long after I had no use for sports, feared the competition with the other boys, my utter failure at it. What seemed so natural to other kids I couldn't even *practice* to achieve. I still walk on the other side of the street when I see boys playing ball in fear that they'll miss a catch and I'll have to throw it awkwardly back. Anyway, I told him I had an earache and a stomach upset. I just did not want to *be* with him. He was furious and took my upstairs cousin instead. Who cared? I hated them both. Convinced I could feel my ear and stomach really hurting now, I put myself to bed and played the abused, misunderstood, sick little boy for no one but myself to see.

12:30 P.M.

I planned to go on a hike today. (Planned, planned!) Left two hours ago. Thought I'd follow the yacht harbors to the bay along San Pedro Road, maybe even work my way around to the Marin County Courthouse, where I'd shoot my way into jail to visit Angela Davis and tell her the *real* reasons why America is trying to kill her. Am sitting now writing this on an old broken-down dock looking out over intermittently blue and murky water.

Walking along the backwaters awhile ago, I realized why I felt so pleased by the view of the boats and marine supply shops there: Sheepshead Bay. Brooklyn. Right back to another good time with my father: Dad taking me to see the strip of fishing boats down at the bay. Our going out in one once. The family occasionally having dinner together at a seafood restaurant facing the water.

I never feel more comfortable about my body than when it's immersed in water. Light instead of leaden. Once I won a swimming trophy at camp which meant more to me than all the goody-goody awards for character that I usually carted home from that God-awful place. I've got water on the brain today. Or does everything go back to water?

I stopped at the supermarket to pick up something for lunch. Always have to have food, don't I? As a child I remember if there were plans that might interrupt my regular schedule at the trough, I'd ask, "But when will we be able to eat?" Very virtuous today, though, buying yogurt and fruit. Then wondering if it would be enough. Would I still be hungry? The ancient deprivations. Cursed the old folks for it. (Talisman.) A new justification for overeating?

During my walk I also stopped to look at some bottle-brush growing along the road, realizing I'd never really seen how they grew, although I'd always liked them since seeing them first on my Fulbright year in Australia. But while I was examining one of the blossoms, I immediately imagined critical eyes staring at me from the passing cars. "Oh, look at the fag at the flowers!" "Oh, my, sensitive, isn't he?" "Who does he think he is—Ferdinand the Bull?" I forced myself to go on looking, trying not to curse myself for my dogged paranoia. And then I had what must have amounted to a small satori. (Can there *be* small satoris?) Anyway, another overwhelming connection: Suddenly it came to me that my paranoia has always been a projection of my *own* self-criticism, my own willingness to condemn myself for feeling what I'm feeling, for having interests that no "real boy from Brooklyn is supposed to have!" Wow, that goes so far and wide and deep. I can see so clearly now how hard I've worked *not* to accept responsibility for my own feelings—so fearful I had no right to them or afraid of the consequences of feeling what I was feeling.

"That girl in the third row is looking at me as though I'm stupid." (*I* think I'm stupid today, damn it.) "That guy hates me because he thinks I'm cruising him." (God help me, I *am* cruising him, and I hate *myself* for it.) Shit, for the first time in my life the most elementary psychological lessons seem to *apply*.

Should I hitchhike the four or five miles back? The mere idea stops me. As a teen-ager in Brewster, and during my year in Australia, I did some hitching. Here in California it's an approved pastime, but what a problem it still presents for me. Every car moving on by is telling me I'm despised. (Once again, my projection of self-hatred.) Then if it stops, oh, the obligation it's bound to impose, the performing I'll feel compelled to do to pay for my ride. Since living out here I've picked up my share of thumb trippers, and expected nothing from them in return. More often than not, I *don't* pick them up because I feel I'll have to give *them* more than a ride—show interest, be helpful, informative, a good man they'll love. Screwed either way. That's how this neurotic survives. I'm too disgusted to trace it all back to its source now. I'll walk home. I need the exercise! (I'm also great at finding the incontrovertible excuse.)

10:00 P.M.

Since it's ten o'clock I feel I can allow myself to write about this extraordinary evening now.

So many times during the last few hours I wanted to rush to this notebook and jot down everything that was occurring to me, every subtle change of mood, until it dawned on me what that would mean: The act of writing is a transformation of present feeling into past fact. By removing myself to paper, inner chaos is all put in order and its experience avoided. No wonder Rhoda said not to write. Oh, yes, quite often this diary has led me *into* feeling, not away, and when that happens I've stopped long enough to get into the feeling as fully as I could. But tonight there was a definite need to use pen and paper as a neat way to feel nothing.

Why? After today's hike and a shower, I found myself without a *plan* again. I did a little crying and moaning, but it was brief and easily dismissed. Waiting around in a stupor until after five o'clock, I felt overcome by a disastrous sense of depression. Not the agonized sadness of therapy, but the old amorphous blues, deepening into frustration and yearning for what I am now beginning to feel doesn't really exist. The yawning void of unscheduled time made me desperately seek to create a plan. "You'll eat at six. Find a movie at seven. Walk home at nine or ten. And be nicely ready for bed."

But there seemed no film worth seeing, and any I chose tonight would be as much of an escape from myself as the bars or the baths or the icebox at home. Then I thought of phoning Stan; only I knew that would be tantamount to saying: "Look what you've done to me, damn you! Look how I'm suffering now! Help me!" Besides, instead of a need for his friendship, I was really hungering for my usual sex with an acceptable stranger. No feelings involved in that, right?

Okay, so I put off the phone call and walked into town for a virtuous salad instead of the fattening foods I craved. An act of will, but okay. The meal was tasty and filling. I didn't miss the french fries. And by then I knew what I had to do tonight: Go home. Sit with this vague depression, this anxious yearning that's taken up so much of my life, and experience it for what it was.

The sense of *needing* to do just that was enough to dissipate some of my bleakness then and there. But I postponed the inevitable awhile longer. Went to a supermarket to reward myself with some fresh cherries for dessert. No cookies, no cake. Dallied at the health food shelves. Looked at the frozen packages as though I were watching a Broadway musical. Coveted nothing, though; merely killing a little time. A leisurely walk back by a different route, eating cherries, and almost feeling happy with myself after those earlier awful hunger pains and that chasm of doubt.

Along the way home I noticed an unusual flower vine. Intricate as a spaceship, the most complex purple blossoms I'd ever seen, inlaid, spiked, cross-stitched, overlaced, with ants working its bearings and wheels. The middle-aged couple on whose fence these flying saucers had landed were just leaving their house. With less than a flash of fear for rejection, I asked after the flower's name.

"Passion vine," said the woman with a pleased smile.

"They're unbelievable."

She was delighted. "Yes, aren't they something?"

I walked on feeling airy and free simply for being able to ask what I wanted to know.

When I reached the Center, I could no longer put off the night. I sat with my pain as I watched the shadows creep up on the eastern hills. Nothing new to record about the agony itself. But this pain, at least, was the *real* pain. This horror, this desolation—the absolute reality of my life.

In all fairness to Dr. M, during my years of psychoanalysis whenever one of those unaccountable depressions came on, we also used to try to trace them to their origin and frequently found them caused by a feeling of my not being justly rewarded for some act I found deserving—if only the living out of another week. Once in a while he'd suggest I try to stay with my depression and not run off to the usual outlets for angry relief. Sometimes I did, but always felt like some medieval page lying facedown on his vigil's crucifix to bring him to knighthood and heaven. More often my stoic deprivation would only make me angrier and angrier until I found greater justification for an inevitable lapse back to a mindless movie, a pizza pie, a drunken bat, a tickle and squirt at the Tubs.

When it grew colder tonight, I returned to my room on the run, recognizing there will be no knighthood, no heaven, crying and calling (unable to scream, still afraid of unsanctioned noise) but feeling fully that endlessly welling grief for never having had enough love, and often fooling myself into thinking if I worked hard enough for it I would find it.

More tears. Deep breaths. The tingling feeling. More pain.

During a lull I wanted to look at my watch—and realized what I was looking for again was elapsed time, hoping it was late enough to end my torture. I laughed and screamed aloud: "It's never going to end! It's there—that emptiness —and it'll always be there! *Now* you know why you're so conscious of the goddamn clock! You think that there's a time limit to this pain! That Mommy will make the hurt go away, that if you wait long enough, are *good* enough, you're going to be granted happiness! That's why your head's always living in the future! Well, you know what your happiness is going to be? Knowing that there's no hope for that kind of happiness and being able to feel your outrage as deeply as you're feeling it now! At least you won't be searching for illusions of relief from that terrible knowledge anymore! At least you'll know the goddamn score! Zero! Zero! Feel that zero! *Feel it!*"

More tears and more.

It came and went, not with greater intensity than it first had, and often with just vaguely hurting lulls. But I knew what the pain was and I sat with it until now.

During the course of the evening while I was still out on the porch, the guy next door said hello to me as he left the house. Contact finally established after a whole week with only a door between us.

Later, when I was in my room, I heard him return. I desperately wanted to knock on his door and say, "Look, we don't have to talk at all, but I was wondering if you wouldn't want to join me by the front window and watch the light go." No seduction. Matter of fact, I thought it might help lead us both to more tears like the group. But I saw from the darkness under his door that his lamp was out, and I was afraid he'd reject the suggestion anyway—or accept it.

No, it wasn't all good clean pain. All too often those lulls began to fill themselves up with new plans for things to write in this journal, imaginary conversations and letters to friends in the future with sentences already styled and restyled—my continual living for later, not now, controlling all with language, escaping presentness, crushing spontaneity with some calculated design.

Despite all that, the evening was of remarkable value. Without irony—my misery was thrilling. And I have no fears that this is just some new sophisticated form of masochism.

Good night, Rhoda Wasserman, wherever you are.

Sunday

Up early as usual. Dallied over breakfast; Sunday paper. Felt athirst for print.

A full week now.

Found myself awhile ago attempting to evaluate more clearly the differences between Intensive Therapy and my experience with orthodox psychoanalysis. (Most likely to convince myself that this won't turn out to be the same waste of time and money and energy.)

Well, certainly not money and time. Three weeks isn't eight years, nor will this cost the thousands of bucks that helped that happy decade slip by. Energy? I've probably already expended more of that during the past week than I have in the past year.

The most obvious difference between the two methods, of course, has been the way in which everything here—all bits of biography, all present conflict—is continually being related back to basic feelings.

With Dr. M I certainly *learned* a great deal about my past and present behavior, but in some essential way I never did manage to feel its *impact* on my life. Direct expressions of deep feeling, in fact, seemed to be discouraged, or at best were symptoms to be analyzed, explained away, put down in the interests of reason, remaining suspect or expected to wither away with understanding. Maybe my well-honed defenses allowed that to happen; maybe it was the limitations of the psychoanalytic technique itself; maybe just my luck to get stuck with a crummy shrink, I'm not sure. But I *do* know that all the standard business I did—the free associating, the dream analysis, the endless acting out and discussion of my transference, the grudging acceptance or violent rejection of Dr. M's interpretations—now seems to me like just so many professionally sanctioned head-trips that did their share to keep me from feeling the deepest sources of my troubles in any crucially liberating way.

And God, it was always so damned defeating, having learned to regard my acting out as idiotic but still feeling unable to stop it. What was the trick, I used to ask Dr. M, that would allow me to *use* all that new insight into my insanities and so prevent me from resorting to them?

From time to time he'd assure me that if I recognized what I was doing often enough, came to understand something of their cause, then eventually I'd realize how needless those defenses and compulsions really were. If I had the courage to risk new ways of behaving, and sticking to the job in spite of the anxiety it would entail, eventually, eventually, I'd be able to replace my old crazy business with something "more appropriate" (his euphemism for "less crazy").

Well, I *believed* that. Worked my ass off for it. It *still* seems a sensible procedure to me. But when I repeatedly failed at it, I had only myself to blame for not trying *hard* enough. And so once more into the breach, dear friends, and once more—failure:

Deliberately denying myself the comforts of the icebox, for instance (having learned that Mommy didn't live there), only eventually to eat up everything in sight when the sense of deprivation became too intense. Feeling like a virtuous boy for a week at a time—dutifully teaching my classes, going to analysis, writing my novel, enduring one more dull blind date—only to find myself overwhelmed by a sudden sense of angry futility at getting nothing in return for so much hard work and running to the Tubs to turn a trick or two or three or four for want of "love." Trying to test myself in front of assorted urinals to see if I could pee without feeling squeamish (now that I'd learned I was really "covertly calling to men," as Dr. M analyzed my dilemma) only to feel constricted once more, humiliated, unrelieved. Willing myself *not* to measure myself against every man I passed on the street—seeing myself better than this one, worse than that—and automatically feeling sexually drawn to the ones I failed to outmatch for whatever figment of my libidinous imagination. Trying to stick it out with this girl, that girl until anxiety ground down to resentment, and resentment provided an angry excuse for escape from yet one more involvement. Trying (when my mother was alive) to set up my own life in the city and finding myself all too often heading homeward on weekends and holidays. Trying (after my mother was dead) not to turn my sister into her surrogate, and finally running off to California when I found myself unable to avoid doing just that. Trying. Trying. Trying.

"Your new knowledge of yourself will provide the impetus and direction for a healthier act of will." That's what analysis seemed to dictate to me. Unfortunately I never learned the knack of *willing* new life into being. Can anything be willed to grow and grow *well?* I couldn't deliberately *think* myself straight, could I? "Every day in every way I'm growing better and better." That only seems to amount to a more elaborate form of repression. "No, I will not run home to Mommy next weekend." Which *still* clutters up your mind with Mother. The cord just gets knotted another way.

No, instead of asking me to feel what I was feeling and accept those feelings as part of me, as primal theory has been telling me to do, my psychoanalyst was constantly asking me in one way or another to be *reasonable.* "Grow up, Mr. Rubin." (Oh, yes, *Mr. Rubin,* for eight years, right by the book.) "Be reasonable. Do the appropriate thing. Can't you see how inappropriate that pattern of behavior is yet? Don't you see by now how childish that feeling is?"

Never, never allowed to be for one instant the screaming little boy who was still wailing away inside despite the best advice, that sad kid secretly dying from some unknown sense of deprivation, and so fearsomely angry for being made to swallow the rage that he'd been swallowing until his guts hurt.

Psychoanalysis

MIKE: That goddamn bastard. I hate him for sitting on the porch all weekend while I spent the whole time working around the farm and following his orders!

DR. M: You're angry with your father again.

MIKE: You bet I'm angry!

DR. M: . . . .

MIKE: What's wrong with being angry?

DR. M.: . . . .

MIKE: Huh? Huh? Am I supposed to feel guilty about it? Talk to me, damn you!

DR. M: . . . .

MIKE: Okay, *don't* talk.

DR. M: Anger has a pattern with you. We always see you being angry when your father puts demands on you.

MIKE: Of course I get angry! Don't I have the right? His demands drive me up the wall!

DR. M: Come now, Mr. Rubin. You know we're not here to make value judgments. Your anger at your father when he puts demands on you is a pattern to be conscious of. It will help you decide whether it is appropriate or not.

MIKE: The anger or the demands?

DR. M: . . . .

Intensive Therapy

MIKE: My father used to sit on the porch and give me orders every damn weekend that I went home to the farm.

RHODA: How did that make you feel?

MIKE: Angry. The goddamn bastard.

RHODA: Tell him.

MIKE: You goddamn bastard! I'm angry at you, Daddy!

RHODA: Feel it. Tell him, Mike. Tell him!

MIKE: I'm angry at you, Daddy! Angry! *Angry!*

RHODA: Tell him why.

MIKE: You're telling me to clean up things again. You're giving me more orders! You're sitting on your fat ass again and making me do your dirty work! And you never took me to the zoo enough! You won't take me to the zoo! Take me to the zoo, Daddy!

RHODA: Why do you want him to do that?

MIKE: I want him to—to give me something for working so hard!

RHODA: Tell him!

MIKE: Give me something, Daddy. I work so hard for you. And you—oh, shit—you don't love me, Daddy! You don't love me! Oh, I hate you for that! I hate you! Love me! Love me, Daddy! Love me, you goddamn bastard! Love me! Oh, God, Rhoda—he won't, he won't—

RHODA: That's right. It's hopeless.

MIKE: But I *need* him so!

RHODA: That's right too!

MIKE: Oh, God—

Oh, shit. I'm crying over this. I have to stop writing awhile.

12:30 P.M.

Well, that was a surprise. There I was trying cockily to dramatize what went on for me in psychoanalysis and what's been going on here—and found myself right back in the thick of feeling again. Ah, the power of ahhht.

Which brings up an equally important difference between the two techniques for me: In this place I seem to be discovering that I *am* my feelings. No matter what those feelings may *be*, that is *me*. And that's not *bad*. My reality —"irrational" as some shrink might view it—is accepted as *valid* because that's where I happen to *be* just then. The spot where I presently *am* is *all* that I am.

I guess the Gestalt people like Perls and the client-centered ones like Rogers, maybe even R. D. Laing, can be thanked for promoting that good bit of sense. What a relief from the abiding burden of shame for my "inappropriate" feelings during psychoanalysis. A shame that never let me clearly see my amorphous frustration as acceptable rage, my anxiety as acceptable fear, my discontent as acceptable sadness.

DR. M: You did that to win your mother's love!

RHODA: You still need your mother's love!

What a world of difference.

Yes, damn it, this week I've begun to realize something I must have been forced to forget: that my problems have to do with my *heart,* not my head, with the visceral needs of the feeling organism that *I am.* This technique is bringing my body back to me. I no longer have to feel like that resentful chattering corpse lying on Dr. M's couch, or the irrepressible wit who tried to charm the pants off Dr. T. I'm a writhing, breathing, screaming being who's feeling the power of his own blood and heartbeat again, who's beginning to feel the ways he was robbed of his right to *have* a body at all.

The influence of the Body Boys again, no doubt—Reich, Lowen. Ms. Ida Rolf as well?

And Rhoda's questions, "What are you doing with your hands? What are you doing with your feet?", her asking me to feel my quivering stomach, to feel my dreadful knots, to let it all out, to break through my—what does Reich call it?—my "structural armor" has helped me make such astoundingly new connections with the origins of my abuse. It's taken me back to my beginnings far more effec-

tively than the talk trips of dream analysis and free association ever did. Its revelations are still very Freudian. But
it's Freud mit Feeling.

And it's been beautiful to begin to find my own way back
to myself without having to feel jeopardized at every turning by an analyst's subtle but pervasive set of value judgments.

Value-free as Dr. M liked to pretend to be—silent analytic
wall and all—how those middle-class standards of his used
to seep through. Once I took a summer job at a community
pool, collecting tickets at the door three evenings a week in
order to make a few bucks and keep me writing during the
day. When I mentioned how boring it was, Dr. M said,
"Why anyone with your education would take a menial job
like that is questionable." I remember dating a girl for a
time who was intriguing to me because of/or despite a
whole host of deep psychological problems. Dr. M's response? "You know by now she's got a lot of difficulties to sort
out and is obviously unmarriageable now. Yet you still insist on wasting your time with her. Why do you think that
is?" His question might well have been valid, but don't tell
me it was value-free. And I bitterly recall how little significance he placed on my writing, never seeing it in itself as a
creditable motivating factor in my choices, the reason why I
continued to teach, the sacrifices of free time I made to go
on with what *I* at least considered important work. Once he
asked me if I'd ever considered going to law school. Talk
about Jewish mothers, Rhoda? Criteria of health for that guy
were marriage, a professional diploma, and a mortgaged
house in Scarsdale.

In a way even Dr. T's values intruded—no matter how
much more deeply humanistic they were. No, he didn't insist on marriage for me, but he certainly did hold high a
Buberish standard of living. The epitome of successful therapy seemed to lie in the ways I could be brought to
establish deep interpersonal relationships. I won't quibble

with that. It's what I very much want for myself. But aside from the fact that I was nowhere near knowing what I-and-thou even *meant*, what I never got from Dr. T was a sense that anyone but I had trouble thou-ing.

Sure, I always chose difficult girls to get involved with (as a handy excuse to run once the going inevitably got rough). That much I'd already accepted. But if only Dr. T had also added a lesson in sociology: The girls I was most likely to meet *were* in their own ways all coercive, demanding, game-playing creatures. No, damn it, that's *not* my imaginary projections of Mother. It's what the girls I knew had been bred by *their* mothers to be. Those girls were the products of their background and the age. And the age, Dr. T, is a sick one. Yeah, sure, if I were "healthy" enough—fearless, self-possessed, accepting—I'd be in a better position to cope with their sad limitations. But now I'm beginning to wonder what the value would *be* for a healthy man in putting up with the limitations of his shortchanged girlfriends. My closest relationships with both men and women have always been the ones in which my sicknesses were most compatible with theirs. *Feh!*

Shit, if there's any value judgment floating around the Center here, it ain't that one's personal fulfillment, one's reason for being comes from *other people*. I seem to hear Rhoda saying that after Mommy and Daddy we really have no one but ourselves to help us to live. No lovers, no friends, no strangers. And if Mother and Father have failed us, well, there's no one left in the world who can take their place, we must make do with ourselves alone. And as for deep interpersonal relationships? Hell, it's beginning to seem to me that they simply cannot exist in any real way unless we are able to need *nothing* of another person, nor feel obliged to give away anything but the gift of what we truly are at any minute of the day or night. And who, may I ask, can put up with that?

5:30 P.M.

A dullish afternoon. Tried to stay with the whole week's wearying pain, but had only sporadic feelings, few tears.

There's a new girl across the hall now: pretty, nervous. I wanted to reassure her that today and tomorrow would be the worst of it. But that's misleading, and might not be true for her. I wonder where I got this Holden Caulfield responsible-for-all-the-kids-in-the-rye complex anyway. (As if I didn't know by now.)

Began to think about the bathroom again and how someone new would be listening to me through the door, fearful she'd walk in on me if I left her latch undone. And here after two good days of feeling free to piss to my heart's content because the previous girl had gone. Boy, I'd like to resolve that someday.

During one of a dozen lulls I looked out the window which, because Rhoda said not to, is still sinful inside me. Blamed myself for cheating on Mommy, but could only laugh when tears were what were needed.

The guilty feeling got worse as I rustled the newspaper for a time and thought that the guy next door would be taking me for a coward, pointing a finger through the keyhole to say, "Naughty boy! Put down that defense against feeling!" And while writing this morning I was sure he was listening to the ball point turn, that he'd soon barge in to shout, "Aha! So, I've caught you at it!" No, Mommy and Daddy never said a word about my excessive masturbation, but I'm sure they must have known. Don't *all* parents know? Don't they have eyes in the back of their heads? Can't their hearts tell when you're doing something wrong?

> He sees you when you're sleeping.
> He knows when you're awake.
> He knows if you've been bad or good
> So be good for goodness sake!

Fuck off, Santa Claus!
Oh, wait, it even gets better:

> Oh, you better not cry
> Better not pout
> Better not lie,
> Better not shout (ha!)

Jesus, they even make you *sing* yourself into sickness.

I heard the guy blow his nose. Fine, that allows me the right to blow mine. But for how long before I'm making measly little sniffles into my tissue paper again? Shh. Shh. Oh, damn it, I wish I could scream!

Did.

Just now I wondered if keeping this journal isn't a serious mistake, if *all* the writing that I've done hasn't been done for all the wrong reasons. As I've been coming to see it now, the very act of putting something down on paper is a suspicious separation from myself. Automatically it turns me into a kind of performer forced to choose the appropriate word, to find correlatives in intellectual concepts for those languageless qualities of emotion, to judge the aptness of a metaphor, the cadence of a thought. Even in a log written as haphazardly as this is, I know a certain vague aesthetic is operating, that I have an unconscious audience if only it's my own critical self busily picking and choosing bits of matter like a magpie building a nest. (Metaphor again and uninspired, but left intact to defy my point, and now defied, more dismal proof of worse self-consciousness.) No matter how slight, I'm coming to loathe that sense of separation from immediate feeling now. Suddenly I can appreciate Tinguely's self-destructing machines, the *objet d'art* that comes apart in the very act of being itself. Those Happenings so popular awhile back and the Yippie street events take on new value for me in their expressed need to be open-ended and free of contrivance. (In theory, at least. Manipulation is always too evident.)

But that's probably all beside the point because what I'm really worrying about now is the basic impulse of my imagination and my commitment of that imaginative process to "creative" writing. All children, I suppose, play games with their imagination—act out fantasies, play house with their dolls, create singsongs full of unconscious desires. Lots of them, like me, even go on to perform them publicly or write them down—those gaudy lies of wish fulfillment of what they consider to be wise and rueful flashes of truth—fleshing it out in fiction and perhaps justifying it all with the Jamesian need to teach us how to live better lives.

When I was very young, I know I kept at writing primarily as an escape. I preferred the pencil to playing with those threatening boys. The fairy-tale plays I wrote as a kid of seven were whole little worlds I could create and control. Solace, diversion, power. And it was pleasant to be praised for them at school. Whether those early fantasies were oblique expressions of yearning after Mama and Papa or harsh judgments on an ungiving world as they later became, I see now that they not only were designed for escape or the means to come to terms with my reality, but also were done in sadness and revenge, as cries for help against nightmare, retreats into comforting lies, struggles against overwhelming emptiness.

As a kid I also loved to act. Why not? The most obvious way to lose one's life is to assume another's, speaking through someone else's mouth, someone else's words, allowing your body to show itself at last because it's not really yours up there on the stage but the character's you are playing. Yet as much as I loved acting and worked at it in college and beyond, even considering at one time to try it professionally, its demands were always much too public for me. My performances were usually marred by an awful edge of self-consciousness, my body much too clumsy for a stage, my voice a weak and uncontrollable instrument.

No, far better for this boy to go back to silence (always silence!), scratching away like a mouse (Mickey again) those stories that tried to make people cry or blamed the world for being cruel.

Well, and so: If my fiction writing has been done largely as a defense, its later aesthetic challenges merely a more sophisticated justification for going on with it, and praise from those nonexistent universal parents the main reward that I sought, do I abandon my creative work now for something more honest? If I learn successfully to confront my inner life now, what value can fiction have for me? If the psychological answers I arrived at through writing will at last be accepted emotionally now that I'm being taught to ask the proper questions, will I have any *need* to write again? Yet I love to write. (Or think I do?) And without it, where do I go?

Ah—so *that's* the problem, you fink! It sure as hell took a long time for you to get to it!

You're trying to plan your future again! That abominable need for certitude. That dead security that kills all sense of the future!

Well, maybe so.

And maybe these new felt truths will simply help me see my fictional situations just that much more fully. At least let me live with that illusion a little while longer.

9:30 P.M.

In San Rafael for supper tonight I came across the guy next door eating an ice-cream cone in front of Baskin-Robbins, whose thirty-one flavors also held out the promise of Mother's milk to me.

"Rewarding yourself?" I asked. My own motive projected again, of course.

He smiled in complete understanding. My projections aren't *always* wrong.

"How's it going?"

"Not too good," he said. "The whole week's been pretty bad. My feelings—I can't seem to get into them deeply enough."

I nodded. But my own feelings were awfully mixed then: empathy for his problem. Worry that the method might have its failures. Mean pleasure for having done better with it than he.

"I've heard it has its ups and downs," I said. "You reach plateaus. I feel that way today."

"It was getting to me on Friday finally. Maybe next week will be better."

Nodded again. "Last night was rough on me. I had an impulse to ask you into my room—just to share the silence."

He looked a little bewildered. (Priest dandling hot-and-bothered buxom young miss: "*Kiss* you? Why, my dear, I shouldn't even be doing *this!*")

Quickly I added, "Your light was out early so I didn't."

"Can't sleep. Get up early as hell but never can fall asleep."

"I'm usually up around five myself. I hope I don't disturb you when I rummage around." (Oh, how patently we betray ourselves.)

He smiled. "I thought I might be disturbing you."

Enough said. "See you back at the ranch—" wanting to walk home with him but afraid of the imposition and pressure it might cause us both. Yes, us *both*, Rhoda, goddamn it!

On the way back the air was filled with hundreds of small dun-colored moths, as though they'd all decided to crawl out of their cocoons together on this last day before summer. Some were already topping others on the bushes. For what? A brief brushing of wings, a minuscule screw, eggs dropped, and death. We don't seem to be born for much else. Then why all this fuss?

Monday

Woke up this early with another connection: the cause of my compulsion to check my mailbox so often at home. I'd always assumed it was a writer's occupational disease—waiting for the latest rejection slip or the all too rare check that meant I could still go on with it. Also a momentary relief from the typewriter's din, another place to run to when the work's rotten and anxiety's already made me drink too much coffee or pushed me to the toilet too many times. But now I see it for what it's really always been: "Oh, boy, the mail's come! Let's see who loves me today! Ah, good old Eva in Missouri, Arnie in New York. What, no letter from my agent? Well, then, it's time for her to go! Mmm, at least the *New Republic* never fails me. Is that all? Is that all there is? No more mail until tomorrow! Maybe the postman'll ring twice. Maybe if I smile he'll bring me good news. Maybe he'll bring me love!"

And right now, at sunup, I'm *still* driving myself with plans for the day—even for pain: "Today I'll try to get into that sex-and-love dichotomy. Today I'll think about my father some more." Even when I've already learned that just by sitting here alone and remaining opened to myself, thoughts will run to important matters of their own accord, the emptiness will roar in enough feelings to fill an ocean floor and flood me with the truth.

I remember when I was still teaching high school English and our reading took us into discussions about family relations, once in a while I'd try to shock a class to consciousness by saying, "All children should be taken from their families immediately after being born! If they're allowed to remain at home, they're bound to be messed up for life!"

(Speaking from experience, of course.)

Some of the injured would agree with bruised smiles. Most, though, would shiver and whine, "How can you *say* that? A child needs his mother and father! Oh, I'd never want that for myself!"

I'd goad them with alternatives, often using the kibbutz or commune as other approaches to child rearing, perhaps more valid for healthy upbringing than the nuclear family. Some would remain skeptical, others at least would concede the possibility. A few were already applying for visas to Israel.

But this morning I'm not so sure that either commune or kibbutz is the best answer. At least not as presently conceived. I remember again my reservations after reading Spiro's *Children of the Kibbutz* and Bettelheim's *Children of the Dream.* As content as those kibbutzniks seemed, growing up without the imposition of Mom and Dad's neurotic shit, some awfully subtle new impositions seemed to be replacing those of parents. Instead of Papa's approval, it's the peer group's love that's sought, and a pressure to conform to the demands of the group for fear of losing peer approval. That seems to me now even more devastating than dealing with two sick adults. Imagine feeling unconsciously compelled to gather clues to the common will in order to learn what's expected of you, when the community might be made up of a dozen or so individuals all with their *own* clue-seeking drives!

Bettelheim claimed to find that kibbutz kids had few strong emotional responses to one another. But is this due to healthy stability or a reaction to emotional deprivation? Aside from educational innovation and increased crop production, no important individual creative acts were in much evidence on the kibbutz that Bettelheim studied. But was *that* due to a healthy lack of necessity or the pressures of neutralized conformity in an anthill of dutiful workers disallowed personal quirks? Bettelheim suggests that a more accurate appraisal of the kibbutz as an alternate society will be forthcoming only when we can study future generations of these communal sabras rather than those who still might be suffering the parental and communal influences of values and fears imported from their devastating European history. Give or take a few more Middle Eastern wars, maybe tomorrow's fully homegrown kibbutznik with more of Israel in his ancestry will be a freer, more flexible, feeling child. Remains to be seen. That is, if the kibbutzim still exist. Recently I read that many of the younger generation are being drawn to the cities for the greater educational and economic opportunities there—and for the bright lights?

Then there's that study I came across a few months ago concerning the importance of the mother's heartbeat on the temperament of her unborn and newborn child. Apparently a rhythmic heartbeat pulsing its life to the fetus, and continuing by its proximity after birth to assure the infant of a stable environment, has a lot to do with the rearing of a secure adult. In *Childhood and Society* Erikson discusses the newborn child's immediate need for basic trust in his world, a sense that his demands are being met, that his cries for food, warmth, safety, can effect the action that will help him. Obviously this fulfillment must come from the reliability of the mother, so why not right down to the comforting beat of her blood? No kibbutz mother or metapelet is in a position to give that kind of ideal attention to her baby, at least not as child rearing is currently handled. Given the *ideal* conditions of economics, leisure, and her own physical and mental health, wouldn't the mother in the nuclear family be in a better position to fulfill this essential job?

And yet I worry about those unforeseen and inevitable

problems even in the most advantaged of homes. My sister's twin boys were forced to spend the first days of their lives in an incubator. Warm as that artificial environment is devised to be, a box sure as hell ain't no mother; soft though the lights and lining, how glaring and cold that place must seem to a baby! Where is the heartbeat for comfort, the human skin to touch? The tragedy of some autistic children has been linked to the experience of the incubator—a machine that might kill much of the organism's essential life in order to keep it alive.

One of my two nephews had an awful time adjusting to being touched as an infant. It took months and months to get him fully to trust another person's body, not to flinch or pull away when being lifted or held. How much that might have had to do with my sister's early mishandling of him, I don't know, but the incubator might have been a stronger factor. Maybe even for his twin brother, whose responsiveness to people is so different; he never seems to get enough cuddling and at times does his sad best to gain an excessive share of attention. Twins might be a special case, yet I suspect that all those jolly big families of eight or ten or twelve sport quite a few emotionally starved children who paste on those grand ingratiating smiles while they're silently screaming their insides out or trying to prove through desperate achievement their exclusive need for parents they never quite had. Ethel Kennedy, I'm watching you.

An aunt of mine complained to me once about her daughter-in-law carrying her baby around in a sling near her breast "like a savage," instead of using a proper carriage. The stupid woman. Of course she was really complaining about her daughter-in-law again for stealing away her son, but as far as that baby is concerned—Fathers, raise your sons high on your shoulders, damn you! Carry them piggyback, let them swing on your arms, cuddle up to you —and don't you dare drop them or do it against their wills! Mothers, breathe deeply, have your blood pressure checked, and hold those kids close to your calmly beating hearts!

1:15 P.M.

The older woman upstairs is gone, some empty air-conditioner boxes stacked against her door. I'm sorry I never knew her name. Or did more than nod to her at the diner. She was a good screamer, whose howling above helped me to cry more than once. But I wish I'd known her story. I've always been interested in other people's lives. Again, I'd assumed that a writer's preoccupation. Now I wonder if it wasn't more out of a need to identify with their strife, as I did with those movie shadows, to puzzle through alien biographies in order to corroborate my own.

Are we turned on to or off by people whose lives reflect our own? Both, I guess. I think of my brother, ten years younger than I, having so little love for me and confessing once that my excessive show of emotion made him nervous. Did he see in me reflections of his own difficulties? His coming from the same fucked-up family would suggest it. He had awful problems with my mother, quite early grew cold toward her, never showing her any feeling, either his anger at her or his unfulfilled need for her. My own depressed and anxious reaction to our sad and stifling household repelled him. Healthy rejection? Or fearful self-preservation?

Early today I put on my freshly laundered sweatshirt and had a Proustian experience. The faint smell of detergent took me smack back to the basement of our house in Brooklyn and the pleasure of sniffing at a basketful of clean clothes folded by dear little Mother's own fretful hands. I write it in irony now (a bad sign) but clung to that sweatshirt like Linus' blanket. It got me into feelings fast.

Still have trouble screaming in my room, though. Am afraid of the noise for the neighbors. Can groan and cry a lot but cannot let myself completely go. (Also feel I should save it up, damn it, so I'll have a good show ready for Rhoda.) She said I could use any of the offices upstairs whenever one was free, but people are coming and going around here from morning 'til night so it's hard to know when to rev up my motor and take off up the stairs.

I thought a lot about child abuse again as I lay on my floor much of the morning (my session isn't until the middle of the afternoon today). An unusual guy I know has been a sailor, an oil rigger, a movie grip, a pothead, a screenwriter, and a thief. The girl he lived with for a while had a baby by him. Sometime after they split up, she went mad and was institutionalized. At the age of three their child was shipped cross-country to New York, where her father was willing enough to keep her in his current cold-water flat.

When I first saw the child, she was covered with fearful running sores, constantly whimpering, barely able to talk and without knowledge of her own name. Her father fed her hot dogs and beans and managed to find girls to sit with the child in exchange for a screw. He earnestly wanted to care for the pathetic thing but seemed incapable of giving her anything she really needed. She nattered and squawled all day long or played odd little games with herself, never being taken out in the air, while her father locked himself in the john to write a screenplay. She'd been reared on a commune, he told me, and the kid's mother had made a mess of her, but the guy seemed to be doing little better, shouting at her to keep still, paying her scant attention.

I wanted to call the authorities. Then felt I had no right to interfere. Aside from the ugliness it might cause, I doubted that any city department would do better by the child. All the guy's other acquaintances sensed the disaster here too, but except for a little advice about food and medicine, what else could you tell a man about his "personal property"? Suddenly the kibbutz doesn't seem so questionable.

Thought too of a college instructor of mine who reared the daughter born to his wife by a previous marriage. While I was at college, the girl was only twelve, a fey thing given to walking alone in the woods. All us college boys were waiting for her to grow up so we could marry the sprite. Years later on a visit to my former teacher, I learned that the girl had wound up in an asylum after whoring around with a hundred men and finally suffering a total collapse. With great passion my teacher declared, "Oh, that ungrateful child! I worked for her! I clothed her! I saw she was fed, Mike!" I'm sure you did, friend. Just that. And told her so too, you ignorant bastard!

After that I remembered the little gifts I always come bearing my niece and nephews when I visit back East. I can spend hours in toy stores trying to find the most appropriate items—imaginative, educational, frivolous, sturdy—and all, I realize now, only to make those kids love me, thinking I won't be enough for them if I enter their house empty-handed. But what do I do next time? Risk bringing no gifts when I've created in them the need to expect something of me more than myself?

Also remembered Laura's salad and wept for being such a fool. One day she appeared at my apartment door with a bundle of groceries. I was panic-stricken. She refused to be cowed by my madness, went into my slip of a kitchen, and whipped together the best chef's salad I'd ever eaten. But I didn't know how to accept it, was scared shit by the obligation it seemed to entail, by the realization that she cared enough about me to surprise me like that, and that I'd somehow have to pay her back for that affection. A goddamn salad! No simple meal that. Monumental! I felt undeserving, ashamed, grateful, afraid. Oh, Mother.

Went to pee, and out in the hall saw the Ex-Girl of the Adjoining John waiting for a private session. I asked her how it was going Out There.

Not bad. Better than she'd hoped. Lots of things had stopped. "I mean I still do all the dishes to get them to love me, but a lot of other things are very different."

"Tell me, is it different because you catch yourself doing something crummy and *will* it away or because it just isn't there?"

"A lot of crazy things—the need to do them—seem just to have disappeared."

I nodded and crossed my fingers. "See you on the floor—"

"Keep with it," she said.

5:30 P.M.

Rough start to today's session. Went in complaining again about my incessant need to organize things, imagining how the sessions should go, so fearful of a life unplanned, of spontaneity, of imperfection. A little talk of that chaos led back to the dark streets of Brooklyn, running home from Hebrew school in the cold winter night, fearful of muggers and kidnappers, back to fears of robbers in the house, ghosts on the back stairs.

Rhoda made me call my parents for help. And as I screamed out for them, I flashed on one particular night when I *did* get my father to search the house. Out in the living room he began to mumble some broken words as I hung back in the hallway. I ran to tell my mother: "There *are* robbers! See! I wasn't making it up! Daddy's talking to them!" My mother sat up in fear only to learn when my father returned to the bedroom that no one had been there at all; he'd just been mumbling in his sleep. Scolding me for making her nervous and afraid and *giving her the runs,* she angrily went off to the toilet. I was making my mother shit! Oh, boy, I screamed about that one for quite a while.

Stayed with all those childhood fears, then centered for a

time on the horrors of my father's meat market with all those hooked carcasses and all the blood, the pretense I made of being Daddy's little boy for the men who worked for him, when inwardly I already hated him, *hated* him! and came down to the market only for the pencils and pads he let me take home from the office, only for the hot sandwich he bought for my lunch at the Greeks'. Pencils and food. The story of my life.

"Pencils and food!" I shouted.

"Not enough for a little boy, is it?" The ubiquitous Rhoda.

"No, God damn it, not enough! Not enough!"

I moaned for the waste. Screamed out my rage.

Began thinking how my mother always kept my father and me apart—never allowing me to say a straight word to him or to make him angry—and realized how similar it must have been in her own life with her own domineering father. I cursed her aloud for not letting me ever show a straight feeling, for coming between him and me, for not allowing herself to express *herself* to him, making *me* believe that that was the way it w̅a̅s supposed to be! Psychoanalysis never revealed that one to me. Nor did it show me what now I suddenly understood: that all my mother's own stifled emotions, those crooked ways of hers to hide her own feelings of grief and rage, showing it only through nervous ticks, screaming annoyance at her children, running off to the movies—all were being done to *herself*, that my father certainly never *asked* her to grieve. Though, who knows if he'd been able to live with her if she'd asserted her own needs like a healthy human being? I'm not sure about that, never will be now, but screamed out my lungs at her for being so crooked with herself, and twisting me up in the same goddamn way!!

Suddenly I felt my whole lifetime of unfairness to my father and sobbed. Then I recalled that my first erotic fantasies had obliquely been about him. Relating him to the picture of an ogre in a book of fairy tales at the age of eight, I'd wanted to crawl up the hairs of the giant's leg.

"Why?" asked Rhoda.

"To get into his arms. To feel his strength. I needed him. His muscles."

"Tell him."

"I can't. It's too embarrassing. Shit, this whole sex-love thing is still such a mess in my mind. I know my mother turned me off women, but that doesn't mean I wanted to sleep with my father, does it?"

"You wanted him to hold you. You needed him. That's a feeling. Feel it!"

Oh, boy, I felt it. Cried out in need of him. Wanted my father to hold me. To hold me. To love me. Protect me. To make me feel loved by him. And behind those tears and screams of need, hating the sense that he never was, never would be mine, that the feeling had to be felt like this and accepted as did the futility of that need ever being fulfilled.

After recovering, I could feel only renewed anger at my mother for destroying a relationship with my father that might have saved me. Then I blamed my father for not being able to stop her from doing it. Not *wanting* to stop her. Shouted it! Then blamed my mother again for ruining my relationship with *all* women—making me so afraid of the involvement, that I'd have to perform for them to keep them happy, be sucked dry, be a sexual athlete, grow weak with dependence, made to feel protective when I couldn't protect myself. She had destroyed my life. I wanted to kill her for it again!

"Say it! Tell her!"

"Die! Die, damn you! Die! Die!"

An endless screaming.

Exhausted at last, I whispered dryly, "Now is she dead?"

"Is she?" Rhoda countered.

"Never."

No more equivocation. I saw her face again and screamed for her death once more, knowing my longing for her would never die but that I loathed her without apology for ruining my life.

"How do you feel, Mike?"

"Good."

10:20 P.M.

An awful session upstairs tonight. Maybe a revealing one. While we waited for the group to begin, one woman, whom I hadn't seen before, started chattering nonstop about having put on twenty pounds since starting therapy six months ago. "Eating to fill the emptiness," she kept repeating. "Eating to fill the void." I panicked at once. If she hadn't come further than *that* in six months, my God, what about me?

During the session I lay in the same room with her, only to find myself listening to her repeated baby squawling, which sounded more like a broken record than anything real. Her noise prevented me from getting into my own grief and made me furious. Only intermittently could I attend to my mother and father and felt oddly at sea when my rage at them wasn't balanced with pleas of need for them too. Either rage—or vacantness. And too much vacantness to feel I was getting anywhere at all. I asked myself about that guilty reaction, related it back in the usual way, but wasn't convinced of anything but my own increasing sense of failure.

Moving to the next room to get away from the annoying sounds of that woman, I found myself connecting her squawling to my mother's early screeching at my sister and me. Although it hardly sounded similar, I wore myself out with raging hatred for it.

Thought then of a lullaby she used to sing to me, some-

thing that's always been good for a nostalgic tear or two.
But again—vacantness.

Decided I was *still* furious and raged against her with
even more intensity than this morning. When the session
was ended, I was still angry and could have gone on with it
in another room but cut it off, almost afraid that I still had
more inside me than I'd figured.

During the wrap-up afterward talk was dominated by the
foul woman, who I suspect also keeps chattering away to fill
that void of hers. But one of her stories was sad: being
pulled by the hair and pushed under a cold-water tap by
her father every time she got angry. An older man added
one of his own: being made to breathe at a natural gas jet as
a home cure for whooping cough and almost dying from it.
Another woman spoke of a panicky incident with a policeman that had occurred that day. A girl spoke of her fear of
a doctor's appointment she had to meet tomorrow.

Once again I began wondering how good this therapy
could be if these people's symptoms were still so evident.
They sound so knowledgeable about their causes; why then
haven't they found quicker relief through feeling the origins of their grief? Or aren't they connected enough yet?
How deep does feeling go? My own anger had deepened tonight, and I know *I'd* turned it off too. But the possibility
of its limitlessness disturbs me so. I thought I'd been feeling
so deeply *already*.

The first summer's night. It'll probably be an anxious
one. Am frightened and can't bring myself to scream it out.

10:45 P.M.

Went upstairs and screamed myself hoarse for five minutes. "I hate you . . . !" "Help me . . . !" But I feel no
less disturbed now.

Against orders I even called Stan to find out why he hadn't shown up for the group tonight. Worried. Wanted him for comfort. Feared he'd been killed on the freeway or something. No answer at home. Will try to sleep.

Tuesday

Woke just now from an odd dream. Feel embarrassed by it and puzzled. First dream I've had here vivid enough to recall:

I'm either host or guest at a big party. A well-known movie actor is there. Apparently we'd once been lovers, although now we live together only as friends (similar to my real situation). As the party winds down, we go to bed to sleep side by side as usual. I begin to feel that I want to make love to him, but the actor has gone "straight" and doesn't want to. I accept that, since the departing guests are still within earshot, which is also inhibiting. Somehow, though, something must have aroused him; now he says he wants to make love to me. (By this time I've reimagined his body into something more suitable to my own desires—less heavy, better built.) I say wait—I have to go to the john first. But when I get there, I can't piss. His waiting for me, the fear of more guests still around create too many pressures. I feel uncomfortable but decide to go back to bed. For some reason there is a urinal or bidet in the bathroom as well as a toilet. It's filled with shit. I complain to myself that some Englishman or Frenchwoman at the party has been too stupid or drunk to know the difference between a bidet and a john. I try to flush the damn thing (once again a urinal), but it's clogged up with feces, which begins flowing all over the floor. Furiously I stand there in the mess, realizing *I'll* be the one who'll have to clean it up tomorrow, not the actor, my roommate, and I'm in no mood for sex with him after all this aggravation.

With material like that Dr. M and I would have had a field day. What does Rhoda want with dreams? I can see obvious elements operating in this one, and some real puzzles. Can't come to any firm conclusions about it and have an aversion to toying around only to find a pat answer. *Are* there answers to dreams anyway? In all those years of psychoanalysis I never did get the hang of what one was supposed to *do* with analyzed dreams. For a while I believed that if you had a revealing one, it resolved a conflict. Expressions of wishes and fears, sure, but I supposed, like writing a book, I was to get some reward—health!—for delivering up a creative act. A good crap? Did Mommy reward me when I shitted well? Are artists all really only anal personalities? When I start mind-fucking like this these days I just get—pissed off.

7:30 A.M.

Damn it, I still can't let that dream go. Feel I have it now and might take it as optimistic—but who knows if that's not just wish fulfillment of a higher order. That "Englishman or Frenchwoman" was really the irritating lady last night. I recalled thinking she looked like a frowsy Irish housewife—loud, dowdy, without grace. And of course, not that lady at all, but a projection of my mother. And my mother? An extension of *me* somehow, the introjected part of her, at least. (Would Fritz Perls be proud?)

The dream was just getting into something important about my homosexuality, or my relationship with Stan, whom I've occasionally associated with that movie actor. Maybe something about the two parts of me too: the part that wants the security of the homosexual encounter, the part that rejects it. The social pressure of the crowd seems important here.

Anyway, before I can get to deal with myself that way, I feel obligated to clean up that woman's shit first. Mother's shit. I make Mother shit, don't I? And Mother still keeps me from myself. Just like that woman did last night.

Those "guests" must have been the group too, each of them filling me with dismay and anger for not being further along in their own therapy. They keep me from *me* too. And since I am a resident of the house—the host but also a guest at the Center—it was my party, and my duty is to keep the place clean. Do their dirty work for them, too.

"I won't clean up your shit!" is what I wanted to shout aloud, and will today. (Planning, planning again instead of doing it!)

"No wonder your sister looks like a piece of shit!" cries that kid from camp again, and again I'm beating him up in defense of my mother's lie, cleaning up her shit for her!

I'm raging now—just thinking about it—and should let loose, but it's too early here. I'm furious with my mother all over again for making me introject her in me and make me clean up her mess before I can get to my own! I have no more tears for her! No more!

Must get into the homosexual thing now:

Stan and I have lived together for three years but have been friends for eight. A "full" (ha) sexual relationship has long since vanished between us. We've survived together as dependent companions, searching for our fleeting sexual involvements elsewhere, running home to each other for protection, forgiveness, assurance of continued affection. All those things I now understand we can't possibly get from anybody but ourselves.

My first attraction to him was sexual, though, the usual father-fantasy ploys. He's a few years older than I, seemed "masculine" to me, intelligent, gentle. Moreover, initially he seemed indifferent to me and hard to reach, but when he did show interest, his sexual responsiveness was overwhelming. I was flattered and amazed to be able to move someone so deeply. And realize now it was just what I wanted to do with Daddy and never did.

Early in our relationship back in New York, I wanted to run out on it, but Dr. M suggested I stick with it awhile as the only way to discover the basis for my anxiety in an active life situation. On doctor's orders I fell in love. I really do love Stan as the most interesting and undemanding friend I have, even though I also realize now that his usual deference to me is the surest sign of his own illness. The worst times of our relationship, in fact, have been when he's most acquiescent to my fearful moods and infantile demands. I almost can't stand his kindness, since it puts me under the gnawing obligation to be as kind to him (shades of Ma). What does the coffee seller say on TV? "You get what you pay for."

What's more, I've often felt compelled to keep our relationship going *because* of that obligation to his kindness, even at times when I feel we're giving each other far too little to keep us together out of anything but the fear of living alone again. Yes, we share good things, common interests and outlook, but our emotional life is such a tangle, everything is so often strained.

Where I display feelings all over the place, he tends to show very little. His attitude has not been so much "Nothing can hurt me" as it's been "I don't really care." Decisions for food, entertainment, friends, etc., all seem to be mine. "I don't really care," he says; anything to keep me happy. Anything to stop him from expressing his own wishes. He must be so frightened it might lose the little he has of me—and doesn't even know it! He had a more fucked-up childhood than mine, and yet unlike my defense, his has been to cloak it all with comical nostalgia that forbids him to feel the abuses against him.

I hate my dependency on him! When he decided to change jobs and leave New York, he begged me to come with him. I'd stopped teaching in order to write full time for a while and had only my complex feelings for my sister to hold me in New York. I didn't want to leave, though, knowing damn well how little Stan and I had operating for us emotionally anymore. I told him one night that I couldn't. He cried like a baby and I heard my father crying again after I finally told him, close to the end, that my mother was going to die. I couldn't stand hurting him. Stan: my father. I couldn't stand losing him. And wept with him. And came to San Francisco with him, feeling a need for his support and protection still, the need not to hurt him, and rationalizing it all with the prospect of a new life, a new novel under way, an adventure, the possibility of finding a more satisfying teaching position, which, luckily, I now have.

But my anger at him for not giving me what I wanted my mother and father to give me and never got I now see shown in so many damned ways. I'm often so angry at him in the house, feeling crazily put upon, doing much of the cleaning and cooking, since I work at home more often, and never feeling properly rewarded with praise for being the good little slave. Then, doing something I consider extra-specially kind in order to wheedle affection from him, which, once achieved, I cannot abide. Just as in the dream —first my trying to win him, failing; then his being aroused and my not wanting to—stalling around the bathroom, my mind turning his body into one that's more excitingly ideal for my fantasies. My God, when we moved into our present apartment and were dividing up household jobs, I just realized that I announced he'd clean the living room and bedroom and study, while I'd do the dirtier work of the kitchen and two bathrooms. I would clean up his shit! In fear of his cleaning up mine! In wanting to make Mommy and Daddy's life more agreeable for them, I took on the toilets again! Boy, this is too painful to be funny.

1:00 P.M.

My session today was overwhelming. Went in saying, "I know talking's a crime around here, but I want to tell you about last night."

Rhoda said, "Go ahead."

Said pretty much what I'd written this morning and started letting out all the rage, feeling it fully and deeply again.

During the ordeal Rhoda asked, "Why didn't you tell the woman last night about how you felt?"

"You mean—during the session?"

"At the wrap-up afterward."

"I didn't think it was allowed or that I should."

"You felt it. You might be surprised how others might have felt the same thing—or not."

"I didn't want to hurt her."

"Who?"

"*Any* woman—no, Mommy."

Tears. Tears. Tears.

"Why not?"

"I was afraid to. I want everybody to love me!"

I-Won't-Take-Your-Shit-Anymore, Mother! became the theme of the day. All my shit stories came pouring out. Once I saw my father's stained underpants and thought, "He can do that, but I can't."

"Tell him."

"You can dirty your underpants, but I *can't,* you bastard!"

I told him all right.

Then I recalled my mother's sometimes lighting matches in the bathroom to dispel the gas, and the pleasure I had in following her example. One day a match set aflame a piece of toilet paper incompletely submerged. The little fire made me think of larger ones. After that I often filled the toilet with tissues and paper and lit them to see the flames in the bowl. Brought my sister into the forbidden game so she might share the blame if Mother found out. Both Mother and Dad were pretty preoccupied at the time— Mother carrying my brother in her, Father recovering from his first cataract operation. I wanted to burn down the toilet! Burn up the shit! Then one evening the laminated seat *did* catch fire and some friends visiting with my parents rushed in from the living room to put out the flames. No damage. No damage? My mother said she couldn't get up quickly now or be frightened because of the baby inside her. My father wasn't supposed to move his head. I didn't do it again. Mmm, I wonder why.

That got me into my feelings about his blindness, the sad history of the poor man's cataracts, glaucoma, detached retinas occupying our lives for years, and finally resulting in his near-total sightlessness when I was about fifteen. Gave more biography than I thought Rhoda would allow; how my father bought a house and new car, spending a lot of money during those intermittent periods of sight between operations, the onset of glaucoma, the detached retina ordeal, all the patching that never held. How we had to be quiet and loving and how I hated to be because I *had* to—and only hated him.

I told him that too. Told him. Told him. Told him.

Spoke out also of my hatred to be with him on the street. My guilt and paranoia over the attention I felt it drew to my own ugliness, his imperfection, his failure for me.

After years and years of thinking it, harboring it inside, I screamed it all out for the first time in my life.

Then I thought about my second novel and how I'd had trouble writing about the mother around whom my fictional family revolves. Never could get her right. The center chapter I'd reserved for her development, as a kind of hub for the family wheel, always turned into bathetic soap opera as I tried to show her in her infinite grace and self-effacement. My editors finally suggested I drop it altogether, keep her in the background of the book as a kind of mythical presence. I followed their advice—a convenient cop-out when in my fear of offending or hurting my real mother and out of a yawning, self-protective ignorance of her nature, I couldn't get at the truth.

I cursed her for making me into a liar for her sake!

She was dead before that book was published, so was my father. Most of it was written during her dying. By writing it I was trying to save her life for me. I lost her and lost much of what that novel might have been.

But I couldn't regret that now.

I didn't want her shit anymore. I refuse to clean up her mess! "No more! No more! I don't want to. I won't, damn you! I won't!"

Still later I flashed on the junior high friends I chose, the guys I saw as class misfits like myself, probably the most interesting kids there, but misfits nevertheless, while I silently envied the rugged athletes from afar or the mature-looking intellectuals who seemed so intimidating. How furious I was when my "short" friend decided not to play the class clown anymore and started lifting weights, even achieving a certain amount of self-assurance as a result. How I ridiculed him for his muscle building only because I felt abandoned and angered with him for trying to change himself while I felt I never could.

Through more tears I recalled how I'd tried to win the older boys in the high school fraternity I pledged for, promptly falling in love with our pledge master, who perfectly fit my fantasy bill. But once accepted as his favorite and a symbol of the fraternity's promising future, I dropped the whole dumb business, never attending meetings, denying the friendship I'd fought for, deliberately making myself the outsider again because of the obligations that *belonging* entailed, wanting lovers not friends after so much work being what I was not!

Thought then too of my counselor at camp my four-teenth summer, a man for whom I still have the warmest regard. He was absolutely everything dear old Dad wasn't—handsome, well built, interested, articulate, sensitive—a guy who played a guitar and sang Socialist folk songs long before they became the fashion. I trailed after him all summer long like a doting puppy, wrote home about him in wildly glowing terms (See, Mom! See, Dad. I've got someone who's interested in me now!). And how noble I was to refuse to include him in my masturbatory fantasies because he was far too sacred for such sinful regard! Sex and love together? Not on your life!

Miraculously that good guy never once rebuffed me. He recognized my crying need for someone, accepted my adoration without feeling oppressed by it, without catering to it out of any sick need of his own, continually kinder to me than any man I'd ever known.

Cried for him—cried for Daddy. Raged at Daddy for not *being* Daddy. Raged at both Mother and Father. Furious again for Mother destroying half my lifetime.

"You won't get the other half!"

"The other half's for you," Rhoda assured me from someplace far, far away.

"Me? I don't even know who I am now."

"You only have yourself."

"I know it—damn it. And I'll find him! Me! Those bastards. They lost him for me! Both of them! Oh, those bastards!"

Then I began to wonder how much I held myself responsible for my father's blindness. I remembered again the day he banged his forehead on a half-opened overhanging garage door. I'd left it that way for my height while cleaning out the garage. He unexpectedly came out to see how I was doing and walked right into it. I didn't see the accident actually happen. And it wasn't until some years later that I learned it had been the cause of another eye operation. For the life of me I still can't make any direct connection in my conscious mind about feeling responsible at the time. But I *must* have in some strange way, since I hated him so and felt so guilty for hating him. Then I recalled my peculiar justification for a spate of excessive masturbation. If I wished deeply enough for it while jerking off, the act would make my father see again! Ah, the archetypal magic of the cock.

Finally I got around to talking to Rhoda about Stan. Mentioned the things I'd written about him and confessed to trying to phone him last night, my worry at his not showing up for the group session.

"How did you know he was supposed to be there?"

"He was scheduled to go to New York on business last week just after I came here. He said he'd be back at the session the following Monday."

"This is your time to worry about *you*, Mike. Not about him. You know, if this therapy is going to work, you might have to consider moving out of the apartment you share with him."

A bombshell.

"I can't do that to him! I'm afraid for myself! It would hurt him so!" I wailed away. Forgot Stan. Began wailing for Mommy, for my need for *her*, not Stan.

"It's something to consider," said Rhoda when I'd calmed down again. "Not necessarily permanently, but for a time. Friends or couples who are in therapy together too often talk away their feelings or go back to the old ways of compensating for their problems. The point is to stay with what you're feeling—and that's hard to do when you feel you have to consider your partner's feelings too. Think about it. And tonight, if he does come to group, I don't want you to talk to him or attend the wrap-up afterward."

"Can't I tell him that?"

"Why?"

"He'll think I've turned against him or something."

"Why deny him *his* intensive experiences by making such allowances?"

That sensible remark was enough to gird me for the ordeal. But I still shake at the thought of leaving him, even if only for a time.

"There are good things we have—as well as bad," I insisted.

"You might get back together."

"Yeah, but I also keep worrying about the homosexuality in it—the dependency I know is there."

"You might not want it on that basis anymore. You'll have to see. You might. Tell me, what are you doing with your time outside the sessions?"

(Why did she want to know that?) "Walking a lot—but I hardly see where I'm going. Sitting in the park looking at the mothers and kids. I want to kill most of the mothers. Um . . . writing." (There, it was out!)

"What are you writing?"

"A journal about this. But I think it keeps me with the feelings. I don't think I'm writing them away. At times, if I do, then I stop. I've been afraid to tell you for fear you'd ask me not to."

"And if I did?"

"I'd go on with it anyway."

"Why?"

"It's important to me. It helps me get into myself more."

"I'd be interested in reading it."

"If I feel I still want to after I get home, I'll type it up. I'm glad you know about it," I added.

"You know, Mike, in the beginning of our sessions you didn't say much. Now, do you notice, your vocabulary has expanded in here?"

"Hell, I'm very verbal. I just didn't know how much talking was allowed."

God, this stuff about Stan won't leave me. I'm sitting in the park now still frightened to death of the possibility that we'll have to split up if only for each other's sake. I feel he won't see that, will take it as my rejection rather than my regard for him. I sense, maybe wrongly, that he hasn't come far enough along in his own therapy to reach the same conclusion. Certainly, when we said good-bye, there was no sense of imminent change in him. And for weeks before I left, he'd been having "plateaus," not getting into things at group. From what he told me, he never did get very far into his own homosexuality during his three weeks of isolation here. To some degree I'm sure he entered therapy only to please *me*. I was the one who told him I was going to try to get an appointment when I learned about the Center's work. If he didn't want to help himself, then screw off! It surprised me when he made his own inquiries. Then ironically, because of our work schedules and the space available here, he went for his three weeks of intensive three months before I did. Maybe that was lucky for me. At least when he returned home, he still seemed taken by the process. There were several good changes I noted during the following weeks: a lot more openness about himself and his feelings; he said that things at his office were going infinitely better; he had a new attitude toward himself. But as my time came nearer, he kept finding excuses not to attend group and seemed preoccupied with emotionless diversions again: business, reading, movies—his usual time killers. A holding action, I think. And there I was getting more and more anxious at my turn coming up. He joined me in overeating. Toward the end we scarcely talked about the therapy or anything of a serious nature. I felt he was closing off his feelings again.

Oh, boy, I'm just now feeling I'll *never* be able to leave him, even for a short while, if he isn't ready for me to go. Father, father again, mother, mother, I know, I *know*. But there are commitments, aren't there? Assumed obligations that must be fulfilled! Shit, the entire ethic of the Western world suddenly seems in doubt. (As though there could be any doubt how fucked up *that* is!)

My God, are *all* our responsibilities—the ones we deny our true feelings to support; that is, the ones that support *our* neurotic needs—conceived out of fear of loss, fear of emptiness, of our reality?

After his wife walked out on him, a friend of mine once complained, "She didn't honor her commitment to me! People ought to honor the obligations they undertake!"

At the cost of their own souls, you twerp?

Stan, Stan—

I think of the living arrangements we have now, the new expenses I couldn't well afford if I moved, even stupidly disappointing the landlord and his wife whose friends we've become, the car I'd have to buy instead of our sharing one, the million little excuses I can find to maintain the *impasse*. But never have I been more convinced that this might have to be done if Stan and I start becoming dishonest about ourselves in support of each other—and never more afraid to hurt a human being I love, even if it's love in my own fucked-up terms. (Maybe even writing this is an attempt to tell him what I can't yet say straight to him.) I dread going home.

6:40 P.M.

Waiting for group to start.

More spleen for Mom: One day I was sitting outside with the young daughter of one of our summer cottage guests. She was on my lap, straddling my knee. My mother quietly said to me that the girl, age eleven, was too old for that. I eased the girl off my lap, not acquiescing against my wishes so much as instantly agreeing with her. My God, who did she think I was, Humbert Humbert? And what was she protecting the girl against? Next year's sexuality, which would arrive on schedule despite my mother and with or without my knee? Jesus Christ, Mother, what the hell frightened you so? You must have been a lousy lay, you pathetic bitch!

Wow, long before that little incident, I must have bought that attitude of hers lock, stock, and barrel. Even today I have qualms about getting too physically close to my niece and nephews while playing with them. I'm afraid I might inadvertently stimulate them sexually at ages eight and five. I fight against that fear and cuddle them anyway, but I'm always slightly anxious that my brother-in-law is going to start to shout, "Unhand my daughter, you sex fiend!" or accuse me of trying to rape his sons.

Have worked out a nice arrangement with the bathroom now. I slam the outer door shut, lock the new girl's connecting one, and piss right into the water! Let her hear, let her hear. Let me take all the time I need to get there! (Hey, maybe something to do with premature ejaculation too— feeling I have to get there fast in order not to take up anyone's time!) But I wouldn't want to bet on this as progress. Whenever I feel more secure in a place, urination becomes less of a trial. Because I'm now senior resident of the floor, the bathroom has become my territorial imperative. Today in the park I shunned the public urinal even though I had use for it. Eventually I'll have to start testing myself again, I guess. "That's my body singing, everybody!" I'll shout as I piss aloud for the whole world to hear.

Hey, just remembered when I asked Rhoda the name of the black therapist today, she laughed and said, "Her name's Miriam. And she's not black. She's tanned and Jewish and has a 'natural.' You're not the first who's made that mistake."

Damn it, and I'd begun to hope that blacks were getting into this new therapy in its early stages. It'd sure as hell help the *real* revolution if they did.

Once in college for a joke I said, "I think I'll write a new Greek tragedy. This guy kills his mother, see, and marries his father." Now I think I was really onto something. *Oedipus Regina,* maybe, or *Electra Rex.* No shit, isn't a concomitant to the Oedipal conflict (whether successfully resolved or neurotically ever-present) a rage at being delivered into one's mother's hands by a deserting father? At least that's what I've been shouting about recently. "Why didn't you save me from her, Daddy?" A basic feeling I never until now knew I had in me.

DEAR PHILIP ROTH:
Forgive me, but the only important line in *Portnoy's Complaint* is the last one: "So [said the doctor] Now vee may perhaps to begin. Yes?"

Laughter is the second husk into which the shucked man crawls.

—Djuna Barnes

10:15 P.M.

Stepping out of my room to go up with the group at 7:30, I saw Stan waiting in the hall. He smiled a little, looking for a smile from me. I *knew* he'd do something like that. But per Rhoda's request, I hardly glanced at him and hurried to an office upstairs opposite the one he chose. It killed me to feel I was hurting him and became my evening's theme, crying for fear of losing him, begging him to save himself, not to miss this chance to become real, to grow well —shouting at him for not allowing me to do the same! One and a half hours of it with little stopping for breath.

Rhoda, working tonight, made me relate it back to Mom and Dad, of course, which I knew and felt and had been including in my fear and anger. But Stan himself still dominated my thoughts.

For some reason I remembered again all the times I hid bread under my pillow as a child. It helped me get it back to Mother more, screaming at her for making me steal bread because she only gave me crumbs of herself. Returned that scream to Stan, blaming him for making me feel like my mother did, taking his crumbs for the whole loaf. A terrible, painful night.

When it was done, I hurried downstairs without sitting in on the wrap-up, as Rhoda had also advised if Stan were there. I spent half an hour weeping alone for myself, my loss, my fear of losing the little I have of him—whom I never had in any real way either. Hated shutting the door on him, practiced shouting "Go away! Save yourself!" if he had the gall to knock on his way out. But almost wanted him to, so that my message to him would be heard, that he *would* try harder to do this thing for himself. Thank God, he didn't come near my door. I'm feeling awfully low now. But I know why.

Oh, my sister, how many times have I heard you or your husband say to your kids: "Go to your room until you're through crying!" Don't do it, please! Let them tell you what it is they're feeling. Help them tell you straight! If they're naughty, ask yourself what you hadn't heard. They were naughty because they needed to *tell you something!* Listen to them! Hear them, *please!* Comfort them, sure, but let them cry until you and they feel what it's really all about. Let them rage if they must. Don't let them beg for your kisses, damn it! Don't *charge* them for your love! Give them your arms for nothing. Let them nuzzle your skin. It's the little you can do for having brought them into this terrifying life.

God damn it, are adults as well as children really merely still and always only fertilized eggs? Embryos still raging at our fathers for causing us to *be* and losing interest as soon as he's done so? Embryos preferring to remain inside our mothers' wombs, raging at them for expelling us to that awful light? Do we spend our whole existence in perpetual need of that first moment when father was full inside mother and mother convulsed us to life, that one brief instant of sentience when we couldn't be anything but certain that we would never die?

SPRING AND FALL:
TO A YOUNG CHILD

by Gerard Manley Hopkins

Margaret, are you grieving
Over Goldengrove unleaving?
Leaves, like the things of man, you
With your fresh thoughts care for, can you?
Ah! as the heart grows older
It will come to such sights colder
By and by, nor spare a sigh
Though worlds of wanwood leafmeal lie;
And yet you *will* weep and know why.
Now no matter, child, the name:
Sorrow's springs are the same.
Nor mouth had, no nor mind, expressed
What heart heard of, ghost guessed:
It is the blight man was born for,
It is Margaret you mourn for.

Wednesday

Slept later than usual, but not easily. Woke still worrying about Stan, the insecurity for me in a possible move, the whole money matter looming large, feeling I'll have to dip into my small savings in order to make the break, and loathing the false sense of security I get from having a little money in the bank. I could swing it, if necessary, but at the cost of so much panic. I still won't give up that penny.

"There are no rewards" is my truism for the day. It keeps ringing in my head with all the impact of divine revelation. That swimming trophy at camp, my published work, my students' responsiveness, applause after a performance, letters from friends, kisses from anyone—my just or surprising reward—none of it does anything but falsely help sustain this sick man's illusion of his reason for being.

It brings a new feeling about boredom too. I'm beginning to think that there's no such thing. To say "God, I'm bored" is really to say "I'm doing what I don't want to do and haven't the inner strength to change that" or "I'm not facing my *real* feelings about the situation" and am hiding my fear of that behind the convenient excuse of boredom. I see myself now "bored stiff" at a party. And I realize how that's because either I'm frightened by the attack or attraction of the people there with whom I feel unable to cope, or that I don't find them interesting at all but am too untrue to myself to say so by leaving, too afraid to assert my real need for need of "love" from them. If I sit alone in my room plagued by inertia or bored edginess, something more profound surely must be bothering me at base. No wonder we fill up our time! Having to live isolated like this has compelled me to deal with moments of what I assumed were utter boredom, and each time I could trace it back to my fear of emptiness, my fear of living unloved.

This "boredom" is very different from the exhausted peace I feel after confronting the truth. I love the good sense of total absorption I sometimes get from my writing, the classes I conduct, the books I read, plays I see, hikes I take. Oh, but the howling sense of ennui when the book is frivolous, the TV imbecilic, the work dishonest, the conversation phony. Isn't that really a warning that I'm deliberately, desperately wasting my precious time again in trying to avoid the central truth of my existence? We are each of us *alone,* damn it. There's nothing to be done about that; no commitment to work, no diversion, no love affair will alter that essential horror. There is no escape but into self-deception and its quiet rattle of panic.

God, that reminds me of a class I once taught on Camus' *The Stranger.*

"Is Meursault the way one should *be* in this world?" was one of the questions I finally asked.

Some of the kids shrugged. Some said, "Why not? That's the way things are."

"What way?"

"The way Meursault sees them. Everyone so disconnected from everyone else. No values to count on. One way of acting as good as any other. Society's demands always so hypocritical and dumb. People—unreliable. Only a momentary engagement of the flesh providing any fun—a roll in the hay, the feel of the sun. Transitory. Not worth one's worry. Why should the death of his ignorant mother bother him? Or even the death of the man he kills? That's where society displays its worst hypocrisy—insisting that Meur-

sault feel what he *doesn't* and pay with his life for not accepting society's mindless modes of acceptable behavior."

Well, not just one student came up with *that*, but
enough contributed to that position for me to ask, "What
about the end, though? What about Meursault waiting in
his cell for death and asking that the one thing to make his
end perfect would be to hear the execration of the crowd as
he goes to the guillotine?"

"Well, that's just to *show* them."

"Show them what?"

"That he doesn't care about them. He's farting in their
faces. It's an act of courage."

"I think it's cowardice," I said. "He needs that crowd to
maintain his stance. Without that crowd to give some
meaning to his meaningless action, he wouldn't know why
he was dying. He couldn't maintain his estrangement. He
would begin to howl for his life. He's *always* needed others
in order not to feel."

"You're telling us that Camus doesn't respect his own
antihero?"

"I guess that's what I am telling you. I have a sneaking
suspicion from having read Camus' other stuff that he de-
spises Meursault even though he might sympathize with his
predicament, since so many of us are trapped in it with
him."

"How, how? Tell us, tell us!" (This remembered class is
getting more and more ideal.)

"Because everything Meursault sees *is* true: Society *is*
hypocritical, tradition-bound, unthinking. People *are* transitory in their affections, their beauty, their commitments.
Like Meursault's mother, they grow old and uninteresting
and probably never gave very much to their sons in the first
place. And like Meursault's mother they probably stage
last-minute love affairs to ward off the fearful specter of
their finiteness. The Arabs are doing nothing more than
that in their silly vendetta. The only way they can maintain
meaning for *their* lives is to flex their stringy muscles and

wield those big knives, risking death itself to give their foolish sense of family "honor" some value. There is no godhead to speak of, except perhaps in the light of the sun, the pleasure of a full belly, and Marie in bed. Even Fernandel can't do much for Meursault but get him into trouble."

"Then you *agree!* Meursault's philosophy, his way of behaving, is the only reasonable way *to* behave in a meaningless universe!"

"You're not listening. Meursault's way of saving himself from that meaninglessness is to cut himself off totally from the full potential of feeling. Yes, he feels Marie and his cock inside her (this class is total fantasy now) and the warmth of the sun. But inside he's as dead as a dried-out clam, seeing below his window only a procession of death as he watches the neighborhood also stupidly filling in the time between the womb and the tomb."

"Then what would you have him do?"

"*Howl* a little, damn it! And by screaming out admit that his heart is *breaking* for the human condition! That's what Anouilh says in his *Antigone*: Tragedy is when you realize there's no struggle, and all you can do about it is shout! Important things get said then when you can embrace your existential dread and feel it utterly without entertaining one iota of hope for changing its nature in any essential way. Meursault is a cop-out and a fink!"

Applause.

Followed by Bronx cheers.

Both—and in that order—inside myself, inside myself, of course.

I really did say a lot of that in that class, but what galls me now is to realize that it was an "intellectual" position I could believe in, without it ever truly entering my heart. *That's* changed. *That's* changed now, believe me.

And Jesus, if that's the case, then I guess I'll never even be able to sit in all honesty through another play. Sure, we all know that 98 percent of our theater is escapist. But I'm thinking about the so-called serious theater. Most of it suddenly seems to me like brilliantly devious ways around coming to grips with our root problems for fear of them.

What plays might still leave me feeling authentic? *Oedipus,* of course, and his buddy *Hamlet.* Ibsen's *Ghosts.* O'Neill's *Long Day's Journey into Night.* A couple of Pinter pauses—but not the rest. Maybe, just maybe Albee's *A Delicate Balance.* Some others I can think of. But I can't even trust Beckett anymore because of his unwillingness to see that all our cosmic hopelessness is really domestic tragedy.

Never before have I felt so deeply the ruthlessness of our biology. Nature doesn't give a shit about us! Her (her? ha!) only impulse is to keep our bodies alive so that we'll produce more bodies, and more. No matter if we warp our souls in order to survive. Biology isn't interested in souls. Souls? A meaningless word. Nothing more than another biological device designed to keep our reproducing bodies alive.

We are made to live. And if we resist living authentically out of fear of our finitude, we are *still* made to live—but at the cost of our own integrity.

That's the only little saving grace our consciousness can allow us: to be able to feel the truth of our predicament—if we have that kind of courage. That's why suicide seems so meaningless to me now. It's only another defense against facing the terror of what it means to be truly alive, the all too understandable impulse to end the horror of that fearful knowledge that we *are* alone and essentially helpless, essentially unloved by anybody but ourselves. But my God, if faced, if truly embraced—I want to write: truth, freedom, reward, health, infinite insight, total sensuality—but I can't believe in prizes or permanence now. If by some miracle within myself I'll be able to achieve a modicum of what this therapy seems to be asking me to feel about my condition—the human condition—then maybe I'll be able

to see more clearly the value of being alive. I don't have a
suicidal thought in my head right now, though my past was
full of them. Yet I've never felt sadder about myself.

11:45 A.M.

During my session just now I began by telling Rhoda
about all these grand existential observations of mine, my
feelings about *le condition humaine* (*la?*). Only to hear
her say: "That's a cop-out, Mike. You can only feel for
yourself."

I argued the point but lost it in tears along the way when
it started to connect itself once again to my own history.

A little later on I returned to it when I heard the guy
next door—whose howls I now recognize—banging away in
the office of his therapist beyond ours. Sometimes there are
three or four patients in individual sessions upstairs at the
same time, and the noise is abominable. But the guy's
efforts made me instantly identify, bringing on another
flood as I thought of all humanity adrift in the same leaky
boat.

"No parent," I insisted, "not even the *healthiest,* in the
best of all possible worlds, can ever give any child enough
love to escape the awful fact that he's essentially alone!"

"Feel that for yourself," Rhoda demanded.

I wonder now if in some measure her unwillingness to accept man's dread of his aloneness as a universal truth rather
than a neurotic symptom isn't *her* cop-out. Oh, maybe she'd
ultimately agree with me, and her efforts to keep me zeroed
in on myself are the needful direction of this therapy, but it
still strikes me that she might have stopped to consider what
I'd said no matter how abstract the sound of it. It *still* seems
important. I'm still wondering if even the loved children
of the world shouldn't come of age through this terrible

knowledge that I'm confronting here. Or does the healthy child, graced by his parents' spontaneous, undemanding love and allowed to express the range of his feelings fully, come to understand this deep sadness of his own accord *without* fear of it? Does he more easily recognize that no matter how lucky he's been in his parents, no matter how minimal his neurotic fears, and how directly expressed his needs, there is still and always more of the same within him? That the emptiness is there, though embraced, accepted, assimilated?

Will the healthy child who knows please stand up?

Jesus, if Rhoda thinks *my* crummy abstractions are a cop-out, how would she handle a mathematician?

Toward the end of the session, Rhoda asked how I was feeling for about the thousandth time.

"Awful," I said.

She let me sit with that another minute, then suggested I take the evening off. I couldn't recollect what day it was. Thought it was yesterday and expected another group session tonight. Wishful thinking? When I realized it was Wednesday, she said, "What will you do?"

"Go to some lousy movie, I guess. Sex is out, right?"

Nothing much new revealed by today's session—but that so necessary and essential repetition of my basic felt needs. Like practicing emotional chin-ups. Exercising the heart.

One bit of biography occurred: Since my mother's death I've kept a few things that belonged to her after we broke up the farm. Mementos I associate with good memories: a string of crystal beads that my father and I once bought for her birthday together. A necklace of ugly tortoiseshell disks which she often wore when I was a child. And a comical perfume bottle with a funny stopper that used to sit on the top of her dresser—a Christmas gift from me. More crumbs, of course, my need to keep together all the little crumbs left of her.

"Do I have to throw them out now?"

"You'll do what you feel like doing."

"Whatever I do, Rhoda, I know I'll never be able to feel the same about them."

1:30 P.M.

Crime, crime! Discovered the San Rafael Public Library. Came in to sniff the books. A pleasant modern place. Will write here awhile.

Old habits die so hard and won't be willed away: While having a great-tasting sandwich in a Swedish bakery at lunch today, I discovered myself already eyeing the pastries in the showcase, wondering what I'd treat myself to for dessert, sacrificing the very fine taste in my mouth for the fantasy of future pleasure. It's always been that way with food for me, and though I find myself tasting things in my mouth more thoroughly these past few days, it's generally been an active act of reminding myself to do so. Home again—that gobbling up what I had in front of me in order to earn "seconds" just to keep that mouth of mine stuffed! No wonder that lady irritated me: "To fill the void. To fill the void," still filling it up just like me with food and words.

Just as with pissing, there was always pressure at our kitchen table. When little, my sister and I generally ate dinner before Mommy and Daddy. I wonder if we were forced to hurry so they could sit down. I feel something of that inside now. I certainly recall when I was older and the family ate together how I gobbled things fast to get away from the scene, wanting to avoid my father at all costs, and made bitter, I suppose, by my mother's preoccupation with him. Besides, there was never any conversation worth hearing at our table. Oh, I listened eagerly when my mother occasionally gossiped (more crumbs) but easily turned off my father's rare opinions, hearing only his growl (even now). After he was blind and began to read via Talking Books, I was even more loath to discuss his work with him. College snot that I was, I hated him more for thinking he could catch up with me now, wanting *me* to educate *him!* (Jesus, I'm going to crack up right here in the library!) I feel so bad about my hating to help him. Well, shit, it was his fault —*your fault*—damn you!

While walking into the center of town I realized I hadn't masturbated since I'd been here. Several heavy fantasies and many fleeting sexual thoughts, though: as always my penchant for appraising people on the street—that guy's face, that one's legs. Girls' bodies too, but not as often. And always in my mind, envy, envy, envy of any physical quality I find attractive.

Most of the time I discover myself seeking out my own humiliation. A bare-chested boy two blocks away, and before I can really see what he looks like, I've fantasied him into a god. That "shouldn't look, shouldn't look!" still dogs me when I'm attracted to a girl. There are plenty of beautiful young people in this town, and it's that time of year when bared unruined bodies are singing to the birds. Though I'm out of the Center only two or three hours a day, the avenue seems a constant parade of sensuality. I avoid trying to look into strangers' eyes here, resisting my endless, habituated cruising, but again, it's been an act of will all week. I pray this need to act out these wishes for Daddy and my deluded dream of finding my perfect self on some street corner will dissipate sometime sooner than my death will do it.

No, I don't want my sensual life to end. I'd still like to appreciate and touch and hold—but something *real,* for God sake, not these chimeras. Am again disturbed, wondering how in the world my homosexual urges will reckon with the possibility of a "new" me. If I have to *deny* them, then it's still only that miserable act of will. If they leave me of their own accord, oh, shit, I'll have to start dating girls again. No, damn it. No more yearning in either direction. If it happens, it happens. The future will take care of itself whether I sit here worrying about it or not.

While walking I also caught my head in the act of forming a phrase: "My mind seems to be emptying, but I feel much fuller for it." I was fashioning that for this notebook and realized again that awful need of mine to project *emotion* into the future too. Instead of writing what I felt *while* I was writing it, I was trying to salvage that good feeling for later. Like the bread I took to bed. A crumb of contentment set in amber and readied to pit against the prospect of gloom. (How's that for a mixed metaphor?) God, how that urge has helped me deny so much of my life! I won't have it! (Act of will?) I'll scream it out until it's part of me! (Planning?)

Ah, I see how I never allow myself to win.

This morning I wondered how Rhoda would handle some uptight mathematician in therapy. It started me thinking about sensibilities and talents and aptitudes. I'd often been told that people were born with different abilities and sensitivities, different capacities of aesthetic appreciation, intellectual, manual skill. Now I'm beginning to wonder. I'm hardly a behaviorist, but certainly such praise as "You seem to be very good with numbers!" at the right age from the right daddy could turn a young experimenting mind more deeply in that direction. I know now more clearly why I was drawn to writing and acting, which were also praised enough to keep me at them. I was very early turned off by arithmetic, I'm sure, by Daddy's awesome ability with numbers, even after he went blind. I still can't even balance a checkbook. My eyes automatically swim before a column of figures. Same holds true of my mechanical skills. On an aptitude test I once scored in the lowest percentile available. Did Daddy's slapping me that day in the car when I fiddled with the buttons or the time we opened the beanbag trying to discover the ways things worked and were punished for it end my interest then and there, just as my early clumsiness and fear of defeat kept me away from sports?

Stan once said to me, "Well, we may have our problems, but at least we were born with the capacity to respond more fully than some people to music and books and plays."

"Born? Our neuroses made us aesthetic!" I said with contempt of my sicknesses.

He couldn't agree, insisted on the inborn traits, the hereditary brain matter. Maybe he was right. I don't want to be written off as a Skinner rat. And any mother can tell you that no two of her children were alike in their crib. So, it could be; only again I wonder, as with the development of our talents and skills, isn't our very capacity to *use* our brains the result of our earliest interaction with experience, parents, success, defeat? The guy who seems indifferent to music—is that more the result of some "saving" action that forces his refusal to respond? The guy who prefers reading nonfiction to fiction—could it be that his greater health doesn't need fantasy to sustain him or, conversely, that his pain is so fearful to him that he *will not,* fearing to respond even to the tears that a serious novel might provoke in him?

All those jocks given sanction by society awhile back to weep over Erich Segal's *Love Story,* that covertly homosexual bonbon. No wonder. A cream puff fantasy with insubstantial shadows of characters and situation on which any scared dreamer could project his own idealized-desexualized girl, vicariously feel the bolstering thrill of winning in competitive adolescent athletics, and the never-never land of reconciliation with dear old dad—all in a narcotic haze of nostalgia.

Jesus, I just remembered seeing Irene Papas as Clytemnestra in a performance of *Iphigenia in Aulis* (add it to the list). While her daughter prepares to sacrifice herself to the winds at the climax of the tragedy, Clytemnestra groans, "Don't leave me!"

I found myself bawling like—*for*—the baby I am.

But did the dry-eyed jock sitting nearby stare stony-eyed because he was healthier than I or too early frozen off to feel the awful truth of Clytemnestra's soul-rending need?

"Aw, crap," I hear someone saying, "you were educated into that appreciation. You studied tragic theory and all that shit in college. You were better read!"

"Something drove me to read!" I answer. "My pain must have been searching for its reasons even then! In that sense, yes, I'm luckier than the jock. I've always been near to it, but never quite knew what it was all about. And I weep for him because he doesn't dare move closer to his own too. A healthy man would be able to weep—and know why!"

"Shit. That jock doesn't want your fucking tears."

"He couldn't bear them, isn't that it? He'd call me a sissy, right? And he'd have America to back him up on that one, approving of his fake unfeeling. Anyway, I'm weeping for myself—not for the jock, not even for Iphigenia and Clytemnestra. For myself!"

"Well, that's what makes horse races, you faggot. Count us jocks out! We don't want your horror!"

"Buddy, you have your own whether you want it or not. And you could probably even get through your whole lifetime without ever really *knowing* it even though it'd still be there."

"That's okay by me!"

"Hell, I don't blame you. I don't even feel sorry for you. I've been that route myself, and I never learned the truth until I was ready for it."

"For *what*, damn you?"

"For myself!"

3:20 P.M.

Moved to the park and still the urge to write is with me. I don't feel it's turning me off myself yet, so I'll go on with it. (Justify my right to do as I please. For Rhoda. For Mommy. Again. *Again,* damn it!)

Just thought of Duncan, the therapist who handled Tuesday night's wrap-up. I got annoyed. Yes, I find him physically attractive, but I dislike the way he pulls at his beard and sucks at his upper lip. He makes me think he's still acting out infantile feelings rather than *feeling* them. What's worse, although he *seems* thoughtful, I sense a preoccupied air about him; that extra second it takes before he delivers a simple answer almost seems an affectation of calm poetic speculation. Maybe I'm being unfair. Maybe he's just checking himself out: "What do I really feel about that?" "What is it I really have to say—if anything?" I like that, if it's true, because I so rarely do it, feeling forced as always to deliver, deliver—what? what's expected of me, what will make me acceptable, loved. Still, I wish he wouldn't take so much damn time being natural!

This morning I noticed the way Rhoda manipulates the session. This is no mean criticism; it's praise. She *does* seem to take me back and forth between tears and rage, tears and rage, prompting a full expression of the range of my feeling needs. She helps me see how inextricably bound love and hate are. Also, she's no longer saying as often "Yes" or "That's right!" like some muted cheerleader sitting behind me. (She still *looks* to me like that Catskill counselor, especially when she wears shorts or slacks. I can see her leading cheers as a teen-ager; only there are fretful lines in her face that tell me she never had much to cheer about. I wonder how long ago she went through this therapy herself, how much time in her life was wasted as it was in mine. [Sorry, Mother, a slip of the soul.]) Her diminishing sideline whispers I take as a sign that I'm on the right track myself, that I feel things for myself more thoroughly and so don't need her encouragement as much. I think she's very gifted in this.

And now my mind-fucking head keeps returning to the human activities I've been drawn to or loathe. Religion, for example. I've always hated its imposition. Not being a Jew so much, though that too—the obligations to it and the peculiar limitations it sometimes caused. But more specifically, the synagogue. My earliest associations with the temple are just memories of a lot of smelly old men, praying in a language I couldn't understand, and the tedium of having to sit and stand and sit and stand for no apparent reason. I went the common route—Hebrew school from ages nine through thirteen, stopping dead on the day I was bar mitzvahed (*sic*). Some of this alienating experience I tried to describe in a novel, especially that frightening run home from Hebrew school in the winter's darkness, and the phoniness I felt in pretending piety for rabbis and relatives.

My folks weren't at all religious. They did their two days a year. The only things I liked about it at all were the presents on Chanukah and watching my mother light *shabbas* candles. She made an ingathering motion with her hands over the flame that was magical to me. And she was so quiet and sad as she rested them over her eyes as she prayed. (Shit on that! *Shit* on it!!)

Anyway, I'm wondering now if, just as I was turned on to music by a mother whom I loved to hear play the piano, I wasn't turned off the temple by a father who found no use for it either—and whom I found no use for—as well as by the whole stern masculine ethic of Judaism itself.

The Old Testament God is an angry vengeful bastard al-

ways demanding all sorts of impossible acts from His children, even forcing them to worship Him against their will.
Daddy demanded the same dumb obedience. I associate
with him the stifling atmosphere of the temple on holidays,
the obligation to attend *his* demand on me, and having to
walk to *schul* dolled up in awful little-man suits to pray in
patent hypocrisy—all an extension of *him*. These are conscious ideas now, as is my sense of Judaism's peculiar attitude toward women—some creature traditionally to be
separated from men, unclean and sinful or sentimentally
sainted. But I'm not sure they weren't operating in their
own doleful way at the time I was subjected to all that ob-
noxious hocus-pocus about God the omnipotent Father.

No doubt if I'd been born and reared a Catholic, I
would've lit on the Madonna at once and lost my life to
Her as I did to Mom.

And the good folk of the world drawn to organized religion even in this day and age? I have to agree with Freud on
that one. Religion *in any form* is nothing more than a symbolic (therefore suspect) expression of the never-ending
need for Mommy, for Daddy, for a false assurance of immortality and community, for fear of the awful truth that
none of our always longed-for security really exists.

After my mother died, my mother's father, who'd ob-
served his orthodox duties most of his adult life, told me
that he couldn't believe in God anymore. I agreed with him
and said it was about time he'd wised up. He didn't like
that but let it pass.

In the last year of his life, when I went to visit him in
Florida, where he ran to escape our tragic farm, I found
him wrapped in his *tallis* and *tefillin* at his morning prayers
as of old.

"I thought you didn't believe in God anymore,
Grandpa," I said at breakfast.

"I don't," he answered.

"Then why are you still praying?"

His mouth opened with a pained and guilty quiver. Uneasily he shrugged his shoulders. "Because it's right," he said.

10:00 P.M.

Skirted death along the freeway to walk to the movies this evening in North San Rafael. Being without a car these weeks has made me more aware how California, if not the rest of America, is designed for those damned machines, the hearts of towns and countryside torn out or stripped to give the automobile its right-of-way. That doesn't mean tomorrow I give up my wheels, but I sure as hell *would* if Life in These United States weren't deliberately laid out to accommodate General Motors and Standard Oil more than it is me.

Nevertheless, with the dry hills to look at and man-made footpaths beaten out in forbidden terrain, I felt good walking in the setting sun and fresh air, reminding me again of the clean clear days I spent in Canberra when that manufactured capital was still known as Six Suburbs in Search of a City. I hope a freeway hasn't yet bored a hole through a heart that had barely begun to beat there.

In order to "take the evening off" as Rhoda suggested, I chose the most insipid movie the county had to offer: *Song of Norway*. At least there'd be a little bastardized Grieg to hear, I thought; I've often missed music this past week. Unfortunately, the horrendous script, the abysmal direction and atrocious performances rendered a dreary score no redeeming service. Even the fjords in that film look phony. Nor could my mind stop evaluating the essence of the story's tedious plot, chock full of parental coercion and youthful self-delusions. If only the story were *conscious* of its own ironies. But, no. These problems are accepted as real! Damn it, I suspected this therapy would spoil these sops! Well, I'll be saving a lot of money, I see.

Worst of all was a sequence at a Christmas party in which Grieg sings to a group of kids a song about trolls to the tune of "In the Hall of the Mountain King" from *Peer Gynt*. The moral: Be good and do what your parents tell you or the trolls will come and get you! Animated monsters start appearing in the woods and ponds to frighten the three little movie brats who imagine themselves into the lurking horrors of the forest. No doubt everyone involved in making this film thought all this was cunning stuff and fit for loving family consumption. Of course, before the sequence is done, the children win out over the trolls. After all, it's *their* fantasy. And another generation of soldiers is born.

Well, what can you expect when we've all been brought up on *Grimms' Fairy Tales* and their ilk? First our parents scare hell out of us, then they tell us stories to sublimate our terrors. Don't get Daddy, get the Giant, Jack! Don't hate Mommy, Gretel, hate the Wicked *Step*-mother or the Witch.

In graduate school I once studied a little about the psycho-sexual significance of such tales as Jack and the Beanstalk and Little Red Ridinghood. Could only agree. Yes, Jack is chopping down Daddy's penis so he can live happily ever after with Mom. Yes, Red Ridinghood is learning all about copulation and birth from that Big Bad Wolf. Rumpelstiltskin is a prick! The Seven Dwarves? Hell, who can't see that Snow White's in dreadful competition with her (Wicked Step-)mother for the love of Daddy and, in psycho-sexual revenge for her near-death, is having a wild old time with all those dirty old men?

A friend of mine has been busy terrifying his two kids these days with chapters out of the *Odyssey* along with other Greek myths. He knows them to be even scarier than those of the Brothers Grimm, but since his kids will be

frightened by children's stories *anyway*, he's decided he
might as well help along their classic education at the same
time.

When he told me this, I enjoyed his wisdom, but now I
wonder. For years I remember I felt chased by the boogeyman, and I suppose I still do, though what a boogeyman
looks like I still don't know. My parents left that up to *my*
imagination. Why not? It was richer in dread for me than
Daddy's might have been.

So many of those awful tales we still tell were products of
nineteenth-century repressions: tyrannical fathers, weak-
willed mothers, schisms between love and sex, grotesquely
dishonest responses to children's inquiries and needs. Those
stories were written by ignorant adults for innocent kids!
And we, poor fools, still perpetuate those terrifying myths
while Walt Disney stockholders make their bucks.

"Come off it," that voice argues now. "Those fairy tales
help kids to release a lot of natural hostility and fear."

"Sure, through *fantasy* rather than directly through life!
Mommy and Daddy need to hear it—not mythical witches
and giants! It's crooked!"

"It's beautiful. It's symbolic! It's artful imagination!"

"It's deceitful! And worse, it's designed to ease the old
folks, you idiot, not the young!"

Many children's authors today recognize this and are
sticking to real situations of plausible conflict or, like Mau-
rice Sendak, are creating original fantasies instead or relying on the old formulas. Still, how many parents, I wonder,
are not quicker to pick up the good old-fashioned kind to
read to their kids, those disastrous object lessons that terrified them into crookedness when *they* were young?

After that damned sequence I could no longer concentrate on the film. My mind kept floating back to Stan. I realized more fully why I bicker with him so, all too often
picking on him for what I consider irksome failings. I want
the perfect father is all. I feel entitled to it since I work so

hard to earn it, don't I? When he doesn't come through—
and how in hell *could* he?—I'm foaming at the mouth to
get what doesn't exist. The way he *takes* it, though, well,
that's another story—*his*.

So, Truism for Today: Neurotics respond to everyone
they meet in their lives the way they were made to respond
to their parents. If not quite true, at least these clichés help
me keep rediscovering my pain.

Lying down now with thoughts dangerously turning to
sex. Once while I was in bed with a girl and having as good
a time as I was capable of, she said with not unflattering
pleasure, "Oh, Michael, don't you hear it? Don't you hear
the jungle?"

I listened for parrots. "No," I said.

"Can't you hear the drums?"

I didn't want to disappoint her. "Yes. I think I do."

Sometime later she married a black guy—to keep on
hearing it all, I guess.

He wears Brooks Brothers suits.

Thursday

Another dream. Was counting on a wet one with a woman because I feel the dam must be about ready to bust, and since I'm not interested in trying my hand at it for the time being, thought nature would provide. No such luck:

I'm part of a large audience watching a black colleague of mine doing African dances on a stage in the midst of a whole troupe of Katherine Dunham-like performers. I find myself apologizing to the people around me because my friend up there used to be less heavy and awkward. In his loincloth his jiggling around looks stupid and clumsy. Then I see his penis escaping his pants. It grows to a ridiculous size. I think to myself, "What the hell can anyone do with that? You can't suck it, you can't even get screwed with it!"

I woke with a morning erection of my own.

The black guy is obviously left over from last night's parting thought, only this one is a teacher and writer with whom I shared an office at school last year. Often I've compared my own career with his and envied him for appearing to be more comfortable with himself than I am. In the dream his unsightly weight and gracelessness, his wish to be a jungle dancer and sexual giant made me feel I was seeing myself up there in a combination of wishes and fears. Rejecting his figure and performance might be a fantasy wish to reject what I've always felt is my own. And yet he is also the "freed" me. Top dog in the audience says: "I'm sorry you see him this way. He really was quite acceptable once upon a time. Now he's an embarrassment." Underdog on the stage: "Shit, man, I'm enjoying myself. I like being free —no matter what you think!" (Of course, if I were doing more Freudian analysis than Fritz, I'd probably have to get into the "feminine" response to the size of the dream-cock, which I don't even pretend to evaluate from the dancer's point of view.) I'd sure as hell love to know what game to believe in.

Shit, I'm still sitting here now worrying about what I'll be facing once I return home. I get scared that I won't be able to take all that I'm learning here back with me, fear that I'll fall into the same convenient traps of accommodation with Stan, doubt I'll be able to perform well up on that stage! That's it. Oh, damn you, Mother, for giving me this awful sense of incompetence! Damn you, Daddy, for letting her *do* that to me! Damn myself for being the dupe of them both and doing to *myself* all the damage they unconsciously demanded.

Performance. It immediately reminds me of sports, my early abysmal fear of playing with other boys. The way I ran from competition. My ingrained sense of failure at every attempt. Team sports especially: the punchball, football, softball ordeal that made life so tough, sensing ridicule on all sides and usually earning it, or feigning indifference or illness to avoid the daily trial at camp.

Eventually I grew to enjoy the more individualized ones: swimming, hiking, bowling. Tennis with a friend. Boxing, naturally, always scared the shit out of me. The few times I was forced to try, I merely stood there paralyzed or cried, making vague attempts at hitting back, no different from the time when I felt put up to that fight at the Hermitage with no father to protect me. As a teen-ager, though, I used to love to wrestle with a particular friend down the block. But that was because it was done in fun and I loved the touch of his body. He filled a lot of masturbatory fantasies.

And now I'm wondering about all those guys who love to watch football these days, the joyful fanaticism that my brother-in-law, for instance, has for the New York Giants, spending a fortune on season tickets, following every word in the papers, the games and instant replays on TV. On the rare occasion when I watch a game the excitement gets to me too, but I don't follow the teams and feel stupid about the names of players, their positions, and plays. A family joke: The "intellectual" is pardoned for his ignorance. I play the clownish egghead for all it's worth.

Yet I can appreciate the appeal that a game like football must have for the spectator as he identifies with the experience on the field. Just like any army, the concept of "team" sanctions violence, legalizes the loss of self at least for a couple of hours a week. In warfare and in football games individual responsibility can be abrogated in one's overwhelming urge to kill someone as uniformly faceless as oneself. What a great weekend release. All that anger and aggression you have to shovel back into yourself during your workaday week can at last be let loose on a Sunday afternoon.

Once while visiting my sister at Syracuse University, we went to a pep rally for the next day's game with Cornell. Standing in front of a roaring bonfire complete with effigy of a burning Cornellian, the university chaplain shouted, "Put aside your religion tomorrow, kids! We're going after blood!" Cheers. Huzzahs.

I wouldn't be surprised if he hadn't gotten the provost's approval for that one. "Sure, Jake, it's better than having to put saltpeter in their chocolate pudding."

And in that battle of Giants, Warriors, Hawks, or whatever totem gods we turn our surrogate fighters into, I think we're back in the land of the Brothers Grimm again. More psycho-sexual fantasies. Proving our potency. The thrust of our helmeted pricks. Playing out our power drives on playing fields when the real enemy—the first father we hate and need so much—is probably killing off *his* father in the same living room as we. Harmless sublimation? A therapeutic thrill? Maybe. Better than killing King Laius for *real*, I guess. Better than My Lai massacres and Charles Manson. Sure. Only I wonder if that old saw, "The Battle of Waterloo was won on the playing fields of Eton," might not be better stated, "The playing fields of Eton were responsible for the Battle of Waterloo." Though, of course, that's not the answer either. The faults rather of French and British rearing systems? Oh, sure, all those traditional ignorances. But then we'd have to search back for the causes of *that* ineptitude—and once again we're right back into primitive realms again, the Wonderful World of Original Need.

I'm mind-fucking again. Mind-fucking. A minute more of it: I'm thinking about the "homosexual" component in play now. (Oh, God, I can already hear my brother-in-law, let alone the jocks, complaining that now I'm out to tar the world with my own perverse brush—the fag-sees-fags-everywhere malady.) But what I'm feeling is that there's nothing to *fear* about that homosexual element in our games, nothing to be ashamed of. Bodies are made to be touched. All that ass-patting. Fine, keep it up, guys. And it doesn't have to be sanctioned by padded shoulders and cheering crowds. That's the costume that our fear of our feelings has made us wear. Wow, I wait for the day when all the guys have told off all the daddies and so can take off their foolish uniforms, no longer needing their primitive masks to mask desire, and can really get down to play. Ha! Unfortunately for me, I just realized that that would be the end to orgies. Since we'll all be in complete possession of our own bodies on that momentous day, we won't have much need to make other men's bodies validate our own. Hence, no more football games, not even naked ones. Shucks. There goes another homosexual fantasy.

1:00 P.M.

The park.

Again this morning's session was filled with almost non-stop emotion: anger and grief, screaming demands and soulful pleas. I seem to find it easier now to stay in touch with myself throughout the hour. No Actors' Studio exercise these. With little trouble I can identify what I'm feeling and why. Rhoda continues to quietly encourage that expression. There seemed very few blank spots today, those moments of unwillingness to feel. Either exhaustion or expression. Hey, the rhythm of authentic life?

No new revelations. Much feeling based on the repetition of old matters. Rhoda still tries to get me to feed back any present biography into the past. More often I do it myself now.

Today I seemed more deeply filled with a sense of despairing waste for so much lost time in my life. I still feel that sadness now.

I found myself screaming out apologies for abusing my sister and brother in ways that I did when we were kids, torturing my sister with ridicule and my brother with threats when it was my parents who drove me to it by blocking themselves off from my needs. A waste of all three children's lives. The utter waste of my parents' own. Rhoda didn't seem to mind today when I wept for humanity while weeping for myself.

One favorite piece of biography called up: From the age of thirteen through sixteen, I was "in love" with a girl named Phyllis. Phyllis—my first Pedestal Lady (that series of worshiped goddesses too holy to be touched). When I finally worked up the courage to ask her out, we went to a dance; later that night, at her door I tried to kiss her. She resisted. With her bright new junior high vocabulary, she said, "Michael, I like you very much, but ours must be a platonic relationship because I find you physically repulsive."

"How did that feel?" asked Rhoda.

I was laughing. "Oh, I accepted it with great grace. She was only saying what I'd been feeling for years about myself. I *was* physically repulsive to myself. I wouldn't even have a *platonic* relationship with me."

"How did it *feel*, Mike?"

"Awful!"

"Say it. Feel it!"

"Awful. Awful! Awful!!"

Oh, boy, but I worked hard to make Phyllis kiss me. Finally did, though it took two whole years. And by that time I'd also fallen in love with some guy she was also dating. Typical. As was my dropping her as soon as something even vaguely began happening between us. Fear of her. Resentment at having had to work so damn hard to win her— like Mom, like Mom—and being too anxious about having to keep pleasing her to let me sustain any impulse to do so. Premature ejaculation, anyone?

Which reminds me of a minor difficulty I still have with Rhoda. Happens less and less as the days go by, but I still occasionally feel I want to win her too, to have her award me with the Best Patient Medal when I leave. Yes, yes, we all know why. But today she laughed at a crack I made and I was all too happy about it. That fawning dog in me said, "Ah! I'm succeeding with her! Charming her with my brilliant repartee." Didn't last more than a second, but long enough to make me feel that the success of this therapy will reveal itself on the day I say something funny and don't give a shit if anyone laughs or not.

Today I also remembered for the first time in thirty years being pinched by one of my earliest baby-sitters, who did it to make me go back to sleep whenever I wanted to stay and sing while looking out the window at the night sky. I wanted to tell my parents but recall being afraid of the consequences—that they might agree with *her* and blame me for not being good.

"Tell them now."

"Margaret's pinching me, Mommy! Margaret's pinching me! Margaret's pinching!"

> Bear with me;
> My heart is in the coffin there with Caesar,
> And I must pause till it come back to me.

At the end of the session I lay weeping quietly. "I'm feeling very sad for myself."

"That's okay," said Rhoda. "No one else can feel that *for* you."

I lay there awhile longer.

"Shall we stop here today?"

I nodded, blew my nose.

"How do you feel?"

"Good. Good and sad."

Went back to my room, cried a little more, took a shower and listened to the guy next door yelling his lungs out in another office upstairs. "Scream it out!" I shouted. "Keep it going! Get it out!"

DEAR DR. GINOTT:

I have a bone to pick with you. That business about saying to your screaming child, "You're feeling angry with Mommy, Billy. Mommy knows and accepts that," leaves much to be desired.

My sister tried your gimmick on her daughter for a while until one day when my niece was raging, that wise child shouted, "Stop telling me what I feel!"

In effect she was saying, "Let me feel it, damn you! Don't turn it off with all your mechanical understanding!"

Jesus, it seems to me now that there's nothing more certain to make one's essential rage move destructively inward than the approach of the *rational* parent. I'm not advocating that mothers share their children's tears (although that might be good for the mother if it's not done to blame the child for provoking them). And I'm certainly not asking the parent to counter her child with any angry outburst of her own. But she sure as hell better let her little one sound it out as fully and as loudly and as long and as boldly as that child has the need to—and within hearing, *listening* to the message of it, damn it, listening to it to discover again what's being said!

All those coldly controlled, rational little beings whom enlightened, well-educated middle-class parents have been rearing these last twenty years. Shit. No wonder so many of them drop out and run to drugs to help them feel something again.

Primer for Perfect Parents

Example #1

SCENE: Six-year-old Nancy comes running into the kitchen crying fearsomely while Mother is kneading whole-grain bread.

(Hold it, Women's Libbers! She takes turns with her husband. They both like healthy foods.)

NANCY: Mommy, the kids are ganging up on me!

MOM (carefully putting down the dough, not panicked if it won't rise right, and calmly sitting with Nancy to let her cry out her grief awhile longer): Why are they doing that?

NANCY (through renewed tears): Because—because they *do!*

MOM: No reason you can think of?

NANCY (whimpering): Because I don't want them playing in our alley!

MOM: Won't they let you play too?

NANCY (whining): No! (A little more crying)

MOM (after it subsides): Why's that?

NANCY (really crying again): *I* don't know! Because it was my turn to be leader.

MOM: And they didn't want you to be?

NANCY: Not all of them—only Josey. She didn't want me to and they listened to her.

MOM: That wasn't fair of them or Josey.

NANCY (crying again): No!

MOM (raising her voice a little): Scream it if you want, because it wasn't fair at all!

NANCY: It wasn't fair! It wasn't fair!

MOM (as Nancy settles against her breast again): An awful lot of things are never the way we want them to be. Mommies and daddies are also sometimes unfair to their very own children—sometimes even without *knowing* it. If I'm ever unfair to you, or Daddy is, you let me know—okay? Tell us right away, right when it's happening. We can't do much about Josey's unfairness or for the other kids following her this time. Maybe, maybe for some reason they're afraid of her. And maybe she was mean today because she couldn't tell *her* parents how she felt about something.

NANCY (running off to play, somewhat pissed): Okay, Mom, cut the lecture. I get the point.

I remember reading somewhere that Japanese syntax operates with a peculiar sense of "play" ingrained in it, an elaborate grammatical obfuscation in which no one directly admits to feeling in polite address. It certainly seems feasible that Japanese gentility and deference are cultural features which could easily seep into their language system. And vice versa.

How we all must be prey to subtle influences like that without our ever knowing it!

In 1984 Orwell proposes that by taking the word "love" as well as all its synonyms out of our language, the concept of love would be effectively removed from our thinking and, to all intents and purposes, from our lives. We would *feel* something, sure: childhood's endless need, procreative physical urges, amorphous longings. But without words to *identify* the feeling, we would certainly not be able to feel what in our former language we deemed "love." And just like the Eskimos, who see *different* colors according to their own language spectrum, *love* as we know it would be diffused into other concepts.

Well, who the hell knows what the word "love" means in our language even now? This therapy seems to be forcing me to find new definitions for a lot of old amorphous feelings that never before had proper names. What portion of what I've called *love* all my life is really only infantile need unfulfilled? How much mere prostatic urge? What small part the pure undemanding enjoyment of another being's separate reality?

Anyway, I'm glad I wasn't born Japanese. I'd hate to be caught in an elaborate language system of politic evasion of my emotional life even more than I am in a language as imprecise in its essences as English seems to be.

My latest harebrained theory: Human neurosis is only another of Nature's many devious ways to assure procreation. If the be-all and end-all of life is merely to keep life going, then Nature has devised us all to give herself as much a chance at that goal as she possibly can.

We already know that Nature makes us nuts to keep us alive; that is, the body survives and reproduces itself often at the expense of our emotional integrity. Ergo: It doesn't seem farfetched to me today that even those defenses which we create to avoid the overwhelming knowledge of our basic physical helplessness, our spiritual purposelessness, and our brief mortality also help Nature get her job done.

Attend: A "cured" individual who can continually acknowledge his emotional needs completely enough and recognize the hopelessness of his position might have very little desire left for encounters with others that are exclusively sexual and escapist. He might infinitely prefer fuller relationships of absolute honesty and be unwilling to sustain any partner's illusions about herself just as he has given up his own illusions. After all, so much of our sexual activity is based on that "saving" behavior: looking for mothers and fathers in our bedmates, being driven to dozens of nameless lovers to allay our anxiety, pushing ourselves into unsatisfactory entanglements for the momentary physical comfort and false psychological security they promise, and when we're inevitably disappointed, searching further afield, and over and over again.

That kind of behavior sure as hell ensures more issue. Who knows, maybe Nature even *wants* us neurotic. Well, if not, then at least she's turned human neurosis to her decided advantage. Never mind the catatonic and the successfully suicidal. Your common garden variety of nut is a great reproducer who more than makes up for the few impotent psychotics left lying around.

The ideal man or woman who is totally whole (*ideal*, I said)—that is, the person who is utterly aware of his feelings at every moment and remains *true* to them, accepting their origin rather than feeling compelled to act them out —might quite probably see the entire world as an involving or uninvolving creation—without distinction of age or sex, the trees and stones as enrapturing as any fetching face. This way lies Buddhism. And isn't that the ultimate ideal of nirvana? Not a cop-out on feeling. But *total* feeling. Total absorption of all feeling. Without samsara, without the need to act out earthly desire.

Janov discusses the lessening need for sexual adventurism as a result of successfully felt therapy. Fewer encounters but far more satisfaction for the self-sufficient man. Nature ain't gonna like that. How long will it take her to work out some new quirk to screw us up for her *own* needs?

10:15 P.M.

Evening group left me worried and fearful again. Found myself concentrating on my father tonight. A heavy repeti-

tion of anger for his not caring enough to save me from my
mother. An awful yearning to feel *his* strength, not hers. I
kept screaming, "I want *you* inside me, not her, not her!" I
cried for need of him but was disturbed to find so few pictures in my mind of those rare times when I felt I had him.
The swim in the rain. The boats at Sheepshead Bay. That
was all. Maybe that emptiness of imagery frightened me too
much. I found myself admitting need but, despite my tears,
felt dead inside. I must get into this more tomorrow with
Rhoda.

Stan wasn't here tonight. Is that what triggered this
worry? Did he stay away because of me, because I shunned
him on Tuesday? It angers me to think he might do something like that—screw himself out of this help to show me
he's annoyed, make me feel guilty for not showing him I
"loved" him enough. Don't know if that's *my* warped per-
ception or the truth. I shudder again for our future.

The worst worry, though, was listening to the people at
the wrap-up, speaking about experiences they are presently
facing without—or so it seems—any greater awareness or
any better behavior than they showed before therapy.
When I complained to Rhoda about this on Tuesday morning, she asked, "Why didn't you tell them that?" I was
afraid to, and still am. Maybe I don't want them to shatter
an illusion I have that things *will* get appreciably better.
Yet, things *seem* to be—at least in my mind (yet to be
proved in action), and it scares the shit out of me to hear of
so much apparent failure. Some of them sound as though
they haven't had three weeks in the house at all! I'm not
looking for magic, just some good changes inside me. I'm
not looking for the end of emptiness, nor even a stoic acceptance of it; I just don't want to be prey to my old sick
defenses anymore, and some of these people still seem to be
saying that they *are*.

The guy next door—who's been looking dour for days—
was screaming with greater freedom tonight and came up

animated and smiling. Good! After group was over, he asked if I wanted to take a walk since he needed to get something to eat. My reaction wasn't resistance to friendship. Normally I would have jumped at such an invitation, if only to please. But tonight, feeling so disturbed, I just wanted to be by myself. It took great courage to say, "I'd like to, but I'm not in the mood tonight." If *he* doesn't understand that and feels I'm rejecting him, well, then, there's no hope for anything here. I have an impulse now to create a situation in which I can return the invitation if only to show him I really care. Why? So that he'll still "love" me. Shit. More to work on. More to do. This job seems so endless.

Friday

6:30 A.M.

I woke filled with the same worries. Dreams disturbed me twice during the night, but I can't recall them now. I know this fear is due to my uncertainty of success here. Maybe I *am* looking for magic after all. Asking for symptoms to drop away of their own accord. Oh, but to have to go on living checking and cross-checking every damn motive for every damn move as I did in the throes of psychoanalysis would be unbearable again.

Well, at least this time I don't have to blame myself for "inappropriate" responses. But ultimately what in the hell's the point of crying out against parents who you know never did and never *can* hear you? I keep having to tell myself that you're just supposed to start howling like King Lear and live with the tragic truth—howling, howling without expecting to get anything out of your daughters anymore, and nothing except honesty from yourself. But by then, damn it, Cordelia's lying dead in your lap. If Lear had gone on living, what would those desireless years have been like for him? I've lived too often with numb resignation to want inertia as an answer. The point is to keep feeling those howling winds still inside you, I guess, and free the fewer daughters left alive from the tyranny of your sick but age-old needs. Oh, but I'm so frightened this morning that all this is mind-fucking theory again, that the Lear inside me will always be banging dishes down on his daughter's table.

1:00 P.M.

At the moment I'm sitting behind the laundromat over-looking the dirty inlet waters and those good Sheepshead Bay smells of some distant sea. Trying to recover, recatch this morning's important session:

In the midst of my general rage and tears, I confessed to Rhoda my fears about last night's group, the sense of failure I felt as I listened to others recounting theirs. One man last night especially had frightened me by relating how panicky he still gets when he has too much time in which to do nothing. So similar to one of my problems, I couldn't help but protest that the therapy wasn't working, *wouldn't* work!

Rhoda delivered a sane little lecture. Therapy is a proc-ess, she said. It's also not over in three weeks' time. There are some areas for some people that are harder for them to approach. It might take them months, years, maybe *never* to get to them. For instance, she's been through the therapy too but still can't seem to lose weight (though ironically she doesn't look heavy to me) and is still working on her feel-ings about food. Nevertheless, other important matters in her life have radically changed, and much of their own ac-cord. That's one of the troubles working with this new ap-proach to therapy. So many people, many who've tried other ways like me, come expecting that this time they are going to get the speedy, complete, magical cure. But each person is very different and demands his own time.

Rhoda explained, however, that every patient who is ac-cepted at the Center goes through the initial three weeks of "intensive" working individually with his therapist for as long as seems necessary each day while he lives isolated in the house or at a nearby motel. Then, only when the therapist feels the patient is ready does he also begin to attend evening group sessions. Nevertheless, the duration of treatment always depends on the individual's own progress and needs. The Center tries to be as flexible as possible in this regard.

After the first three weeks many patients often continue in individual sessions once or twice a week for as long as seems advisable. More often, others continue on in the group situation as they see fit for several months more. The point is, Rhoda said, to keep you as close to your feelings as possible. That's not always so easy to do in the outside world. And once you're at large again, your vulnerable state can lead to new and distressing connections which might best be gone into in a supervised situation. Sometimes people continue coming back on occasion just because this is the only place available to them where they can fully express their feelings without scaring the neighbors. Lots of times old patients stop by to use an available office for work on their own. And the Center will be open to me this way too.

That reassured me. I realized again how lucky I was to have been able to "get with" my inner emotions even from the first session here. There are some people—like the guy next door—who took *days* to be willing to risk rage and tears, to make those awful connections. And I suspect there are others who probably can't do it at all—and run away.

I *know* good things are going on inside me, and I'd count myself pretty lucky with even one-tenth of my self-destructive symptoms gone. It's my wild need for reassurance and perfection that I must still "feel out" in order to confront more fully.

During the session today I did feel more deeply than ever before that major parental conspiracy against me.

As an early reader of Freud, by the age of fourteen I'd already accepted the concept of the Oedipus complex. "Oh, sure, I love my mother and hate my father—probably too much of each." Yet, of course, my heart never really bought it. Moreover, it was largely misunderstood.

Later on, when I was busy reading case studies in college, trying to determine the cause of my homosexual impulses, I'd underline all the standard explanations: victim of over-possessive mother. Abandoned by father too soon. Mother too demanding—frightening the sexual nature of the child. Father a tyrant—overpowering. Father too weak—in-effectual for satisfactory identification. Reasonable enough, all of it. I searched my own past for examples to prove it, yet it never seemed to provide really solid evidence. After all, as far as I could tell, my mother *wasn't* too demanding. If anything, I *wanted* her to demand more of me so I could fulfill her wishes and prove my love. She was hardly over-possessive; she scarcely hovered at all! My father was, yes, overbearing, but . . . manageable, easily escaped. Nor was his strength ineffectual, and God help him, he was certainly around all too often for *my* comfort.

Sorry to say, more than eight years of psychoanalysis never proved to me much more than those case studies did. I simply was exhorted to stop relying on my foolishly child-ish impulses, to abandon my parents and go my own way or accept them as they were and stop complaining.

Now, though, getting in touch with my true feelings about it all has forced me to do a hell of a lot of rethinking:

For example, this is the very first time in my life I've ever felt my mother to be anything less than a saint. Oh, sure, I could complain about her faults in the past, but I always managed to find excuses for them. All the guilt and self-hatred I'd felt for myself were usually blamed on dear old dad. Moreover, though I was vaguely aware that I shared my mother's secret suffering, never did I realize until now how deeply this identification went, how I had to become her in attitude, manner, mood, out of a futile effort to win her. How I had to be quiet and dutiful, that good little boy waiting to be awarded the crumbs of her affection. And how my tentative involvement with other women always withered away because I was still trying to satisfy my early need for a loving mother, unconsciously maintaining fidelity to that gruesome lost cause.

Last night, during group, I had a common experience when Ruth, one of the trainees, came near to listen and encourage me. She's an attractive girl, and I immediately felt threatened by her. No, not because I had to perform for her as I'd felt I had to once with Miriam, but because I sensed the old excessive demands of Mother to be what I wasn't— good, quiet, sensitive, sparing of her feelings, untruthful to my own.

"She really got your balls, didn't she?" Rhoda asked this morning when I told her some of this.

Hard as I tried to deny it, I felt the truth of that for the first time too. Though I'd heard it before, read it in countless books, now at last the idea of psychological castration began to make emotional sense to me. My balls are my feelings, and in her sad, unconscious, stupid, pitiful way, my mother demanded them as the price for the little love she could offer me. *That* never being enough, I offered myself all the more completely in the vain belief that if I gave enough, finally, finally, so would she.

But that was only half the story. Since being here I've also grown more emotionally aware of my basic need for my father. The need for a man who cared enough at the right time to save my jeopardized life. He didn't. He couldn't. God knows why not, but that's not my business. Still, that little boy inside me *felt—feels*—that lack more than he's ever dared admit before.

Sometime during our session today I complained about Duncan, who handled last night's wrap-up—how distant and cold I found him.

"Tell him."

"Who?"

"Tell Duncan."

"I want you closer, Duncan! I want you to care! I want you to love me!" I screamed.

Crying it out like that brought it miraculously back to my father again. It was *his* cold distance, his abandoning me to my mother that I felt so deeply once more.

All this, then, combined to produce this startling new revelation: I saw my parents committing their early crime against me *together.* For the first time I understood the damn tangle from *both* sides. The double bind. Her inability. His inability. My mess produced by the necessary belief that if I loved one enough or hated the other enough, the two of them would finally hear me and make it better.

I know now that somewhere inside there will be a piece of me that will always want them, always hate them, always fear and always need them. *That emptiness of not having had them will always be there!* Oh, God, that's awful. But I'll be damned if I'll waste the rest of my life looking for them anymore. They exist no place! No place! That's terrible, damn it, tragic! But that's what I can no longer deny by acting out my need. And that's what I have to live feeling as fully as I can from here on out.

2:30 P.M.

Back at the OK Corral:

Still feel like writing and exempt from guilt for it, though that may be due to the weekend upon us and Rhoda's advice to do as I wished provided I don't talk to anyone about my feelings. Have no plans. And will practice doing what I wish to do *as* I wish it—at least for as long as I can.

Thinking about classes in the fall: Oh, boy, would I love to walk in there *neutrally* for a change, without seeing each batch of new students as potential conquests, potential threats, to be able to prepare adequately but without the need for excessive mental rehearsal, to have my cluttered mind cleared enough to feel spontaneous, honest, and hopefully (rotten word) of some egoless responsiveness to those people.

Feeling. To feel my real needs at all times without having to act out those self-destructive symbols I've turned them into. That's the goal. But as soon as I write "goal," the ideal collapses. I think of the goallessness of nirvana. Nirvana means "above the wind." Jesus, that sounds awfully empty. We incipient Buddhists need a new word for ideal living. Something that suggests: "with-the-wind-known-for-what-it-is-and-forever-blowing-through." I'll check it out with Moondog or Krishnamurti. I don't want Allen Ginsberg near me.

Shit, at times it seems so petty and foolish to refeel these long-forgotten griefs: that damned beanbag, the broken promise of a trip into the city. Yet, no matter how meager the event, if the memory of its hurting is still there, I'm beginning to see how it must be worth refeeling! Besides, there's just not enough in my memory to offset those countless little murders with any remembrances of unsolicited, unearned love.

Most modern neurotics, I've read, don't get sick all at once à la Freud's Victorian traumatics. It's the Chinese water torture for us: a drop at a time hurting where it hurts until we become spongy with pain and sometimes even learn to welcome it in order to allay our deepest dread of what it truly means.

For instance, I never remember either of my parents ever reading to me. Maybe that's why I read very well as soon as I could. Stories—my escape from reality, books—the means to get there when the radio wasn't on or the movies had to wait until Saturday.

I do recall one time when I was legitimately sick in bed (the only times when I felt my mother was ever particularly caring) that she read me parts of a Walt Disney comic book. By then I could have read it myself, but I preferred her doing it for me. In that issue the publishers were offering a reduced rate as a subscription gimmick for the first some-odd children who could most neatly paste pictures of the cartoon characters around Mickey Mouse's birthday table. With my mother's help I worked hard cutting and pasting the party scene together, and as a reward, she sent away for a subscription. The picture neatly done or not, the magazine began to arrive (no doubt for anyone who'd sent in the dough). But neatness won the day with Mom and Mickey Mouse. Neatness brought her to my bed. Because Mom had made that little event feel so good to me, I asked her to keep up my subscription long after I'd grown bored with Walt Disney and was already looking for fathers and myself in Captain Marvel and Billy Batson, in Superman and Jimmy Olson, Batman and Robin, Plastic Man, The Green Hornet, and the whole sick muscle-bound crew.

My generation's penchant for comic books! God, we all spent hours reading them, trading them, stealing them. The bloodier the better, the more robust and spectacular the heroes, the happier we were. Pop critics nowadays speculate that the current revival of interest in the 1940's comic book comes out of our nostalgic need to recapture our lost youth. Maybe. But if we'd had our youth in the first place, maybe we wouldn't have to be so damned nostalgic about it. How many boys tried to identify with those primary-colored flying jocks because they had such puny men to model themselves after at home? How many boys had to kill through grim fantasy those many villains with Father's face —The Joker, The Penguin, Mr. Mind—because dear old dad wouldn't dare allow them any direct expression of rage, of regretful need? And how many boys like me tried to find in those winged and virtuous musclemen the protective and loving father who'd spiritually never even flown *near* them?

Primer for Perfect Parents

Example #2

> SCENE: Late at night. Five-year-old Johnny, who wakes from a nightmare, screams for his father. In Perfect Households kids call indiscriminately for mothers and fathers. Both are terrific on all occasions.
>
> DAD (coming into Johnny's bedroom quickly but unpanicked, and certainly without irritation): Johnny, what is it?
>
> JOHNNY (crying): That awful man! He has purple eyes and leafy scales down his back! He's coming at me!
>
> DAD (holding Johnny and letting him feel full terror): Are you still dreaming now?
>
> JOHNNY: No, but I can still see him!
>
> DAD (still holding him close but allowing him to experience his monster): What's he doing?
>
> JOHNNY (resentfully): Chasing me. Chasing me into the house through a lot of dirty old leaves. He wants to get me!
>
> DAD: Anything else?
>
> JOHNNY: No. But now he's—he's looking at me through his glasses!
>
> DAD: Oh. Like anybody you know?
>
> JOHNNY: Like—like—
>
> DAD (a little louder): If you can't say it, scream it!
>
> JOHNNY: Like you! Like you! Like you!
>
> DAD (holding Johnny close as the boy cries again): Wow, I must've really scared you bad to make you have a dream about me that way.
>
> JOHNNY: You sure the fuck did, you cock-sucker!
>
> DAD: When—do you remember?
>
> JOHNNY: In the yard—you yelled at me for jumping in the leaves we raked up.
>
> DAD: Oh, yeah. Boy, that was dumb of me. They could've been raked up again. But I was tired then and thought of

all that damned work. Listen, whenever I do something like that to scare you, you be sure to tell me right then and there so maybe you won't have to dream about it, okay?

Johnny nods as he falls asleep in Dad's arms.

9:30 P.M.

Spent the afternoon lying around, not particularly trying to connect with much; dozed, took a long walk through one of the prettier areas of homes near Dominican College, which looks like a sanitarium for sick nuns. The walk, sun, flowers along the way were enough to keep me content. Returning around 5:00, I saw the long night awaiting me, but with no obligation to keep the deathwatch again, and no inclination to do so, I decided to take a bus to another flick. Wrong bus. Wound up in Sausalito, which, under any other circumstances, would have been enjoyable. Only, it frightened me to be near so many people and my own renewed potential for sick yearning.

I walked a little, watched some crabs scuttling like two dozen Prufrocks under the bay-side boulders, but it was too chilly to remain too long by the water. The City Across the Bay was completely shrouded in its inevitable summer fog. I'll miss the reliable warmth of San Rafael when I return to San Francisco. Browsing in a bookstore held me for some time, but suddenly I just felt I had to get back to more familiar territory, the aged convict wanting to remain in jail.

Had to wait close to an hour for a bus but, oddly enough, didn't mind. Most of the time I'm furious about getting no place fast. Began to feel hungry, but preferred waiting rather than attempting a Sausalito tourist trap or a tacky beanery, or worse, the gay bar and restaurant I felt inclined to peek into. More than once I wanted to wander over there for a drink and God knows what else.

Finally was relieved to take the rambling route back here via the local line, the small-town life along the way—Larkspur, Ross, San Anselmo—suddenly holding great charm for this inveterate city boy. Fancied myself spending the rest of my days cultivating passion vines and organic vegetables, never seeing another living soul, and not caring to. For me that's quite a switch in fantasies.

This mood persisted throughout supper and the mile walk back to the manse. Didn't and don't feel blue about staying in tonight. Bought a book which I'll read awhile: Turgenev's *Fathers and Sons*. The title was irresistible. And ever since disliking it in college I've been promising myself to reread it someday.

The new girl across the hall was sitting by her window when I walked up the drive. This may be her Night of Trial. The guy next door seems to be gone for the evening. I feel slightly abandoned. Had a fantasy that the girl would open her door and say, "Keep me company." Not at all threatened, but certain it would be the wrong thing for her, I'd say, "I'd love to, I really would, but I don't think that would be doing you a favor tonight. Keep with it." Always Mama's little helper.

Okay: a good book, the stars above. On such a night what else do I need to keep content? (You really wanna know?)

Saturday

8:30 A.M.

Gray but mild morning. Breakfast and newspaper at the Sad Café. I'm a regular there now too. Feel easy about coming in each day and being greeted by the waitress like an old friend. She asks no questions. Probably has surmised why I'm around so often, since many of us loonies take meals there, coming and going in our three-week cycles. Stan told me he never looked up from his plate during his term here, and the waitresses like good nurses discreetly left him to his gloom, silently serving him warm sugared milk and one piece of french toast—the baby foods he found himself craving. It's still a surprise for me to find that kind of undemanding friendliness out here in California. The haste and indifference or downright hostility of New York City never did much but reinforce my paranoid fears of an uncaring world.

Another dream last night, and a familiar one coming at the wrong time: Almost every year, just a day or two before the fall term begins, I usually have my Terrified Teacher Dream. There I am trying to keep in control a bunch of hate-filled students who finally overrun me like a pack of rats. Its annual recurrence has become a grim joke: but in a way, its absurdity helps allay the lurking anxiety I feel each year before entering a classroom, where my rank fears never prove out.

In last night's version I'm getting ready to teach again

but am told by my current department chairman that instead of the usual creative writing course designed for twenty select students in a seminar, I'll have to teach composition skills to more than two hundred unwilling souls in business administration. I'm petrified, panicked by this new plan, the extra work required of me (therapy?) but feel eager to collect new materials, even missing a slew of useless department meetings to do so, which enrages my boss.

That's all I can remember. My most important feeling about it has to do with asserting myself regarding the imposition of those teachers' meetings (perhaps the group sessions as opposed to the private). I didn't give a damn about attending. My work at preparing new lessons seemed more important. I felt no need to be the dutiful little boy soliciting my superior's love. A fantasy of progress presaging new behavior—or more wish fulfillment?

Yesterday I thought I might rent a car today and drive up to Point Reyes for a hike or take a series of connecting buses over to Stinson Beach. But the weather looks too uncertain for either now. Ordinarily it'd bother hell out of me not to be able to fulfill a plan, but now I know I could just as contentedly spend the day walking around the neighborhood, reading, writing, crying, screaming. Might go into SF just for a change of scene, but again, like Sausalito last night, its easy traps scare me. I associate so much unfulfilled longing with the cities I know, the constant appraisal of men on the street as possible partners in bed, so much yearning to be regarded as such myself. I dread finding myself prey to that lie again. Moreover, I have an urge to go home, see Stan, get my mail, feel the old false security of our apartment, talk all this out with him instead of keeping these important feelings mine.

Last night I fell asleep over *Fathers and Sons* after fifteen pages. I'm afraid I still won't like it. Fifteen years of studying and teaching have changed the reasons why though, so I can easily continue with an interested if critical eye. It seems as good a way as any to spend some of the day.

(Oh, shit, I'm planning again, aren't I? Oh, shit.)

In the paper this morning, as there seems to be most every day now, the Gay Liberation Front was holding another protest march, this time in Sacramento. The usual demands: legalization of homosexual acts between consenting adults, no police harassment, no job jeopardy, no government security curtailments, no social charges of immorality.

I'm all for it.

However, I still can't reconcile myself to the purple-feathered and sequined queens who usually make up part of those parades, or even the straightest-looking of the lot when they carry signs proclaiming, I'M GAY AND PROUD OF IT! The new breed. It annoys me. Not on any moral premise or out of any old sense of associative shame. But for the patent need it expresses to make society sanction sickness.

"Homosexuality is not a sickness! It's a preference!" the Gay Libber exclaims.

But every time I try to reconcile myself to that point of view, my own history can only let me see it as a preference *arising* out of sickness. Damn it, I can understand all too well that desire, can concede the need for it that might never die in me, can recognize and have enjoyed the real physical pleasure that sometimes comes of it. (Nature, in her shrewd attempt to keep us alive, has neatly left us with *that* capacity too; our perversions are often quite satisfying.)

Nevertheless, under it all I simply can't seem to accept homosexual activity as much more than illusory, a self-deception unconsciously sought and consciously practiced to help the soul that feels less than complete from dying entirely. No doubt a lot of heterosexual activity is based on similar lies, the same kinds of secret struggles, hostilities, role playing, humiliations, dreams, feigned helplessness, feigned strength, as is common in homosexual behavior. But that doesn't make either any ideal. "I'm straight and proud of it!" sounds as self-deceiving.

In my own experience I've never met a homosexual who would let his partner be *himself*. Whether demands remained unspoken or were shouted from suicidal parapets, whether affection was gobbled up like chocolate-covered goobers or was cynically rejected for fear of it, the worst perversion always lies in the prevailing urge to fashion one's partner to suit one's own sad needs.

It's a rare affair when compensatory needs are so compatible and fantasies so mutually sustained that a homosexual couple can remain responsive to each other on every level— social and sexual—for very long a time. Again, I suppose the same can be said of heterosexuality. But in either situation that endless search for specific specters of love is basically unbearable. As is some neurotics' inability to feel even the illusion of warmth of another. Or my own emotionally barren contact with strange bodies, a hole to push a cock into or a hole offered for one, anyone's. God, it's all such a sad crime against one's original capacity for joy.

I'm not blaming the homosexual himself for treating himself or others as mere objects of fantasy. Nor could I blame the heterosexual man for fooling himself in similar ways with women. Either has been forced to it for very real reasons. And the worst that happens to either? Oh, nothing so very much, really: They live out their lives with less pleasure than they might, and inwardly twist with the agony of knowing to some degree that something is missing again. Or effectively narcotize themselves against that sense of loss, and so lose even more of what remained of their feelings. Our capacity to cope seems boundless.

Hell, the least "society" can do through the sick strictures of law, education, and religion is let the homosexual alone. Straight or gay, it's hard enough to live with illusions without the harassment of other self-deceivers who happen to be in positions of civil or "moral" authority.

But that's what all the rules are about, aren't they? Vain legalities or social demands conceived and executed by those who fear something in themselves—not necessarily homosexual, no, but some inner weakness, some irreparable loss of power—Daddy's strength, Mommy's love—that craves the illusion of law and order, demands more and more authority in order not to have to recognize that inner helplessness, all that chaos.

Even so, I'm convinced that with all the legal rights in the world and all the social acceptance achieved, the homosexual won't feel any the more fulfilled. He might cruise the streets without fear of the fuzz, but he's still endlessly cruising. He might fuck to his heart's content or get fucked, but the more promiscuous his behavior, the more he attests to his own frantic acting out of his loss. He might establish his own church, but he's still looking for Big Daddy up there in the sky. He might publish his own rag sheets, camp through gay soirees, write his own song lyrics, doll himself up in his own comforting costumes—whether it's feathers or leather or a particular cut of jeans—but once again that need to be identified and to identify with a larger organization other than to get some specific job done is a dead give-away that he is *not* his own man, that his soul is still acting out its essential longing for union with something more secure than his own belief in himself. And that action is the central lie for me now.

"If we could just *learn* not to hate ourselves quite so much!" Michael cries near the end of *The Boys in the Band*. How can we *not* hate ourselves, Michael? We were forced to it, and no act of will is going to change that self-loathing until we feel ourselves into its source.

"1950 fag!" shouts a member of the current crop. "We don't have those hang-ups! We're not ashamed of ourselves!

We'll wear our beads in public and show our asses for anyone who wants to see!"

"Look, I repeat, I respect your protest for equal rights.
But I just can't support its illusion of health—any more
than I can the sickness of those who deny those rights to
anyone else."

And now once more I find myself wondering about the
nature of love and sex altogether. Is it *ever* anything but
compensatory? Anything *ever* but just a little fun? Samsara.
The pleasures of the sexual experience are real enough,
sure, but the foundations of those desires—neurotic or not
—seem nothing more than Nature's insidious way of getting us to do her work. Our instinct to protect our young is
also Nature's doing. Then at base, I mean without hang-
ups, aren't our blood-tickled nerves and our warm effusions
really indiscriminate of any specific object? Child, woman,
man—all can fill our hearts and stir our flesh if we have
been freed enough to allow ourselves to let them. We love
the look of a loved child and feel an impulse to touch his or
her flawless skin. We love a loved grandmother's face and
want to test our smoother fingertips against her wrinkled
cheek. We love our loved father's beard and muscle, want
to run our hand in the rough grain and along his protrud-
ing forearm vein. We love our loved mother's soft neck and
breasts, want to kiss them and bury our face in their per-
fumed warmth. We love our loved women for bringing
something of that first love back to us again. We love our
loved men for the same primary reason. All love involves
our bodies. Abstract love, platonic love, religious devotions,
organizational fidelity—are all bullshit in their refusal to
recognize that the body *is* the spirit and the spirit is the
body. Oh, how we fear to acknowledge our body's involvement with all the people we love. The fraternities and football teams we devise to divert our attention from the truth.
The beauty salons and sororities. The unions we join, the

country clubs, cocktail parties, theaters, games—all excuses to see without being accused of seeing, to touch without feeling condemned for touching.

"Wait a minute! You're advocating that my daughter be raped in the street by any son of a bitch who feels free enough to admit what he's feeling?"

"Don't be a schmuck. A guy as honest and real as that would automatically allow your daughter the right to her *own* feelings—her complete integrity. Rape has nothing to do with love—body or soul. It's a power play. I might be content just to look at your little girl because she's pleasurable to behold. I might even want to stroke her soft bright hair. But I'd make dead sure I wasn't even doing *that* against her will. More likely my instinct to protect her would make me more caring of *her* needs than of my own at that moment. But I'd *know* at least what my guilt-free impulse was all about, and how much I'd enjoy acting on my affection for her to the extent that it moves me to do so. Anyway, I doubt if I'd linger long on your daughter when the whole avenue is a constant feast for my blood. What's more, there'd probably be someone in my life who shared similar feelings for me and with whom I could most fully share mine. Maybe even more than one—"

"I knew it! I knew it! The end of marriage! The end of the nuclear family! You and all that Margaret Mead shit! Don't think I haven't read *The Harrad Experiment*! Filth! Filth!"

"Take it easy, take it easy. There's a great deal to be said for the nuclear family—at least regarding the original and exclusive needs of a child. It's true, I admit, I believe marriage laws should be abolished, but that takes us more into the realm of economics and cultural anthropology, not psychological health, and I'm not ready to think about that now. But how about a baby contract? If you're proved well enough to agree to conceive one—"

"There's a police state brewing in your mind! I suspected as much! Whether it's the CIA or the Mental

Health Association, you're planning to make *new* laws, *new* rules—bed-tapping techniques to make sure no sick kids get born!"

"I don't want sick kids, true. And I don't want sick parents having them. But you've got a point."

"And what about all those crazy geniuses that would never be nuts enough to create something worthwhile? No more Beethovens! No more Burt Bacharachs!"

"Burt will have to speak for himself. But why should anyone stay sick just so you can buy records? These are tough questions you're asking me. Let me think about it. Meanwhile, did I tell you that I like your smile? It reminds me of my father's. I don't have to touch it or kiss your mouth because my father was a loving enough man not to make me feel I have to try to find an illusory shadow of him in you. Besides, my deeper affections lie elsewhere. But your smile fills me with that same warm feeling I have for my dad, and yet behind that sensation there's also a terrible sense of loss —a sense of inevitable sadness—that ever-present need for my father to save me from the dark truth of our human condition."

"Pervert."

2:00 P.M.

Spent the rest of the morning reading *Fathers and Sons*. Really enjoying it now despite what I feel are many false notes. There's the nineteenth-century style to contend with, of course, but that's easily accepted as convention, absorbed as history. A translation too that I suspect is crummy. No, it's Turgenev's "positional" characters that annoy me at times when he sacrifices his psychological attention to get to his philosophic debates. And a plot which, so far, is only an excuse to set scenes for more abstract disputation. Ah, but such discussions! I'm embarrassed and delighted to see

Turgenev asking some of the same questions over one hundred years ago that I've been asking today.

The liberals branded him conservative for this book and the conservatives suspected him of subversion. It seems to me that the expressed values of both his new nihilists and his old aristocrats are fairly much in balance, though I could see why a socialist like Herzen would be upset. The thorough nihilist—Bazarov—simply has no heart. He is the reverse side of the Romantic coin. His destructive indifference and scientific detachment are as inauthentic as any Byronic excess of emotion. Each leads to its own disillusionment. And yet he is so *right* in so much of his criticism of the old institutions. *Old?* He could be complaining about America today. And though the aristocratic Kirsanovs have the edge on him in compassion, their mindless nostalgia and wasting regret for what never was are equally self-deluding.

I see where I'm now going to be judging all fictional characters relative to my ideal Intensive Man. Bad for books. Good for me.

Am sitting in the library now trying not to be too attracted to two good-looking men who just came in. Or, since I am, trying again to trace that feeling to its source, and to see them as attractive without the need to project my wild needs on them. But right now I feel that all of this is just another form of sublimation. I can't stand the idea of becoming a closet queen in my old age. That's like Oscar Levant saying he knew Doris Day before she became a virgin. Or a monk in the mountains turning his sex drive to the service of God. I've the urge to refute all my wisest advice right now and fuck the day away with some guy who'd like that too. Some guy, some guy, some guy—see? It hasn't anything to do with being truly human or wanting to encounter another complete human being! Any warm object with the right body will do!

Shit, I feel as though I'm merely trying to manufacture some new brand of humanistic Puritanism for myself: "No, no, I couldn't go to bed with you, Charlie. I'm not interested in the *real* you, only a fantasy of father or my idealized self. And so, you see, that wouldn't be fair to either of us!" That way lies celibacy! Doesn't Rhoda know that a stiff prick has no conscience! Damn it, either that desire of mine borne of anxiety and unfulfillment withers away of its own accord or this therapy is full of shit! This lost little boy will be damned before he turns himself into a big bad policeman.

Fuck it, again I'm demanding too much of myself, I see. I can't possibly ask two short weeks of therapy, no matter how intense, to undo a whole lifetime of need!

10:20 P.M.

Late this afternoon I talked with the guy next door. We both confessed to a sense of sin for it but compared notes for a few minutes anyway. He feels as into it all now as I do but reminded me of the very hard time he'd had starting. Having had no previous analysis, vaguely aware of a host of amorphous problems, he suspects it was more difficult for him to make honest contact with himself than it might have been for me.

Stan also had no previous therapy but his experience differed from either of ours—an initial overwhelming opening that flooded him far more fully with physical ills and hysterics, then a sudden stopping after ten days and a kind of stalemate which, the last I heard, he said he was just beginning to overcome. It had to do with his fear of approaching his deepest fears. I pray he's worked into them by now, though I doubt it, considering the interruptions to therapy he's manufactured for himself lately.

Now that my neighbor has got into things, he's worried about the possible changes it might make in his marriage and his relationship with his folks. He says he feels that things can only go better at home, but I have my doubts about that. I suspect that neurotics can settle down only with people who are compatible with their problems. It would take a rare kind of mate to accept his or her companion's sudden end to established quirks. Besides, if the partner were honestly "whole" to begin with, he or she would never have dug that neurotic mate in the first place. That delicate balance of neurotic compromise and compensation is necessarily unsettled by any kind of successful therapy, isn't it? If a marriage is still to work, I can't see how one spouse can undertake the treatment without the other. At least my neighbor's wife knows where to go if things start getting rough. He's also worried about being able to keep his mouth shut when his father comes visiting him later this summer. He knows that his ranting and raving against years of abuse won't change the old man; yet if he's honest now, he certainly won't be able to play his father's games anymore, though any new show of strength will detonate the explosions he hopes to defuse by keeping still.

These problems are no different from the ones psychoanalysis creates if, slowly and willfully, a patient begins shedding old adjustments for a try at new ways. But this newer feeling-approach seems to elicit a far more swift and compelling need to drop old habits, and I suspect the impact on those unprepared for it can be all the more devastating.

Decided to see the movie I missed last night. *Plaza Suite*. A decent choice since, despite its selling short every serious idea in its commercial-minded head, it inadvertently presented a comprehensive brief against the institution of marriage. Right up my alley tonight. The short subject with it was far more reprehensible: lying propaganda in the guise of a travelog telling me how progressive the Island of Taiwan is—"the Republic of China" in case I'd forgotten —with its jugglers on TV, its beauty contests, its traffic glut, its modern consumership, garish cities, and children dressed in army uniforms preparing to march, if need be, against that Ugly Red Menace on the Mainland. A deliberate and ugly falsification of Taiwanese history and current political life. And of course scattered applause from the gullible suckers who spent their money to be fed this shit by our unsubtle government machinery.

Trying to evaluate my day now. Except for those sudden panicky doubts in the library this afternoon, it passed by with no great emotional highs or lows. At times I felt I should deliberately set aside some minutes for a good cry, but my Geiger counter of crackling sadness was turned on throughout most of the day, and I certainly didn't do anything deliberate to avoid any radioactive fields of feeling.

Of course there's still a sense of being under house arrest here, or at least a silent pact to behave—*i.e.*, not resort to my old devices—which, once I'm released next Friday, might automatically tempt me to new disasters. I must, I must keep in mind that this therapy is not finished when I leave the Center. I've learned the means for staying close to my pain now, and the deeper I can keep with it, the better my chances for change.

Sunday

3:30 A.M.

Shit, if I wrote this dream for a novel, it would be criti-
cized as contrived. A nocturnal emission just woke me. And
the fantasy to help it along? One chaste kiss wrenched from
a disinclined James Dean, followed by Walter Matthau ac-
cusing me of being a faggot while I'm trying to help his
daughter—Phyllis, Phyllis of my fourteenth year!—to work
up the courage to run off and start her own life. "Why are
you only her platonic friend?" Walter grumbles. "Not
true!" I protest. "I once loved her but she said I was physically repulsive!" My solace? James Dean, I guess. Hell, I'm
reliving my fucking adolescence! Now, if I can get back just
a little further, say, into the womb—

10:15 A.M.

A morning in the park to watch the Fathers and Sons.
So far this Secret Sleuth of Child Abuse surmises that all
seems well.
("Things are seldom what they seem/ Skim milk mas-
querades as cream." G. & S., I think.)
Woke again at 7:00 A.M. vaguely depressed and preoccupied by my wet dream. A relief for the groin, but not this
soul.
The James Dean I saw last night was the one from his

role in *East of Eden* in a scene that breaks me up every time I've seen that film. Cal is rejected by his father, Adam Trask, for his birthday gift of money which the ignorant self-righteous father-of-us-all considers ill-gotten gain. In inarticulate desperation Cal tries to embrace his father and explain his motive, his need for his father's love, but Adam has long ago written Cal off as the "bad" son in favor of Aaron, the "good" one.

Might James Dean be me? Perls would say, "Sure!" If so, then what kind of autoeroticism was behind that kiss? I immediately think of another movie, Cocteau's *Blood of a Poet,* in which the artist discovers a living mouth on the palm of his hand. Slowly he begins applying his hand to the most sensitive parts of his body and swoons in self-perpetuated ecstasy. Great symbol for the artistic ego— proper *amour-propre.* I really dug that scene when I first saw that film in college. That's all I'd need to live a decent life, I decided then, the ability to give myself my own blow jobs.

Maybe last night's kiss was a recognition of the mere masturbatory function of the dream. Maybe it was my own body asking for itself to be loved—for itself. Maybe it was purely homosexual. But isn't *that* only an elaborate word for the crying need for self-love too?

Walter Matthau, of course, came right out of *Plaza Suite.* But no matter what the role, he's always made me uncomfortable on the screen because of his vague resemblance to my father. There is a certain look of uncompromising disgust which his carpetbag of a face sometimes assumes for comic effect. It holds no comedy for me. It's my father's disdain. Well, I suppose few fathers can face the fact that they've had a hand in producing those traits in their sons that they've been brought up to despise. But Walter is playing top dog in this dream. "Why are you only her platonic friend?" he asks. He is asking for the relationship to be complete with Phyllis. And I say that the Phyllis part of me considers me physically repulsive. "I loved her once but—" Once upon a time I loved myself . . . but now it all gets too complicated, or I'm getting too afraid to play the Fritz Perls game or the Freud game . . .

And anyway it was pleasant seeing Phyllis again after all those years. Obviously she had a greater effect on my psychic life than I'd ever dreamed. But I feel a little spooked by it too. It reminds me of a college friend who killed himself during our junior year. Sometimes I still think of him, but it's always his face at nineteen I see, as I did Phyllis' at fourteen, while I seem to be the only character who's getting any older.

One father is reading his Sunday paper while pushing his daughter's swing. I'm not sure she minds his divided attention or not. I don't blame him for being bored by his uninspiring job. He doesn't seem unkind, smiles, helps, but talks to his child in a somewhat abstracted way, his mind still on the news.

On another set of swings, a second father, too priggishly dressed and sounding almost like a grade school teacher to the three children he's with, is pushing and swinging along with them. I like his genuine involvement, yet there's a textbook air about it that's suspicious to me. Nevertheless, he's preferable to the newspaper reader, who just advised his three-year-old to say "May I?" instead of screaming to get off the swing.

Oh, boy, I've just spent almost ten minutes swinging a group of little girls who begged me to push them! Did it with overwhelming pleasure. Not one dirty thought as I touched a variety of six-, seven-, and eight-year-old bottoms. They asked for my name and began calling, "Mike! Push me! Push *me!*" until my arms gave out. I sympathize with the newspaper reader again. Yet when I tired, I told them so and suggested they pump on their own awhile—which they accepted with thanks. They're off at the slides now.

For the first time in years I feel as though I might make a passable father.

Which again brings up the question of this notebook as another form of wish fulfillment. I hate so much to write about failure in here, desperately wanting to believe the therapy is working, that I wonder if I'm not to some degree deliberately shaping experience to fit an unconscious dream of success. Another form of *willing*. I've no doubts that neurosis is stronger than will; so, if there's no improvement it'll only be a matter of time before disillusionment muddies up any positive lines written out here.

But God, I'd hate to have to burn this notebook as just so much more self-deception. I've been trying to record the events of these unusual days as honestly as I see and feel them, but my egoistic organism is such a self-preserving bastard that I'll never be able *ever* to tell the degree to which illusions are operative even here. An old truth hits home: The human species can never fully know its own kind simply because a species cannot possibly fully measure itself. Hell, neither can it measure anything *else* for that matter, except by its own arbitrarily imposed systems of analysis—that old scientific ruse. All our tests and measurements, all our elaborate apparatus are by their very invention contingent upon our nature, and in our fearful search for security, whether domestic or cosmic (the same need writ small and large), we rarely wish to acknowledge that devastating universal illusion.

Damn it, I *must* face the possibility that my homosexual "preference" will *not* end after I leave the Center. Three weeks, three months, three years might not be enough to dissolve the latent and active habits of thirty-six years. "Not all the perfumes of Arabia . . ." The saving grace of Shakespeare and my poor fooling aside, that will be a very hard truth to face. I'm not inalterably opposed to a homosexual life in the future. Only, even in its best moments I've always thought it second-best. No, not because of the social prejudices, although of course they're always present, but because it seems to sell short my body and my soul. Cocks are constructed for cunts and vice versa, any spice of variety notwithstanding. Moreover, despite some intense physical and psychic pleasure, in my homosexual experience that pleasure has always been surrounded by anxiety and regret. (Hell, who knows if that in itself didn't for some sick reason *increase* its value for me?) Nevertheless, I continued an active homosexual life as a convenient way to express my needs, allay my fears, court approval and seek a compromise with the reality of my emotional limitations. Now, though, all my understanding of homosexuality's compensatory nature is a much greater felt truth. And if I fall into its familiar ease again, it can be only with a greater repugnance for myself (a new crime!) and a greater sense of regret for knowing it to be not so much a compromise for me anymore but abject self-deception.

Oh, God, another father is not handling at all well his little son's fear of a swing! The boy won't attempt one whose height is really more suitable for him, but his father doesn't seem to care. The boy's younger sister is swinging nicely on one the same height as his, and the father is indicating this by a disregard for his son's declaration that he's swinging higher.

The boy's physical cowardice reminds me of my own. His father's indifference *my* father's.

"Hey, Daddy, watch how fast I go!" the boy shouts now.

The father, who's trying to force them on to another activity (one no doubt more minimally interesting to himself), wants them both to come along. The little girl protests with tears. The boy rushes after his father, who's now returned to the swings at his daughter's bidding. Now he stands dutiful but inattentive to both.

Jesus, if he's offered to take them to the park—*their* play-

ground, *their* time for activity with him—why must he
make it so difficult for them? Doesn't he realize what's riding
on his generous and honest interest? And if he can't muster
it up this morning, for whatever good reason—last night's
boozing, trouble with the missus—isn't there some way,
some way not to increase his children's unconscious suffering because of his own inadequacy? *No, of course not!!*

Shit, the father took the daughter to the slides; the boy
was left behind swinging high and still trying to attract
Daddy's attention with a loud singsong, then shouts of
"Daddy, look!" finally jumping off the swing to chase after
the father, who's walked off holding his daughter's hand.

Okay, okay, the inevitable sibling rivalry, but would that
be so intense if Daddy had originally paid proper attention
to his son, or made allowances for the trauma of a newborn
baby entering the house? During the last fifteen minutes
he's certainly spent far less time with the boy, and his little
girl seems much more self-sufficient. Is it too farfetched to expect a parent to be able to read his children's *individual*
needs more accurately? That bastard there is obviously responding to his *own*. He must do that, I suppose—but not
at this time, not as a father, not at his own son's expense!

"Do you have to go *sssst?* Yes or no?" asks another father
now, ex-Army captain type, cropped hair, basso voice, and
obviously embarrassed about saying the dirty word aloud.

"I think so," says his little boy, nodding sheepishly on the
way to the public urinal.

Good luck, sonny.

That fuck-up is *still* across the park with his daughter
while the boy now sits forlornly on the lower swing repeating, "Daddy, Daddy, Daddy . . ."

I'm not making this up, damn it! It's happening right before my eyes! I'm holding back a sudden swell of tears.
What can I do? Rush to the swing to push the kid, which
would probably frighten him to death, or create hostility in

his father, and at best give the boy only a sorry substitute for what he needs? Or get down on my knees to describe the human condition to the kid, telling him the last thing in the world he wants to hear: that his fucking father doesn't love him enough! Or hurry over to the father, and like some psychologically crazed Jeremiah, berate him for his betrayal, or pedantically explain it, or beat the hell out of him—or *God knows what???*

"Push me, Daddy!"

"Get on the higher one," the father stipulates.

The boy goes. Tries it—doesn't seem too frightened. But stops as soon as the father turns away after registering again only the scantest interest in his son's brave attempt to do his bidding. Back to the lower swing now, calling, "Push me, Daddy!"

He doesn't want to go high! He doesn't even want to be pushed! He wants to be *loved,* you fucker!

The father comes over at last and pushes, but with the question: "How come you switched swings?"

The boy doesn't answer. It would be a forced confession of cowardice. And he's fool enough now to be happy that his bastard of a father is near him for a little. Stay with him, please, damn you! Don't desert him again. Your daughter's perfectly content over there, not even looking for you. Push *him.* Push *him!* Not too high!

Damn it, you pushed too *hard!*

The boy's afraid now. He scuffs his shoes to stop.

"What are you doing to your shoes?" the fuck-up complains.

"I want to go on the slide." The boy runs away from his father.

The father looks at the sky.

I'm the only one crying around here!

Ex-Army captain type back. He's okay. His little boy seems to like his independence, which he asserts with lots of shouting allowed; without any testing hostility between them. Father seems playful when needed, patient, watchful of his child's wishes. Okay. It's a wise father who knows his own child. I like him. He has a sturdy kind of kindness. Attractive figure, tall and balding with glasses softening his face, reliable and good-humored. I wish he'd been *my* father. That *sssst* for piss a cultural legacy not necessarily the beginning of the boy's inhibition. The kid's mother might be another story. But the father's okay.

That other father I'd like to kill.

Just pushed the little girls again and received a round of lovely good-byes.

Also stopped in at the public urinal. Empty of men and/or boys, thank God, but considering that even getting inside one is usually enough to stop me from going, I *sssst'd* with very little trouble.

What a morning.

1:30 P.M.

Have stopped to rest while climbing through the local woods, the smell of dry grass and pungent gum trees as heady as ever. Lots of poison oak too, so I'll probably end my three weeks here scratching. Overlooking Marin County Courthouse now—and testing the rifle range, to see if I can avenge Angela Davis from here, or arrange *her* escape. Another shoot-out? More victims. Leading to *more* panicky injustice. Leading to *more* blood. All simply desperate forms of "acting out." Hardly the *cure* for America's neuroses.

I thought I was through with biography by now, but a few more scraps occurred to me along the way up here. Nothing to hold against Mom or Dad exactly, but instances of my own crooked ways of trying to tell them something was wrong.

Twice as a kid I wrote forbidden words—expressions of anger I couldn't let out straight. And both on wood.

Once on Halloween night at age eleven I wrote SHIT on my grandmother's front door. I hated that critical, cranky woman; what's more, I was sure my mother wasn't very partial to her. The next day I confessed to the crime and was made to wash the word off the door, but its shadow remained there long after anybody else could see it but me. It tickled me.

The other time was earlier; I etched 7734 into an expensive end table and blamed it on my sister. Inverted, the numbers are supposed to look something like HELL. I certainly knew it was wrong to scratch up a table, but I did it anyway. My mother put a picture under the glass top to hide the mark after polishing some of it out—but we both knew it was still there. It never made me very happy.

Ah, so there was power in words, I see. A word could hurt. A pen could tell things—even when I couldn't.

In college it always amazed me to learn that some of my friends had played hookey many times during their high school careers. I never did. Even when our secondary school teachers went on strike, and Lincoln High came to free the slaves of Madison, I stayed in school that day—good little Michael running messages to and from the general office. God, I hate that fink.

Only once did I skip Hebrew school. One Sunday morning I spent the time sitting in a nearby playground. Unfortunately, my teacher lived on our block, and wouldn't you know it, while we all were outside on the front steps later that spring day, he walked by with his family.

"Moshe, why weren't you in school this morning?"

"I was sick," I lied, looking away from my mother.

As soon as he was gone, she said, "For that we're not going to the rodeo next week."

Shit. Another excuse to break a promise. And never a
question as to *why* I'd skipped school or an attempt to sympathize with the overwhelming apathy I felt for that whole
dull obligation. You fucking mother, *you* didn't want to go
to the rodeo! Liar! Hypocrite!

Oh, shit, now I remember another time when I found
myself defending her: The principal of our primary school,
one of those old 1930's Irish battle-axes who maintained
those fortresses, called our class down for a talk one day.
"What do you do to help your mothers at home?" she asked,
and those who didn't snicker delivered their simpering little sweetnesses. My turn came and I said, "I always get my
own breakfast. I sometimes make it for my sister too." For
as long as I could remember I was doing that, even thought
I preferred it that way so that my mother could sleep late.
Like the little mouse again I'd noiselessly scratch around
the kitchen. "But that's awful," said the Bitch of Erin.
"Mothers should always get their children's breakfasts."
She had the gall to say that in front of my whole class! I was
mortified, stunned. I choked back a protest. She was insult-
ing my mother! I wanted to strangle her! But it's not until
right now, this very moment, that I've ever questioned the
point she raised, that I ever admitted that I *did* feel deprived of my mother in the early mornings as she slept on
in her bedroom and allowed me to rummage around on my
own, and made me feel I was "grown up" to do so, forcing
me to justify to myself that deprivation, to uphold her subtle neglect as honorable, her *right,* and my duty to be
bound by it.
Oh, but I would have done anything to make her happy.
One day she took my sister and me to see a revival of *The
Wizard of Oz.* I'd seen it before at the age of five, but my
sister never had. I told her that the Emerald City would be
so brilliantly green, she'd have to shut her eyes. She didn't.
We were fourteen and eleven then, and I found myself
bored with a lot of it. Not enough magic anymore.

After the movie my mother asked us to choose a place for lunch. I suggested a restaurant I'd been to with an uncle; a glorified hamburger joint with phony Western decor that seemed unique for me at the time. But the place was noisy with kids, and the service slow. Mother was disappointed. She said, "I was hoping to take you to a nice quiet place where the three of us would be alone together for a change." This was during all the strains of my father's eye operations, my brother only a year old. My heart sank. My mother wanted to be alone with us! For the first time in ages! And I'd ruined our chance. I'd made her unhappy! My imagination immediately conceived a cool blue booth where just the three of us would sit by ourselves all afternoon, just enjoying each other's company. This open table in a garish purple room with waiters wearing phony cowboy gear was a crime against my mother's deepest wishes for us. I'd ruined her day, my day—my life.

And to realize now that even if that day had worked out well, it would never have made a difference—

Oh, boy, this is a great place to cry—these woods. . . .

The Wizard of Oz. My God, that one and *Ziegfeld Girl* probably made me gay. M-G-M I demand reparations! Fantasy—and Judy Garland.

One night years later at the Palace, while listening to Garland singing out her sick quivering soul, some black queen behind me screamed, "Tell them for us, Judy! Tell them!"

I sneered in disgust of him, abhorring the truth of his pathetic need—and mine. No wonder Garland was so popular with the boys. Her voice was Longing itself. She shared our agony and could shout it out for all of us: "I'm afraid. Help me! I need love!"

No doubt our reverence was also due to the role she played in the childhood of my generation: the lost little girl from Kansas trying to find her way home from Oz, the would-be showgirl winning the world's applause with her final production number, the dreamer pining for the boy next door, the clown feigning happiness to hide her broken heart while that flitty Ann Rutherford won Andy Hardy once again. Our problems, ours.

What's more, we never had to worry about Judy grown-up. Essentially she remained a little girl, one whom we could identify with and protect like the baby sister inside us while we watched Gene Kelly wiggle his ass.

Our other great suffering sister—Bette Davis. Give or take Luise Rainer, Joan Crawford, Ida Lupino, *et al.* Warner Brothers also knew what brought in the bread. Oh, those tearjerkers that Mother loved! Bette's larger-than-life emotions, her bitter wit to mask her secret pain. She taught us our defensive repartee. And like Judy she presented no sexual threat. (Sorry, Bette.) Underneath the devouring, demanding woman, we instinctively knew, was a weak and needy thing who showed women up for the bitches we unconsciously believed they were, as critical of them as she was convincing. Mae West, Harlow, the later Garbo (though I only got to know them through revivals) did much the same, I guess. Drag queens all. Tragic like Garbo, comic like Harlow and West, but never a threat. Not like Carole Lombard, Lana Turner, Goddard, Hayworth, Lake, Sheridan—those women who seemed to demand a certain reciprocity, who wanted to play for keeps. That's frightening. Sex and love together? Wow. Spooky. We'd much rather camp around in costumes by Adrian and die young like Garbo in *Camille* or Davis in *Dark Victory* still dreaming of the perfect love we'd lost.

9:10 P.M.

A long, long night.

After stopping for that rest in the woods, I continued walking along the ridges of several more hills this afternoon. Fine views of the county, the bay, Mt. Tamalpais.

The warmth and the wild flowers and the smell of the hay finally got to me. I stripped in the sun and all too soon began to feel my penis stir. Despite last night's release, I masturbated—fast and without an iota of imagery. Small pleasure but great relief. Yet all day I'd fought against it because I knew I'd have to write it down, loathed admitting to "failure," and felt I'd be breaking Rhoda's Rules of Order. Who knows, maybe it was a healthy rebellion. Since I'm prone to following orders to please Mom, maybe breaking one did me a service (no pun intended). Or is that just my power to rationalize. Without the benefit of fantasy the act left me feeling not too faggoty, and it felt great to lie naked in the sun. I really think I'm beginning to feel I don't have to hate my body so much. What's more, since I recently learned that jerking off doesn't grow warts, I had no regrets, just a fearful concern for the time when all the vain wish-fulfilling imagery might return.

My neighbor moved upstairs and a new guy is now next door. I expect they prefer to keep the new customers on the ground floor away from the racket at least until they're acclimated. This one, young and Clark Kentish-looking (uh-oh), meeting me in the hallway, asked about restaurants in the area. I told him what I could but, as much as I wanted to go on talking, hurried into my room for fear of breaking his isolation. My impulse was to assure him that tonight would probably be hell for him, but it was all in the best interests of tomorrow. Yet even that might have assuaged his anxiety, and it seemed to me important not to give him a clue of what's to come. He's been quietly coughing from time to time and I feel my own early anxiety again in what I assume is his.

At around 7, after an early supper, I went upstairs to scream and cry. Couldn't sustain it alone for more than half an hour, but that time was good. Came downstairs to sit and watch the night fall, to try to keep with the pain. Right now it's a quiet sadness with an occasional tear or two—but

the night seems endless because of it, and even escaping
into this notebook, as I know I've just done, hasn't eased
my discomfort over the truth or my fears of the future.
Back to watching the sky—and no doubt an early retreat to
bed.

God, no more dreams, *please.*

Monday

8:15 A.M.

Several. Only one recalled with any clarity. But nothing devastating and nothing I don't already know:

In this one that black writer-teacher and I are sharing an apartment with two bathrooms (this house? the office we shared at school?). This time he's normal-looking, *himself,* and as open and friendly as always. My problem seems to be to keep out of his way—my own demand—the fear of his coming upon me while I'm urinating, bathing, etc. I keep having to anticipate which bathroom will momentarily be the more private and am always sure I'm guessing wrong. In he comes with students, and lugging in office furniture, to catch me with my pants unzipped (fear of his seeing this journal? the guy I see as "normal and together" hating me for my perversions? laughing at me?).

So often I've envied this guy. A good writer who has great rapport with his students. I've not done badly myself in that department, I think, but it seems to come to him so much more easily than it does to me. Nor is it solicited in the way I secretly beg for attention and love and work so hard to earn it. Several times last term our unscheduled office hours conflicted and I willingly shuffled away while he held a conference, not begrudging him the time or space, merely envious that he seemed so *necessary* to his students, so wanted.

If that guy is a projection of the better side of *me,* the

side that might be *easy* with himself, then maybe the dream is showing me how I am my own worst enemy, how *I* interfere with all my fears and wants from being at home with myself. I don't know. It could just as easily be reversed: The guy as projection might be an unattainable ideal, a standard of perfection with which I continue to dog myself instead of allowing myself to be me. That's the trouble with these dream games; they always seem up for grabs. I wish I knew better ways of getting into them so I could be *sure* of my existential stance (ha-ha).

The urination business is obvious to me at least. As always my fear of the forbidden shameful noises issuing from my unwholesome body. Thinking about that, I just realized I never saw my father piss. As a little kid I wondered about the massive size of his penis, but much later, during his blindness when I occasionally had to help him bathe, I saw his penis again and realized it was nothing spectacular. Satisfaction in that. Jack the Giant Killer. Jack and the Beanstalk.

Should fathers piss for their sons? Well, I doubt if they fastidiously should *not*. Although I saw my father naked often enough later on, when I was little I have the feeling he deliberately kept his body concealed from me, which may have contributed to my own sense of shame.

More important, I'm sure, was my wretchedness whenever I heard my mother urinating in the bathroom. This is tied up with adolescence though. Once I learned what women "did," urinating seemed just as forbidden a thing to hear or see as sex. If I heard my mother piddling, it was as good as raping her. That dirty book from junior high kept popping into my mind. Percy gets an erection upon hearing his aunt urinating. "Don't tell your mother, Percy. She's been saving you for herself." Well, as Rhoda said, "She got your balls all right." Jesus, and I didn't even know it was hurting.

DEAR JONATHAN SWIFT:
Yes, you poor fuck-up, Celia shits!

Thinking back on the weekend, I realize that my moments of anxiety and depression are always related to my fear of failure. Even last night's dream reiterated that theme. Failure in any action—this therapy, my writing, pissing, sexual performance, altruistic impulses, conversation. The attendant anxiety is always due to a need for love and the fear that I won't be rewarded with it. To merit love one must be perfect, perform well, succeed. No matter how many times that's been disproved to me, the compulsion to create those harsh terms for love has never left me. That was a learned thing, wasn't it? Mother taught it to me. Father let her. I rarely tried earning my father's love. Fulfilling his demands wasn't worth his meager rewards. But Mother? Ah, Mother held the Promise at Dawn. Did Romain Gary ever understand that the mama he idolized in his biography was really a demanding, lethal, castrating bitch? Oh, how we sentimentalize those early crimes against us in dread fear of recognizing what they truly mean.

Perfection. The need to be perfect. I remember now attending a workshop on Artistic Blocks at Albert Ellis' Institute for Rational Therapy in New York. Each week two or three of us would talk with the therapist before the group about a specific instance of creative block. Aside from the fact that many of the people were untalented (but suffered a dumb compunction to prove themselves artistically because of some past imposition), the major reason for paralysis seemed due to our varying fears of failure. One's whole life depended on producing the perfect painting, the perfect poem. The therapist was a pleasant young man who apparently had suffered the same thing until Albert Ellis called him a silly shit often enough to make him realize that his latest short story was not *him*, that *he* wasn't those sheets of paper coming out of the typewriter.

Nice home truths. I believed it—every rational moment of my day. Only, reasonable moments like that are pretty rare for the fucked-up. Artistic impulses are not at base "ra-

tional," Albert. One's performance might very well be—
with all sorts of judgmental modes immediately set in operation—but that first *need* to set pen to paper, paint to plas-
terboard, is as emotional as my childish need for alliteration.
Along with that sheet of foolscap one's whole past goes into
that typewriter, and no rational process—except one of
self-deluding will—is going to make a nut believe that his
potential salvation isn't riding on the graceful balance of
that last sentence. That's Mommy's love you're trying to
earn with that little poem, with that bowel movement, with
that noiseless pissing. It damned well *better* be perfect or
Mommy won't even sniff at it! And when you feel it's not—
oh, well, you knew it all along anyway, didn't you? You
never really *were* worthy of Mother's love, were you? Eat
your heart out, kiddo. There's always next time, and next
time, and next time to try to earn her affection (or the
world's when it won't work with her) with your perfect
paragraph, your perfect turds. Forget the fact that it never
existed and never will! Aesthetes turn to esoteric problems
of form and style only in secret despair or in terror of their
mounting suspicion that the work of art they produced to
win love and prove theirs will never be enough. Never.
Never.

Primer for Perfect Parents

Example #3

> SCENE: One summer evening. After a picnic in a lovely
> field, our Perfect Parents are lying outside on a soft quilt
> with their two children, Danny and Suzy, between them.
> They all are watching the stars begin to appear above.
> Daddy has been helping Danny look through a small
> telescope. Suzy has already had a turn but wants another,
> slightly annoyed with Daddy's attention to Danny.
> SUZY: I want to look again!
> DADDY: Hold on. It's Danny's turn. You'll have it in a
> minute.

MOMMY: The stars look pretty good to me even without the telescope.

SUZY (unconvinced): Don't con me, Mother. (Pause.) Today Judy said she had a better bike than mine.

MOMMY: Oh? Why did she say that?

DANNY (still looking through the telescope): Because it is.

SUZY (ready to cry): See?

DADDY: What kind does she have?

SUZY: A two-wheeler with trainer wheels. She said it cost more than fifty dollars.

DADDY: Wow. That's a lot of money. I guess it probably is a better bike than yours.

SUZY: Well, why can't *I* have one like hers?

MOMMY: Because we can't afford it just now. We were hoping you could do with the one you have for another year or so. You'll be taller by then and will need a regular two-wheeler then anyway.

SUZY: Will it be as good as Judy's?

MOMMY: It'll be a good bike that'll help you get where you want to go. What's all this about being as good as Judy's?

SUZY: All her things are better than mine!

MOMMY: Do you believe that?

SUZY (hesitant): Well, she always *says* so!

DADDY (a little too coyly for my taste): I wonder why—

MOMMY: Maybe she doesn't feel that *she's* so good. Maybe that's it, Suzy. An awful lot of people go around saying that the things they own are better than other people's because they're afraid that *they're* not—not inside themselves. A person isn't the thing he *owns,* you know. That never makes anyone feel any better about himself inside. Not really.

DADDY: Do you feel that way inside yourself? That you're not so good?

SUZY: Sometimes.

MOMMY: Me too. But not too often. Because I've learned that I'm the only one I have, and that's good enough for me or *has* to be—at least I feel that way most of the time.

DANNY: Hey, look. A shooting star!

SUZY: Where, where?

DADDY: We missed that one. We'd better watch carefully. There'll probably be more tonight.

The family watches in silence for a while, the telescope laid aside, the sky too spectacular for the sops of science.

SUZY: It's so big. Where does it stop?
DANNY: It doesn't. It goes on and on forever.
DADDY: As far as we know. There are a couple of theories—

Unfortunately he's ready to expound. Fortunately Suzy is feeling the sky's immensity deeply enough to hold her own, and interrupts:

SUZY: It makes me feel so small.
DANNY: Like a worm. You're a worm!
SUZY: I'm not!
DADDY: And you, Danny? Are you much bigger than that? Am I? Or Mommy? I'm afraid we're all just about the size of worms when it comes to looking at the sky up there.
SUZY: That's scary.
DANNY: It sure is.
MOMMY: For me too. That really makes me feel small and lonely and lost sometimes.
SUZY (snuggling closer): I don't feel lonely when I'm with you, Mommy. You'll stay with me, won't you?
MOMMY: I'll sure as hell try. For as long as I can manage it, and as long as you feel you need me.
SUZY (sleepily): I'll always need you.
MOMMY: I suppose in a way you always will. (Reflectively) I still need my mother too sometimes—and she—she lives in Chicago.
DADDY: And you, Danny? Do you feel the same way?
DANNY: Well, right now I do. But according to the Primer for Perfect Parents, you offer me a certain necessary security which, however generous, will never be enough. Secretly I already know that. I've got the both of you now to give me comfort and strength, of course, but neither of you is going to last forever, and you feel just as scared as I do about your finitude. It's nice lying out

here looking at the stars and even feeling spooky about it. That's the score. I don't have to wear an Army uniform or become a bank president to show the world I'm not afraid. I'm scared shitless—the same as everybody else.

DADDY: You're also in danger of mind-fucking, kiddo. Don't talk away your feelings.

DANNY: Okay, Dad. How about a communal scream for old time's sake?

DADDY: That can be a cop-out too. Just hold my hand, if you want, and let's suffer a little in silence, okay? It's too nice a night for noise.

SUZY: Oh, look! A shooting star!

Mommy looks up at the universe and down at her drowsy children. She quietly begins to weep for herself as she takes her husband's hand.

Writing that little scene made me realize another, perhaps even more defeating motive for picking on Stan so often. Not only do I pester the life out of him to be in some sense the all-attentive mother and father I never had, but also because I see him as my possession, as an essential part of me, I want him to be perfect—the best bicycle on the block. When he's not—collar crooked, a sentence slurred— it's reflecting on me. It means I'm no good, not perfect, the possessor of secondhand, damaged (like Daddy) goods.

Once more I see the blind man I had to help down the street reflecting so poorly on me, my father not the best, handicapped just as I felt I was, and my hating him for it so. Stan is absentminded on the street (a real problem of his, I believe) but I'm furious when I'm forced to remind him to look where he's going. Taking care of Daddy again when Daddy should be taking care of me. And it's more proof that I own nothing worth showing off, which I needed so desperately for feeling there was nothing worthwhile in me. And why? Damn it, because they never made me feel worth a good goddamn when I most needed that assumption to set my life straight. Not even the touch

of my own skin! My body a nuisance, noisy, smelly, value-
less, not worth a caress!

Once in a violent rage I broke a favorite but scratched record of mine. It was no longer perfect. I hated it for that.
Nothing I owned was any good, nothing! If I did own it, it
would turn to shit. To this day buying clothes is a trial for
me. I can't stand to see myself in a salesroom mirror, certain
to feel disappointed and ugly. And when I finally break
down and buy something, as soon as it's home, I decide it's
all wrong. Rarely do I feel comfortable in what I wear.

There's a nice unspoken bit of stage business in *Boys in
the Band*: During Michael's first scene with Donald, almost
unaware of it, he needlessly changes his sweater after checking his appearance in a mirror one more time. That constant discontent hit where it hurts. That vague, vain belief
that our clothes and our goods, the very people we sur-
round ourselves with will validate us by making up for
what we feel we so lack.

What else has my homosexual search for my perfect
counterpart been about, if not that? The handsome, well-
built, clean-cut, all-American boy was the one I first saw
receiving the world's unqualified adulation. If I could be
him, or at least hold him close, *own* something of him in a
vain attempt to incorporate his body into mine, *I* would be
somewhat beautiful too, wouldn't I? I too would have the
admiration of all the girls, the approval of all the boys, my
father's respect, my mother's love.

God, I hate them for making me hate me! *Of course* they
didn't know! Of course not! They weren't evil people. In
many ways they all were too damned typical of their generation! But that makes the little boy inside me no happier
about it! And now at least I have a relieving sense that
there's no longer any need to forgive them for it!

2:00 P.M.

Rhoda was a half hour late today. Whether deliberately or not doesn't matter, though I suspect it was planned. And it did its dirty work well. By the time she knocked on my door I was quivering with need of her.

"Go into it," she said immediately. "Go into the feeling."

The session, which started at 1:00, was short and sweet. For the next forty-five minutes I might as well have been in my crib again, screaming for my mother, crying for her, hating her for not coming to me when I needed her to. My grief seemed boundless and the intermittent realizations that she was never coming, never had, never could—at least not often enough to make me feel secure—were appalling. I doubt if I'll ever recover from it. How she could have been so far off base is beyond me. But it doesn't matter now —that kind of mind-fucking inquiry. I felt my visceral need for her more profoundly than ever before. A baby and a little boy were crying for her up in that office. Me.

During the session I flashed on a feeling that there really is no such thing as *love* at all. Not for a mommy, anyway. Just pure and simple NEED. To deny an infant and child that biological necessity is the worst crime any human being can commit.

"See that little boy holding onto Mommy's hand," said Rhoda at one point.

I wanted to grab up in my arms my own three-year-old body and run away from that ungiving woman as far as I could go. Who else could give him what he needs now but me?

6:30 P.M.

All afternoon passed close to that pain. It seemed—*seems* —insupportable still to have been so stupidly neglected. Again, my older mind keeps saying, "Yes, but she didn't *know*."

That still doesn't appease that kid abandoned in his crib too long. I cannot mistrust my feelings in this. But I do mistrust the concept of the single "primal" event, at least in my case. No, this must have been a slow accumulation of enough unconscious instances—though maybe that colic-filled first week of life was what started it off—to keep the dismal action going. Why else would that little kid have gone on torturing himself in pursuit of her, and why would this big kid still be crying about it? I'm not that good a fantasist. Out of the mores of that decade's child-rearing techniques, or out of her own massive difficulties, a mistrust in her own instincts maybe, my mother managed to make a terrible mistake and continued making it. The man in me can forgive her, sure; the boy who's always been my more honest part never can.

God, it's amazing what I'll do to keep resisting such crucial truth even now. All day I've been fitfully dozing, feeling bone-weary, only to wake crying like that neglected kid again. And a great desire for sweets. Apple pie and chocolate cake. Wouldn't you know it—Mother was great at baking those. Eat enough of her cooking and you could almost convince yourself she loved you. I resisted buying anything like it at supper just now, but the craving remains.

Those damned sweets. How many children have been reared on the promise of sugar: "If you'll be quiet, you can have a piece of candy." Training us like circus ponies. I'm not so sure that children's penchant for candy and cake is all that natural. I remember those experiments with children being left to select their meals from tables of natural food, and how they chose surprisingly well-balanced diets. How many parents' consciences are put to rest by giving children sweets instead of themselves? "Rochelle, take a Hershey bar!" a Jewish grandmother once called from the back of the five-and-dime where I worked one summer. At the time it seemed an ethnic ugliness that made me shudder with scorn. Now I think I'd slug that old cunt for fooling the child into thinking a candy bar can give her love.

I read somewhere that alcoholics are generally sweet-prone kids. Simple body chemistry? Maybe, only I've got a hunch now that the candy-eating child, like me, gobbling up Milky Ways, O'Henry's and Mars Bars in those darkened movie houses, and that sucking, chewing, engorging incipient alcoholic are craving a more vital kind of carbohydrate to keep their bodies from admitting they're dead.

Oh, God, I think again of the role I've cast Stan into, not only as feeder of this child, but my secret anger when he's five minutes late getting home from work. As with Dr. M and Rhoda this morning: fury whenever I'm kept waiting. As with those kids at the train station that day. And my always being early—that deliberate way of making sure I'd earned the right to be angry. No, the *hope* in that—that if I'm early, they'll come sooner. That's it, the pain will stop sooner. Happiness, relief will begin sooner, sooner! For thirty-six years I've been calling for Mother from that fucking crib and she's never going to come on time! She's never going to answer me! Never! I have to live with *that*— *THAT!*—and never again imagine that someone else can do for me what that sick and frightened woman never did! Who *wants* to believe it? Not I, damn it. But I have to. I *do!* And the admission once again forces me to tears.

9:25 P.M.

Evening group just over. Almost at once I relived this morning's pain with the same intensity, the same rage of need, the same despair of finding love. Physical symptoms returned upstairs, my knotted stomach, a headache, the need to vomit up my feeling. I was a squawling kid again, and twice found myself dozing, only to begin again. An hour and a half of it—fitful weeping for a coda.

Rhoda was working tonight. She stayed with me for a while and rested her hand on my head for a few moments. I haven't had any tenderness from a woman like that since . . . I was a sick little boy. As I bitterly wept for myself, I remembered holding my mother's hand several times during that year she was dying, knowing she was dying and trying to imprint the feel of her hand in mine because I knew it soon would be dead, just sitting on the couch at home and holding her hand, trying to indicate to her that I loved her but never really being sure that she knew what I was trying to say. "You have a beautiful nose," I said to her on her deathbed for fear my telling her I loved her would make her more miserable than she was that awful night— and knowing now the far more devastating truth behind it all.

Well, I'm sure my disillusionment is just about complete, but during the wrap-up I confessed to the group of my fear of having to support my sister's illusions about our mother, the fear of losing my sister in the bargain, since I know we both revered my mother in much the same idiotic way.

One of the women told me she'd gone through the same thing, and the Ex-Girl Across the Hall said she'd had to face that with her brother recently. Both agreed that if other members of the family were lost as a result of one's new honesty, then one never really had them in the first place.

God, I pray that's not true of my sister. We suffered so much together for the sake of our parents, I hope we can still be friends after this. Having none of my own I would hate to lose her children, and I'd hate to hurt her. But I won't be party to any fantasy about my mother's goodness anymore. Her awful death and difficult life of sick, self-imposed responsibility has done too much to mask the loss that all three of her children sustained during the most crucial time of *our* lives!

One woman tonight also assured me that leaving the house after her three weeks had proved not quite as terrifying as she'd imagined. That is, she didn't readily fall into her old traps. New problems to face, yes, reconciling your changes with a world that expects you to return unchanged. That's scary but healthy. Easier to bear than the fear of being the same despite all one's agony here.

Well, I'm exhausted. I need a hot shower. It's been a long terrible day for which I'm glad.

Tuesday

8:45 A.M.

Woke feeling spent but well. No blues or worries, renewed conviction that I was getting somewhere, but a slight
weariness of having to plunge into that emotional abyss
again today. Those sessions are physically as well as psychologically draining. It takes me time to make contact
with those deep feelings. My body resists submitting itself
to the rack. Good old Nature working right along to keep
me screwed for her own pleasure.

The new guy next door seems to have disappeared after
his first day. Is it my writer's habit or my own sickness for
assurance that makes me want to know why? I wonder if I
shouldn't have followed my initial instinct on Sunday and
given him the benefit of my experience. Hell, playing Holden Caulfield to the kids on the edge of the rye again. Well,
if so, it's one of the least disagreeable aspects of my ills. Was
the first day of isolation too rough for him? Couldn't he get
anywhere during his first session? Was that decision to leave
his own, or mutually agreed upon, or his therapist's demand? Each person here is unique, I know, but I still have
this dumb need to see in anyone's possible failure my own
fate. I want everyone to succeed if only to ensure my own
success. Again, that old sense of incompetence, my inability
to believe in myself—that I, in myself, can bring about any
effective change without the whole world's approval and
support. I must do more work on this.

Once again, I'm furious with Nature's way of protecting us from the truth. Last year, a girl I was somewhat involved with against my will (for practical as well as neurotic reasons; she's crazier than I) appeared at my apartment in tears.

"What's wrong with me, Mike?" she bawled. "Why can't I keep my friends? Why am I still so tied up with my parents? Why do all the guys run out on me?"

It was the first time I heard her ask such searching questions of herself. Aha, I thought, at last we can begin to be honest with each other. As delicately as I could, this old Freudian tried to tell her what I felt was true: She suffered from an unhealthy attachment to her father, a damaging self-centeredness arising out of sad self-hatred, leaving her dissatisfied with her friends, her work, her wardrobe. Her symptoms were all my own. Maybe that's why we managed to get along as well as we did. In propping up her ego I supported mine. Yet I also despised her for having the same set of problems.

After my lovely analysis, not all of it off base, I gently suggested that she try to get some professional help.

I never saw anyone get well so fast. Sniffing back her tears, she rose high in her seat. "Oh, don't be silly. I always get depressed this way when I'm late with my period."

Shit, it takes guts to admit you're hurting. But I'm convinced that the person who *least* needs the help that this therapy might offer would be the least resistant to it. The healthiest person should be able to value this kind of strategic contact with himself, and would probably profit by that exposure to raw feeling if only to re-prove to himself what he has already felt and accepted in an informal way.

While reading the newspaper at breakfast I noticed a good-looking athlete on the sports pages. "No wonder he's an athlete," I automatically said to myself. "Look at that jaw." The proper chin of a Micky Finn, which I've always associated with the tough and active, the kind of strong open face I envied as a high school boy, still do, immediately assuming that those heroes own the world.

Cultural illusions, psychological illusions. The dozens of perfect physical specimens I've tricked with have proved that a lie often enough.

Yet, I'm still not sure if there isn't one strong element of truth in it too:

When in college I first came across Sheldon's work on varieties of physique in our psych. courses—the endomorph, mesomorph, ectomorph classifications and the personality-related viscero-, somato-, cerebrotonic types—I immediately bought the fatalism implied by its conclusions: You Are What Your Body Type Makes You.

In my own case I felt stuck somewhere between meso- and endomorphic, leaning toward the viscerotonic in temperament. In my sorrier moments I could feel my bones melting like wax toward the more completely endomorphic, my muscles waterlogged sponges cushioning the hippo inside.

Now I'm wondering how much more society rather than physiology must be held accountable for the growth of our bodies. Our particular society most highly approves of the mesomorphs. The sturdy child with the best coordination generally receives far more applause in America for his appearance and action than does the narrow-boned child or the wider one, the clumsy, the slow. Doesn't it follow then that the so-called inborn nervous energy of the cerebrotonic, the sluggishness of the viscero, might be merely the influence of his earliest handling, his reactions to deprivation, rather than the irreversible laws of heredity? Everything after simply reinforces those earliest suppositions of society. The jock becomes a jock because jockdom is both easy for him and the way that wins him his love. Parents approve. The crowd cheers.

Is there such a thing as a natural born leader, a universally admired prototype to whom our instincts automatically draw us? Ardrey makes an interesting case for that in

The Social Contract in his discussion of the alpha fish. Or is that alpha a different hero for different cultures? Under ideal conditions, for instance, in some mythical shtetl that knew no fearful pogrom or in an Israel that suffered no paranoia, would the physically unfit little Jewish boy, genuinely, generously regarded by both parents and made to feel secure in *himself* rather than in his scholarship, would that boy be free of even the remotest unstated wish to be born with bigger bones? (Would, indeed, he even be a physically unfit little Jewish scholar under such perfect conditions?) Or would he in the deepest recess of his heart have to admit to an instinctive need to identify with, envy, and serve as beta the sturdier alpha in the cottage down the lane?

Well, whether instinctive or cultural, Joe Palooka and Li'l Abner still reign supreme in my America. Call them Jim Plunkett or Astronaut, if you will, they're alphas all. And in this country at least the slower, heavier child or the quirky thin one is born with an immediate disadvantage. How subtly that measure of disapproval begins to be felt. How swiftly it builds itself into the body. The tapeworm of doubt grabs for the guts. And how soon the less-than-ideal American boy finds himself something of an emotional eunuch as he discovers himself in second place. Which is not to say that the alpha-male hasn't sold his mess of real feelings to maintain his birthright too.

1:50 P.M.

Disconcerting session. Something unsatisfying. A sense of much unfinished business.

I recounted an unusual amount of biography today: my early terror of playing games with other boys, the fights I avoided or lost, my sense of absolute inevitability when at seven a classmate let the wind take hold of the script to a fairy tale play I'd spent hours diligently hunting-and-pecking out on our typewriter the previous day.

We got into my clumsiness too. Rhoda made me feel my dread of people laughing at the way I walked, my inability to run fast or climb a fence or throw a ball straight, my awful fear of my body not functioning as I wished it to. I screamed out my fears, my need for help.

My urinating problem rose again. I recalled the tremendous pressure I'd felt one day when Joel and I went into the city on our own and, after the planetarium show, hurried to the men's room. The place was mobbed. I was twelve, so there must have been a sexual component burgeoning then, but my most vivid impression was that pressure to perform —to hurry up and pee while all those men's eyes were on me, impatiently waiting in line, making me feel incompetent to do my work in time.

Rhoda made me relive the agony of that pressure. I screamed out my fear of it, recalling again those early times of not being allowed to wake my parents by getting up early to pee, to be as quiet about it as possible for fear of their yelling at me, for having to hold it in, having somehow inside myself to apologize for the room I took up, the noise I made, the smell of me.

Again Rhoda made me get angry at them for that.

"God damn it, what do you *want* from me! I have to go! Let me go! Let me pee! Let me pee!"

I remembered too so often being constipated as a child. "And so was my mother. She used to live on mineral oil, Rhoda. It probably helped kill her."

Which made me cry in rage again at being forced to identify with her sickness in order to win her.

I remembered once hearing that my father used to bundle me up tight in a blanket to show me off to the "boys down at the market" when I was still a baby. And also seeing pictures of myself at the age of two or three wrapped up in a heavy coat, my arms almost useless in the sweaters stuffed inside the coat. I felt a sense of utter helplessness. That little kid—*me*—trussed up like a turkey without being able to use his arms or legs to keep himself from falling. I relived the sensation today.

Yet somehow something wasn't completely clicking. I was desperate to make more solemn connections but couldn't.

We got into my sense of shame for liking to act on the stage, to play the piano, to dance. All three activities abruptly stopped for a while during my early teens when the pressure to "behave like a boy" grew too strong. Those pastimes were wrong!

"Why were they wrong?"

"Boys in Brooklyn don't do things like dance or play the piano. You're a sissy if you do!"

"Who said so?"

"I don't know. The other boys. I knew it. I even knew it was wrong to play with Margery across the street when I was five. But I liked it because I was afraid to *be* with the boys. I couldn't do what they could do, didn't *want* to for fear of not being able to, always got out of playing war by pretending to be wounded."

"Who said those other things were wrong?"

I tried to say that my parents disapproved, but I can't recall that they did. My mother and her two brothers all were musicians. Music wasn't disapproved. My acting lessons were granted. I couldn't *feel* any connections. But the dancing, that compensation for my clumsiness, I don't think was liked very much. I can't tell, but I think my mother's eyes told me that was wrong. Maybe, maybe. I just can't tell.

I went into my hateful camp experiences. Six wasted summers in that competitive sports-crazed jungle prison, and I had to wrench out a passable time by acting in plays or associating with the camp misfits, feeling both activities reprehensible, unapproved. Never did I dare suggest an alternative to my parents, too afraid of their disapproval to announce that I wouldn't go, that I hated the sports and the competition, that I loathed them for sending me away each summer! It was costing them a lot of money, wasn't it? It was an excellent camp. It wasn't supposed to be a punishment. My parents thought they were being good to me! When I think of the kinds of experiences that I later discovered existed—farm-work camps, hosteling trips, music, study, travel programs—it makes me want to vomit for all the suffering their ignorance caused me.

I felt so incompetent, so unworthy of doing much with my life that I never even entertained the idea of going to college until my senior year of high school. No, my parents weren't the usual Jewish kind crying "Be a doctor! Be a lawyer!" Decisions were left to me, although my father did have the absymal idea of turning me into a butcher on a couple of occasions. My highest aspiration in high school: secretarial work, maybe in a library. I even took a shorthand course to prepare myself for a third-rate livelihood.

Only when the friends I made while living for that brief time in our own house on Avenue R began to talk of college did I wonder if I might qualify too. That house. How I loved it. I finally seemed to be making headway with a few friends at the age of fifteen, finding kids who shared my "offbeat" interests in the theater, in books, then had to move to Brewster to start all over again in a place where no one would be caught dead with a book in his hand.

My parents saw my unhappiness then. I was acting it out all over the place. They even suggested I stay with my grandfather and aunt back on 13th Street for that final year so I might finish high school in Brooklyn. But I couldn't bring myself to do it.

"You couldn't leave your mother," Rhoda told me.

"I was sixteen years old, damn it!"

"How old are you now, Mike?"

"Thirty-six."

"You still need your mother!"

I began to cry. "I'm six years old inside, six months, six days."

"Maybe if you'd had her the way you'd needed her, you wouldn't be so anymore."

"I think healthy people always need their mothers too. Only they're able to *know* it."

"Well, anyway, you needed yours. You still do."

The session ended on that sorry note, but I feel no closer to solving my enigma today. Moreover Rhoda's unwillingness to see this problem as universal rather than neurotic undermines all my fancy theories. I guess I can't be concerned with humanity just now, not when my own seems so damned jeopardized.

While having lunch today I wallowed again through my fears of pissing and shitting. Nice topic for the table. Suddenly I suffered a phantom panic that the restaurant was going to close before I was through eating. God damn it! What else must have caused that but my earliest training. Was Mother stingy with her breast? Did she take away the bottle too soon? Did I have to get it all in before it stopped coming?

All this sounds so patently Freudian I almost want to laugh. But never during my work with Dr. M were these possibilities even remotely considered. And now they make the gravest sense. My unanswered cry for help and that unconscious sense of my own ineffectiveness in eliciting a response from my crib. My need to urinate and defecate—but only on command. And *not* to do it for fear of reprisal. Mean feeding patterns applied? Well, maybe these in themselves didn't do the whole job, but they sure seem to have gone a long way in screwing up that little boy's future, with nothing or not very much to counteract that early mishandling. His whole life was predicated on it.

5:10 P.M.

For the past two hours I've been brooding in my room, trying to recall the earliest and specific men in my life with whom I tried to identify, whose love I tried to win:

Alan, the boy next door on 15th Street, who took me to Saturday matinees, let me rummage around in his junk-filled basement, played with me when he had the time. I loved him and was also deeply impressed by his older brother, a soldier in uniform who'd been overseas.

These were the war years. There weren't many men in our neighborhood except for a few overworked or alienating fathers like my own.

Some teen-ager I recall jumped off the roof of his house in a homemade parachute. And a few months later when he was rejected by the Army, hung himself in his basement. Ah, the war years. Nothing like it to separate the men from the boys. Macho America.

Then there were my mother's two brothers. I hardly knew the younger one, who was either overseas or in Pittsburgh. But the older one, a classical musician, stayed with us often. He let me listen to him practice his clarinet and help him clean the instrument when he was done. (Sure, sure, blowing and cleaning out cocks, we know, we know.)

Up in the country at the Hermitage, ages six, seven, eight, there were only women and children, except for weekends when those uninterested fathers arrived to play pinochle and preferred to be left undisturbed by their kids.

Camp at the age of nine—1944. Again, most of the younger men were off fighting the war. My counselor was middle-aged, almost like a grandfather. Next bunk, though, was a handsome junior counselor. Even now I can see myself ogling him and not knowing why, just knowing he was the person I wanted to be with—wanted to *be*—handsome, strong-looking, gently concerned with his charges. I wished I'd been in his bunk.

That summer, age nine, was really my first real contact with unfrightening and interested men. My father's men friends never seemed any more comfortable to be with than he was, except for one who reared two daughters and whom we didn't see very often. So it was camp, despite my hatred for the place, where I first met sympathetic men who made it all the more awful, seeing the possibility of love there and feeding off them in my craving for a father's affection.

Big deal. Does that solve the problem? How long do I have to shout "I need you, Daddy?" to stop the need. Oh, God, this damn therapy is still trying to teach me that the need will never stop, and once again I'm afraid, knowing the potency of that craving, the momentary relief from that longing which is so easily available to me. Damned to act out that terrible need for the rest of my unnatural life—

6:45 P.M.

Rushed out after writing that. Suddenly I had to eat and knew damn well why. I was practically sprinting down the street to get away from the awful pain still with me. Food the simplest solution. And all the hundreds of diets I've been on have always played right into the same sickness! Starve yourself, feel your stomach's emptiness—then you'll have the *right* to eat! You'll have the right to ease your pain!

I wolfed down supper, barely tasting it, suppressing indigestion, and hurried back here almost feeling faint. But not faint enough to stop me from buying something gooey and sweet at last. At last! With conscious irony I chose something as close to the Mallomars of my youth as I could find. Mallomars. Do they make those anymore? Mallomars— those chocolate marshmallow mommies! Those soft, sweet breasts you could swallow in one fat gulp! I lay you odds, anyone you catch eating Mallomars after the age of—at *any* age—is sick! I knew damn well they wouldn't assuage a fucking thing, but all the same I shoved the tasteless cakes down my throat and only made my teeth ache.

Oh, God, as I sit here waiting for group to start, the truth of this afternoon's brooding keeps coming back! All those older boys, all those counselors, all the hundreds of men I've been to bed with since—hell, I could go to bed with a thousand more but *still* I'll never find the father I never really had, or the beautiful *me* that Mother might love! But what else can I do? I hate myself so! I've always hated myself! I walk down the street looking for people to relieve me of me. I loathe myself so. I loathe myself! When I make love, it's not to play the woman. Nor even the little boy. But to do all the loving, to possess, not to be possessed, to want to merge myself with, to be the body I'm with, to love it as I was never allowed to love my own! How could I learn to hate myself so? How could they have done that to me! I hate them for it! Hate them! I keep hating myself! I keep wanting to die now! Not to be me! Oh, God, this is terrible, *terrible!*

I know I'm screaming in silence here. I sit trembling, wishing for group to start so I could howl it out.

9:30 P.M.

Just finished. A large crowd tonight and only two therapists available. It was forty-five minutes or more before Dr. Rosen got around to me. I'd been screaming my lungs out and found myself brutally slapping at myself, hitting my arms and legs with utter contempt, over and over again, an awful painful self-flagellation, certain there was nothing inside me to make myself *be* myself, that I would be doomed to search for myself until I died—search for me in other men even though other men could never give me myself no matter how long I looked. When Dr. Rosen finally came around, I raged at him for not coming sooner, for not stopping me from hitting myself, and then begged to die.

He told me to think back to the little boy I'd been and see that boy again as clearly as I could. The usual routine which in seconds had me crying once more for the Daddy-Who-Wasn't, to be able to hold him, to be loved by him, to share his strength. But nothing came for *myself*. I cried again that there was not enough inside me, that I felt like nothing, that I hated myself so, that I had to *beat* myself.

Dr. Rosen said, "Was there anything wrong with that little boy?"

"He felt like a girl!" I insisted.

"Who made him feel like a girl?"

"*He* did. He made *himself!*"

"Not himself. He couldn't do that to himself. Someone did that to him. He was born being okay."

"But it happened so early—even in his crib. He never had a chance."

"Right. Even in his crib."

And I knew Dr. Rosen was saying what Rhoda had also been telling me all these terrible days that once I'm really ready to accept the fact that they did that to me, and *not* myself, once I'm ready to stop protecting them, I'll be better able to stop hating myself, I'll be better able to begin to find that I'm enough in myself, that *I'm enough!*

For a long time I lay there feeling that message in silence, gathering stamina for the assault I knew had to come. Finally I let loose again torrents of abuse, unforgiving rage condemning both my parents for destroying me, for making me hate myself, for wasting my life. I told them I'd be damned if I'd let them take what was left of it. That I loathed them. That they fed me promises of love—all lies. That they gave me nothing of value, not even crumbs, and I'd wasted too much time believing in them. That I'd loved them as much as I could, and *still* it had never been enough for them, *never*. That I might not be much, but that was all I had and I couldn't go on hating myself for them. To protect *them!* That they gave me even less than the little I still thought *I* was. That there was no reason to go on looking for myself in other men because I'm only here inside me and there's no place else *but* me. That I'd be damned before I'd hurt myself again!

The group was a marvel during our wrap-up. I told them readily about my feelings and began to cry in front of them. Others wept with me for themselves. Still others, open and honest and healthy, admitted how hard it was to be out in a world where people whom they once thought had loved them now *blamed* them for being themselves.

Stan was in the group tonight. He began to cry too as he spoke about being held by a great-uncle of his, the only man in his family who ever did that for him. For a brief moment I resented his bawling before everyone, until I realized he was only being honest in his feelings, that he was *himself* now and not an extension of me, that I was using one of my worst habits again in hoping he'd be the more perfect and manly representative of me. If that's all the effort it takes to be honest with myself, well, suddenly I feel I'm halfway there.

He also told a funny story to the group about a man he met the other night at our neighbor's house, a rational therapist who became furious when Stan suggested that his theories sounded too much like the power of positive thinking. Others spoke of their encounters with traditional analysts. One boy said that a Jungian he knew announced that this kind of emotionally based therapy was good only for stupid people.

That set a woman screaming: "For the first time in my life, after years of their garbage, I feel normal—and they want to take it away!"

That made me recall my own encounter with a psychiatrist at a party last month. When I asked him if he'd read Janov's book *The Primal Scream*, he said, "Nope, but I've heard enough about it not to want to. It's just a lot of glorified encounter group stuff. A fad. It won't last."

Dr. Rosen said he'd come up against the same attitude. So many insight therapists have too much vested interest in maintaining what they have. It's annoying, but understandable, I suppose. All that education they've undergone; their financial and professional status might be opened to question if a therapy of this nature caught on. And what about those untapped emotions of their own?

Well, the millennium is not around the corner, and until then I don't intend to go to feel-ins with Bernard Gunther and William Schutz, but I think it's only a matter of time before more people discover this approach to therapy as an effective and valid alternative to the more traditional ways of helping the psychologically sick and ailing.

Wednesday

Thought I'd sleep well last night, but my mind kept turning the evening over. Found myself fitfully weeping and ruminating for hours. Woke up around seven feeling unrested and glum again.

My gloominess, I know, is due to the weight of that awful reiteration last night. Right now it seems the hardest reality I'll ever have to face. I find myself continually called on to repeat it, to be better able to draw it into my heart: Your mother and father fucked you up, Michael, not *you!* You cannot afford to hurt yourself anymore! They made you hate your life, turned you into a whore in your useless search for what never existed, and all the forgiveness you feel compelled to lavish on them for *their* own ignorance and illness only makes it harder for you to accept yourself!

But my mother's sad eyes continue to interfere. I can more easily call my father to accounts. It's the illusory belief in my mother's good care that's still so terribly strong in me. No matter how closely I examine the damaging ways she neglected me, made me hate my body, made me feel there was nothing I could do to win her, and wrapped me up in her own personality so that I lost my own, the felt truth of it all again becomes unbearable. What follows is always such an awful, awful emptiness—and a hollow return to myself which is all the more terrifying.

I must keep at it! I want to! I've been there several times

already. And any return from it now would be a lie and a worse kind of loss.

I guess there's plenty of sadness in store for me. I'll never recover from the truth of their strategic neglect. But that sadness, God damn it, might finally help me live a life that's no longer just some muddy salvage operation.

DEAR MARTIN BUBER:
    Another old Chasidic saying: "If my therapist isn't for me, who is?"

DEAR MOSES HERZOG:
    See what your letter writing started.

As I piddled away in the bathroom this morning, I realized that I don't have to piss for the whole world to hear. The sickness of an exhibitionist, who needs it? As long as I can piss for myself without caring who hears, I'll be okay.

12:30 P.M.

I feel wonderful. Wonderful and sad. The content of today's session was no more revealing than the best of them, no less emotional.

Most of my time was spent repeating last night's last half hour: the rage, the fear, the need. And reasserting my new determination not to let that old self-hatred ever get such an upper hand again. How can I if I pause long enough to feel my way back to its origin?

No new biography today, but one brief flash of my father teaching me how to ride a bike when I was around thirteen, a rare good feeling of being with him. All too late, much too little. I cried a great deal about him today and blamed him once more for turning me into a whore in search of him.

Rhoda and I spent more time talking to each other than

has been usual. I spoke about my appreciation of the group, how real those people allow me to be, and how good it was to see others last night so unashamed of their feelings. I told her about my reaction to Stan's crying and felt that through again for a few more minutes.

Later, she offered some information about herself. Before undergoing her own intensive therapy and subsequent training here, she'd been employed as a psychiatric social worker and a school guidance consultant through the state's protective services for children. All five therapists, including two psychiatrists, now working at the Center are licensed by the state; the trainees, who have had others kinds of professional counseling experience, will help expand the staff once they have completed the Center's internship program and satisfied any additional state requirements. Rhoda's husband Al is co-director of the place with Dr. Rosen and, now I realize, also my next-door neighbor's therapist.

When Rhoda told me she and Al are the parents of three children, I said, "My God, if they had *you* for parents and *still* have problems, what hope is there for the rest of us?"

"That's *now,*" she insisted. "Too late. I was a rotten parent before my own therapy. A typical Jewish mother, never letting my kids breathe, making them feel guilty, not allowing them to live."

"I'm not sure that's necessarily Jewish."

She laughed. "Well, Jews seem to have cornered the market on it."

"But Jews aren't too far away from their feelings—at least culturally. Some of the WASP's I know would never dare cry. They're so tight and dry—or pretend to be."

That brought up the whole question of popular rearing patterns and cultural constraints. I raised the question about how much my own mother might have just been responding to the 1930's edict against indulging an infant's demands, following doctors' orders about toilet training and feeding.

"A mother has feelings. If a baby cries, you pick him up and see what's wrong, or hold him. If your mother used doctors' orders as her excuse, something wasn't right with her."

After a time I confessed to my unhappiness at the disappearance of the new guy next door. We went into the feelings I noted earlier. Then Rhoda said, "He wasn't ready for therapy. He hadn't bargained for this."

That bothered me. Shouldn't a valid therapy be able to have perfected methods to reach the most recalcitrant? Then I thought of psychoanalysis, and client-centered therapy, and pure Gestalt, and realized that the person has to be hurting enough to want to be helped, that he'll get no place unless he's ready, truly ready for it.

I asked how old Rhoda felt a person had to be for this particular kind of therapy. Would children or college-aged people respond more readily, let's say, than middle-aged people? She had her doubts. In many cases with the young they're still too hopeful, she said; they haven't been knocked around enough, haven't yet suffered from the longings that a separation from home can bring about.

Then Rhoda talked about some of her own intensive experiences that still grab her during the normal course of her day. Recently a song she'd heard on the radio made her think of her mother's aging and she started to cry for that earliest need of her. A relative made her angry enough last week at some old wrong to allow her a fit of quiet rage in her living room. Even some of the things I'd cried about there in her office had at times hit responsive chords in her, she said, and made her weep for herself behind me.

I told her that my problem about urinating had somewhat eased up, but since this was still in the security of the house, I couldn't trust it. Whenever the anxiety arose, she said, I should try to feel it all the way through to its source again.

"Sure, I can see myself having a good scream in a public john."

She laughed. "As soon as possible then."

"And the men? I'm so afraid I'll still have all those old feelings for men."

"You may. The longing might be there maybe even after it no longer has to be acted out. Just feel it fully—feel who it is you're really searching for, what it is you really need and admit that feeling as deeply as you can."

This, in essence, is her advice for my inevitable encounters with future anxiety and fear. Unlike psychoanalysis, it's not to *know* and so be better prepared to guard yourself *against* your panic, or to *will* your terrors away with reasoning; it's to feel your fear to the very source of its unfulfilled need until your bowels cry out with the agony you never allowed yourself to admit. The impulse to move that need into compensating self-destructive action might then dissipate, disappear, growing useless for being defused.

Since Rhoda has to go out of town on Friday, she told me I could return home after our early meeting tomorrow. She feels I know how to get into myself well enough now so that we could postpone our next private session until Tuesday. But I must return also for the evening group tomorrow night. I panicked a little and asked her if I could stay at the center throughout the day if I wished. The choice was left up to me. Next month I'll be seeing her privately once a week and will attend evening groups twice weekly.

I'm not sure if I'll go home tomorrow or wait until Friday morning. I'll see what my feelings are then. For the first time in my life I feel freed of having to make those protective little plans of mine. It's a wonderful feeling, wonderful.

3:15 P.M.

I'm back in my room now after an hour watching the antics in the park, that unending tragic carnival. The constant critic, I sat there applauding this mother, chiding that one, loving each little kid, and oddly enough, often receiving smiles as they ran by. "Watch me!" one shouted as he went down the slide. "Did you see?" he asked.

"I sure did!"

Full of himself he ran off while I blew another Kleenex to bits.

It seems so *easy* to give those willing, open children exactly what they need, and I know goddamn well it's *not*. But we're beginning to know *why*, right?

I'm the first one to admit how stupid I am about political and economic theories, but I'll be damned if I'll be able to buy any social analysis that neglects our basic emotional needs anymore. This therapy is leading me to believe that all the ills of this world—poverty, prejudice, exploitation, war, dictatorship, and the willing submission to it—generate out of our earliest domestic unfulfillment and/or ignorant patterns of rearing. No matter how "democratic," the institutions we conceive are still only flimsy defenses against the basic conditions of our existence on earth or, at best, sad bastions to ward off the more violent defense mechanisms of a far more frightened enemy.

I don't think I'll ever be able to pledge my loyalty to any institution from here on out—no country, no church, no political party, no school. Each in its own way denies me myself. Each in its own way is a vain attempt to fight the dark. Each in its own way gives me a false assurance of my importance, even an illusion of immortality if I'm fool enough to believe in the group's greatest lie.

Granted, the goals of a group might be noble ones—building a new nation, sharing unselfishly with others—but even at their best I suspect they offer a kind of sop to cosmic fear that in its most ruthless forms Communism provides, religion, corporate visions, unions, fraternities, armies, boys-in-the-band—*any* organization that prearranges structure and imposes its own meaning on your life.

Maybe I'm fighting biology with this attitude, I don't know. Tiger's *Men in Groups* and Ardrey's *The Social Contract* suggest group activity as biological necessity. But I'm becoming convinced in these last few days that the healthiest animal among us remains an essential anarchist. The most authentic man or woman will stay flexibly uncommitted to any organization, committee, or group, using them only when they serve to help him achieve a specific and realizable goal. Once that goal is satisfied or perhaps recognized as unattainable, the "compleat" human being will leave that particular group behind, abhorring its fearsome blood-demand of absolute fidelity, not taken in by the carrot of security it offers, the illusory promise that if only we sing the group's rallying songs out of key, or don't break that circle of linked arms, we too will never have to face the chasm of fear beneath those dancing feet, we too will be able to shut out the darkness with our shouting.

By its very nature the group must demand fidelity. And in that its inherent oppression lies. No group can actively support the independence of its members for very long. Let one person stray too far and he will fill the others who cling with the dread of dissolution. Call him revisionist, defector, heretic, traitor—and he is all the more clearly exposing the fear of those whose desperate certitude he's undermined.

"Man, you ain't been black," a new militant scoffs. "We have a need for banning together. It's the only way we're going to get what we've been denied!"

"I've been forced to hate myself as fully as any black man has, and—"

"You don't know what it's like to be black!"

"Damn right I don't. I can only feel *myself*. But listen, in *feeling* myself, I can feel myself in you, my own desperation, my own degradation, my own anger, my own needs. Don't think you're unique in that because of the social injustices you've been made to suffer. Ninety-nine percent of the world feels the same way as you, I suspect, if they'd only let themselves know it. And that's just the reason why they try to keep *you* where you are. To save their own illusions about themselves. That's why you were enslaved, that's why you're still bound by economic and political treachery."

"No more! No more! We're changing that, you hear?"

"I have no quarrel with that. I respect your rage as I respect my own now. But you must also see this: Just like any other group raging for its just rights—Women's Libbers, Gay Libbers, Chicanos, whoever, *any* human being demanding his freedom—even if you fulfill your goal in your own way and are able to forge your own life-style, your new-found freedom will be just as illusory unless you are also willing to embrace the universal terror. Whether you're gunning to become the next decade's middle-class Jew or some newly minted nation, as soon as you've arrived there, believe you've made it, hell, you've screwed yourself as royally as any neurotic immigrant who thought money in the bank and a fancy car in the garage meant the security of his soul.

"I insist again that the healthiest man among us, the one who had the most responsive mother, the most reliable father, has somewhere in his life suffered the same essential loss as you and I have. His only difference is his ability to probe that emptiness utterly and accept its frightening clamor without any illusions of identification with any soul-saving group. It's he who can fully feel the total hopelessness of believing that he really ever*had* or ever *will* have anyone or anything that could serve him better than himself."

9:50 P.M.

I knew it, I knew it—movies will never be the same.

Late this afternoon I took the bus into SF to see Jules Feiffer's *Carnal Knowledge*. Enjoyed it a lot—fine performances, Nichols' directing with unmodish economy, minimal

decor and music deftly suggesting entire decades. The
script a gem of precision, Feiffer at his sardonic best—and
ultimately as depressing as all get-out. Then what's the reservation? Well, this picture portrays as accurately as any
I've ever seen the psycho-sexual self-delusions of my generation. (As always the heterosexual mechanisms are dismally
similar to the homosexual.) But, but it portrays, it *illus-
trates*—and never really gets to the root of the problem. It's
all perfectly shown symptomology. When it *does* obliquely
probe into causes, it never gets further than a slim argument against America's cultural absurdities: our schizo-
phrenic distinction between love and sex (not only in
America, but probably in all of western Europe dating back
to the time of Eleanor of Aquitaine), our awful obligation
to play preordained roles as "men" and "women," our dismal double standard of morality and meager compensation
of marriage, the incredible servile function that woman is
made to perform as man's housewife and whore. Yes, all
these abominations are graphically revealed, but at base,
the reason Jonathan saw all women as ball-busters and
Sandy envisioned them as either sinners or saints has more
to do with Mom than with America. And Mom—even as a
suggested cause—is reduced to one brief allusion ("I've
been through the good little boy bit") that is no more than
a passing joke. Accurate too; that is, the characters' inability to see through to causes. But not if Feiffer doesn't make
us see the truth that his two protagonists are so desperately
eluding.

Well, I guess I go only to frivolous flicks from now on.
The thoughtful ones frustrate me as they skirt around the
awful issue. Puns intended.

Before and after the movie I had a little time to walk,
and managed to promenade Polk Strasse—Vaseline Alley
West—without needing or soliciting the attention of a
dozen available tricks there. Had to do a little folk-cursing
to center the blame at times, and those times always in-

truded when a particular gait, a head of hair, a squared wrist made me doubt the value of my own again. I'm not out to win any records for health, but I think at least I've got down pat the knack of not despising myself quite so much. It promises to be a sexless future. Who knows, maybe a more companionable one. I hesitate to write a "more loving one" because I'll be damned if I know what love means anymore.

Thursday

Just came down from a very early session to accommodate Rhoda's weekend away. A fortuitous hour. The house was quiet, the other residents still asleep, and so again I was afraid to make noise. I felt it thoroughly, then blasted back at it. Must have waked the dead. And didn't care.

We went over events that never seem to exhaust their feeling potential: goody-goody grammar school obedience, the importance of the kitchen in my mother's house, my waiting there like a lapdog for the scraps of her attention.

Most important was Rhoda's request for me to get back into the fears I felt in that house on 13th Street: the ghosts in the cellar, the robbers at the back windows or in the living room, the kidnappers waiting outside the front door, my cousin upstairs marauding me in the vestibule, frightening me with the horrors that lurked down the back stairwell. I felt them all again and realized how forbiddden it had been to express those fears to my parents. "You should be ashamed of yourself!" I could hear them say and, so obedient to Mother's wishes, was ashamed, rarely allowing myself to express one goddamn legitimate emotion.

"How do you feel?" Rhoda inevitably asked when I'd been through it.

"Like I have a lot to do yet."

And I do. More fully now I can appreciate those people in group still telling stories of their vestigial terrors. Three weeks is not enough time, not for me, anyway. No doubt a lifetime won't be enough to dissolve all the neurotic acting out of those early injustices. But at least I have a firmer sense of direction now. I seem to know what and why I'm feeling what I feel almost every minute of the day.

Have still to decide whether to leave this morning and return tonight for group, or to stay the day and leave tomorrow. I feel inclined to remain. This place has been good to me. And although I know I'm postponing the inevitable, one more day's reflection and unfettered sense of freedom to feel, unencumbered by old pressures, doesn't strike me as cowardly.

This morning I kissed Rhoda good-bye and she kissed me. I wanted to cry then, but didn't. I'll do that now.

1:30 P.M.

Haven't been able to shake this morning's memories of childhood fears. As hard as they are to bear, I don't intend to. If they're sticking with me like this, then they're worth feeling through. It's a shock to me to remember all I'd never really forgotten, the terror that house and neighborhood held for me—killers in every shadow, every noise a threat. God knows where that insecurity and lack of trust ultimately began, but short of the dawn of man, I'll bet they went back at least to my fucking crib. And the silence I imposed upon myself so that Mother wouldn't grieve, the shame imposed upon *me* so that I would blame myself for all those fears, well, the answer's obvious to me by now, but the pain is as fresh as it ever was, and all the harder to bear since I feel it with the heavy weight of its ultimate implication, the cruel disservice I was forced to perform on myself. And that's enough to make me mad. And that's when I have to scream and weep the way I never did when it would have been wise to do so—and was so utterly impossible!

9:45 P.M.

Surprises still to come. Although my heavy emotions during group tonight ran through many of the old themes, I began to concentrate on my problems with time again. I found myself shouting, "Don't rush me!" A response to a vague feeling of being pushed to finish meals, finish shitting, finish taking up room. "Hurry up and finish!" I heard my mother say, saw my father once again coming in for supper, making me rush from the table. Panic over schoolwork, arithmetic problems especially, seems related to this now, never having been given enough time—not even to learn to walk properly, or run, or throw a ball, no one having the time to teach me the skill, or caring to.

Immediately I flashed on my urination problem again, that pressure to finish up fast, a sense of someone waiting at the door and my having no right to take up space at the toilet. The same suddenly seemed true of my problems in bed, wanting to rush to a climax for fear I was already boring my partner, that all pleasurable activity—eating, shitting, studying, fucking—must be finished fast to allow someone else a turn, that all those activities were somehow *wrong* to begin with and therefore had to be hurried through, unexamined, hidden, that I'd better get my pleasure in *fast* because sure as hell something was going to come along and stop it if I didn't finish quick!

I screamed out my anger at that imposition! Raged against my mother for causing it, for my father for being party to it. And now will no doubt become a master of the slow-motion screw. No bets accepted. But at least I feel more deeply the right not to rush!

Al Wasserman, Rhoda's husband, whom I've not worked with before in group, was on call tonight. He stayed with me awhile, encouraging me, and at one point asked, "Why are your fists clenched?"

I didn't realize they were. I felt them then, felt their anger and a worse imprisoning sense of not being able to move, not being allowed to. "I have to move! I have to move!" I shouted.

Al said, "Do it!"

I flailed around in a deeper physical frenzy than I've ever experienced in my life. Liberating. Exhausting. And giving me a deeper sense of the restrictions I'd imposed on my body to please my folks, the constricted guts they'd given me in return, the clumsiness, hatred, and shame that it led to.

I doubt if that recognition now turns me into a gazelle, but I'll be damned if I'll ever have to feel as tight inside as I've been all my life. At least I know more fully now how to recognize my body's clues. I mustn't be afraid to feel that physical need again!

Finally, a funny flash: I'm not sure how valid it is, but it seems to connect. Again I remembered that day my mother dragged me back to the dentist after I'd sneaked home. And I shouted out my fear of the physical pain, blamed her for telling me I should be ashamed of myself instead of doing what any normal mother would do—comfort me or at least try to assure me that the dentist's dirty work had to be done. But tonight I also recalled that after the ordeal was over, my mother read to me the peculiar things I'd said under the anesthetic. She'd copied them down on a slip of paper, and though I scarcely remembered saying them, they'd made her laugh, pleased her. She even read them to my father that night and to the neighbors upstairs. I can't recall the words that elicited this unusual response from her, but I wonder now if pleasing Mother with words wasn't embedded then and there as one of my earliest impulses to continue to write them down. (And is that another reason for having to give it up now?)

"Neurosis is the inability to express need," Al said during our wrap-up. He blamed neurotic parents for doing their damnedest to shut off their children's feelings to suit their own. Their motive? A child's candid expression of feeling inevitably brings parents closer to their own pain, which, as neurotics, they're unable to confront.

He also spoke of the risk we might allow ourselves to undertake by expressing those needs to our parents and family now that we've recognized them for what they are and can feel them straight again. Not, of course, to expect them to be fulfilled, but to make the painful opportunity to experience our parents' reaction and test our own new-felt feelings against them. "See how it feels to you now that you know what it's all about when that cold bastard of a father reacts after you tell him you need him and always have needed him."

The thought made more than one person in the room shiver with dread. I'm glad I'm saved from that trial. No, damn it, I'm not. It would be good to say it—if only out of vengeance—though I have the sneaking suspicion that if I'd said that during the last sad years of my father's life, he and I both would've dissolved in tears.

Though suddenly I'm petrified to think what that admission might have meant to him: more reasons to exploit me, to make new demands, to turn my need to his own advantage. Oh, boy, what courage I would need then to express my rage. I can just hear him saying, "But I thought you just said you *needed* me!"

"Not to be your slave, you bastard! Not to be *used* by you! For you to love me with no price tag attached!"

Al told us that tension always means you're close to a feeling. It should be a signal to let it all hang out. He mentioned Reich's *Character Analysis* and its astute observations about the body's reflection of our deepmost states of being. Worth reading, he wryly muttered, "for those who still have the mind-fucking need to read." I had to laugh at that, knowing how often I'd buried myself in books as a substitute for feeling the real mess of *my* life.

A good evening. I feel relaxed and confident.

Friday

6:30 A.M.

Up at the crack of dawn again and still feeling fine. In an hour or so I'll catch a bus to San Francisco. I'm in no rush. The New Me. Ha. How long it lasts, who knows? Damn it, there's so much more for me to do. But now at least I can *feel* what I'm doing and must be done.

Well, so, I may be leaving now to encounter for the millionth time the reality of experience—but certainly *not* to forge in the smithy of my soul the uncreated conscience of my race. I'm just beginning to find my *own,* damn it.

And the future? Will I be able to pee in public? Will I go straight? Will I give up going to movies? Will I leave the bright lights of Broadway where I have reigned for the last fifteen years as the world's most beloved musical comedy star to become a saffron-robed monk baking pumpernickel somewhere in Tibet? I guess I'll find out.